A MASTERS IN MOTHERHOOD

(FROM THE UNIVERSITY OF LIFE)

Gill Arthey

Copyright © 3P Publishing
First published in 2015.
This edition published in 2019
3P Publishing
C E C, London Road
Corby
NN17 5EU

A catalogue number for this book is available
from the British Library

ISBN 978-1-911559-62-7

This book is dedicated to the memory of my lovely dad Peter, to dear sweet James who will never be forgotten and to the wonderful 'Auntie Pat.'

Acknowledgments go to:

My family and friends, for allowing me to write about them.

Eddie, for putting up with me burning the midnight oil and for understanding my total obsession with writing this.

To Sarah for her constant encouragement when the seeds of the idea began and for letting me write in the peace of her lovely Scottish home.

To Mike Hutton for his advice, ideas, encouragement and interest.

Joan, for putting my punctuation into some sort of order and for proof reading the manuscript. Also, for her wealth of technical knowhow, without which I would have been lost.

Special thanks to Rosanne who worked so hard to get all her illustrations completed. I really enjoyed our afternoon drawing sessions as we illustrated this together.

To Mum for helping me with my apostrophes and for reading my first draft manuscript. Also for her constant support and devotion to our family.

To dear Pat who was endless in her support and interest, right up to her last few days.

To Sally O-J from the Literary Consultancy.

To our new friend Sue, retired midwife and until August a total stranger, who has read and given great and encouraging feedback about the manuscript. This has given me the confidence to go ahead and publish.

Thanks go to my youngest son Michael for doing the cover design and for cleaning up and sizing the images.

And lastly to all my friends who have put up with me banging on about my passion for writing.

Thank you everyone.

Something about the Author

Gill was born in London, on 12th July 1958. As an only child, she led a very happy, active and varied childhood.

A love of books was instilled at an early age - with a father involved in the publishing industry; books were always part of family life.

At the age of seven she travelled with her parents to live in Africa for a year, while her father worked for a Christian publishing company. They settled into rural Northamptonshire when she was 13, where she later met her husband, Eddie, at a young farmers' club meeting.

Riding instruction was her chosen career after leaving school. With a few years spent working for the NHS she soon returned to her first love - working freelance caring for horses and teaching, until the arrival of the triplets.

This is the first novel Gill has had published, although not her first attempt to write. At the age of 12 she wrote a book full of advice for parents of horse mad girls, followed by several other efforts to write equestrian literature!

Gill is still happily living in Northamptonshire, where her interest in horses is shared by her husband, and now grown up children.

MODULE 1:
OBSTETRICS AND GENETICS

'Mrs. Feodora Vassilyev had her first child in 1725. She went on to have sixty-nine children from twenty-seven births. Sixteen pairs of twins, seven sets of triplets and four sets of quads'.

The hairs on the back of my neck stood up as I read that opening paragraph. All the magazines were strewn untidily across the waiting room table, so I picked one up at random and opened it on an equally random page. My eyes casually scanned the text, but slowly the information I read sank in. It went on to quote the percentages of parents having natural multiple pregnancies. 24.7% of births were natural twins, 5.8% were natural triplets and 0.8% were natural quads. Was I about to become one of these percentages? A statistic - an odd phenomenon - like this poor Russian woman who had beaten all odds and statistical records with her tremendous efforts.

But this was not the sort of thing I needed to be reading at this moment in time, and with no insurance policies or even the bookie's odds to make us a fortune, I had put this thought to the back of my mind. On the other hand though, could reading this be an omen? Or was it just some kind of freaky coincidence? I closed the offending article, quickly placed it back on the untidy pile and sat waiting to be called.

It was early in the month of May, and the year was 1983 - obviously a time well before the invention of the internet, and its informative spawn Google. In my case ignorance was bliss, and certainly peace of mind was achieved by my being relatively un-informed.

Now I was standing half undressed in the hospital cubical, gazing down at my rapidly expanding abdomen, wondering if an alien was about to burst from within. Muffled voices permeated the thin plasterboard walls from the waiting room behind, reminiscent of the quiet chattering of the Canada Geese that flocked to the water-filled lagoons in the stone quarry behind our house. The crisp, clean gown felt harsh against my skin as I slipped it over my shoulders and quickly tied the cotton ribbons in front of me. Once suitably covered I sat on the chair in the corner of the cubicle, lost in my thoughts.

Our GP's phone call on Friday night had left me feeling shocked and concerned. He had called to say that my blood test results for the Alfa-Foetal protein levels were back and my dates were, in fact, correct rather than his, which had put me a month in advance of mine. 'I'm sending you for a scan on Monday' he said, 'you're just too big to be having one baby. I'm sure you must be having twins as the AFP levels are very high, which usually occurs in a twin pregnancy. Well, it can also indicate a problem - Spina Bifida or Down's Syndrome.' He told me this fact almost as an afterthought. 'So we'll have to repeat the blood test again when you reach sixteen weeks.' I was completely shell-shocked by his cheery message, which he delivered to me like a boxer's punch to the solar plexus. 'But what if there's something wrong with the baby?' I asked in a small voice. 'Oh I don't think you'll have to worry about that,' he said chirpily, I know there are no twins in the family, but they have to start somewhere don't they? He chuckled, 'Let me know how you get on.' I heard the phone click - then he was gone. Oh my goodness, how on earth would we cope with twins? The thought quite horrified me. But even worse was the niggling thought that our child may have a problem, and the ensuing difficult decisions that would have to be made if that were to be the case.

'Mrs Arthey!' A faceless voice called. I got up and padded barefoot towards the doorway, feeling as though I were about to be thrown into a den of lions. A tall girl with a ponytail and a nice smile greeted me. She was probably a little older than my twenty-four and three quarters years, although it was very difficult to tell as, like me, she wore no makeup and her hair was tied up with a thin piece of ribbon. 'Date check, it says here?' she smiled enquiringly. 'Well my GP thinks I might be having twins, and I've got a very high AFP level, so I'm really quite concerned there's something wrong with the baby.' 'Ok', she said calmly, 'Let's have a little look shall we? Hop up on the bed and get yourself comfy.'

I lay back in the darkened room ready for the scan. She shook the squeezy bottle that contained the gel and apologised as I flinched when the cold clear liquid hit my exposed stomach. Having drunk two pints of water two hours before the scan, I felt as if I could quite easily burst, and then the cold gel seemed to bring about an even stronger urge to relieve myself, as by now I had a near to bursting bladder. The scanning head rolled swiftly and smoothly back and forth over the bump, resonating blurry pictures on the small screen beside my head, angled so that both myself and the radiographer could see. 'The baby's very small,' she remarked as she continued her journey around my abdomen. Little bits that I thought could be a baby came into view, and then faded away again as she moved swiftly on. But wait a minute - there was the same bit I had just seen a moment ago, this time in another place. I enquired, 'So is it twins then?' 'Just a few minutes longer and I'll be able to tell you,' she answered. But a few minutes passed and I was none the wiser. By now a worried expression had appeared on her face, her cheerful chattering had stopped, being replaced by a frown of deep concentration. I asked again, 'So is it twins?' With that she jumped up. 'I'm just going to fetch my senior.' Well that confirmed it, there must be something really wrong.

I lay there waiting to take the terrible news as she returned with her colleague - a woman in her early forties, and obviously with a wealth of experience. She repeated the same process as her junior had done, hovering once or twice over one spot, then another, occasionally looking over her shoulder to catch the eye of her partner in crime, who in turn glanced back knowingly, raising their eyebrows in a silent language they shared. I asked again, this time wording it another way. 'So is there something wrong with the baby?' The older woman turned to her junior. 'Well go on then, have the courage of your convictions and tell her.' I had the overwhelming desire to cover my ears, like a child not wanting to hear it was bedtime. 'We think you're having triplets.' 'WHAT?' I half sat up, propping myself on my elbows, staring at the screen hoping for the information to become clear. 'We think we can see triplets, but we'll have to get the consultant radiographer to confirm it. Can we go and tell your husband, he can come through now?' The excitement at their discovery was tangible in their voices now that it was all out in the open, seemingly oblivious to my complete and utter shock.

Eddie came to join me; he smiled, 'We're having twins then?' 'No, it's triplets.' I answered. I could hear myself telling Eddie our news, but it was as if someone else's voice was speaking; in fact it must have been someone else. The voice I could hear sounded calm, matter of fact even. Whereas the one deep inside my head was screaming out – NOOOOOO this can't be happening, it must be a bad dream! The women had obviously decided to refrain from telling Eddie; probably having second thoughts about delivering the news in such a public domain, with other parents all waiting for the first view of their progeny. Upon the impact of the news, he sat promptly down on the bed, putting his head in his hands. 'But how are we going to cope, I mean three all at once, how on earth has this happened?' With an A level in biology I was rather surprised he was asking me this question.

I couldn't help but think of the woman who walked across our path when we visited my sister-in-law in Lincoln hospital, just two days after she had given birth to her first child - a son, William. It was earlier on in the year - February 28th. This woman was absolutely enormous as she waddled across the corridor in front of us to go into the patients' sitting room. 'See that lady there,' said my brother-in-law in a loud whisper, 'Well she's having triplets. Phew, can you imagine it? I mean what a nightmare that would be.' He had shaken his head and given a little chuckle. Now I was beginning to wonder whether a case of triplets could be catching, like a nasty cold. No, worse, more like a bad dose of flu! I must have just been pregnant, although only by a couple of weeks, but I was certainly blissfully unaware of the fact at this stage.

The consultant radiographer had now appeared; a smiley, ginger-haired man, who very swiftly confirmed that yes, indeed it was triplets. Although a little small for their dates, they all looked fine healthy beings, with strong heart beats, all spines intact and all appeared to have their own little amniotic sac. We were able to enjoy a brief guided tour around our ready-made family, whilst some quick measurements were taken.

***

Word spread fast as we knew one or two people who worked in the hospital, and once the senior radiographer had been for his coffee break and related the tale, it became grapevine news.

Eddie and I drank a cup of tea made for us by the department, as we, of course, by now held celebrity status. We smiled and laughed with the ladies, and chuckled to ourselves at our wondrous news, feeling quite elated by our new-found fame. Eventually we emerged into the sunlight, still full of laughter and merriment as we made our way back to our respective cars. Eddie to return to work and I to drive around in a daydream, dropping in on friends to share our remarkable news.

My mother had made a strange remark when I phoned her after having the conversation with our GP. 'Well darling,' she said, 'Prepare yourself for triplets and then twins wouldn't seem so bad.' I couldn't help but wonder how my mother had such insight, so I couldn't wait to phone her when she was back home from her art class later in the day to ask her this very question. It appears that she had seen my father's sister, aunty Kay, who had suddenly announced on hearing the fact that I was getting rather large for my dates, that she had forgotten to tell us some essential information. 'Apparently your father and aunty Kay's great grandmother was a triplet,' mum told me. The information had been passed to my cousin, but my aunty had forgotten every word about it when I became pregnant, until mum revealed my rapidly increasing size. Needless to say, triplets' chance of survival, over a hundred years ago was far less likely, with no ultrasound or neo natal units. My great, great grandmother was the lucky one, as she was the only one to survive.

Later on that evening Eddie and I decided we must visit his ninety-three year old grandmother to tell her our surprising news. She lived alternately with my parents-in-law and Eddie's aunt and uncle, which was where she was at the time. Grandma was such a sweet, little old lady, and in spite of her age was still very with it. Her hair was white and tightly permed, and her false teeth had a life all of their own as they often tried to make a break for freedom. Her hearing aid whistled loudly, almost matching the volume of the last night at the proms. We both thought the world of her and I think she felt the same about us too.

Although she was a great grandmother five times over, she was now extremely proud and excited that her only grandson was also going to become a father. But our latest news would be a huge shock for her. So Eddie crouched down next to her chair and took her hand in his before beginning. 'Grandma, we have something to tell you.' She leant further forward in order to make hearing a little easier. 'Ooh do you dear, how exciting.' Eddie leant a little nearer still, 'We're having triplets, grandma.' Grandma frowned a little and then moved even closer, her teeth clicked and jumped ominously and her hearing aid whistled for all it was worth. 'What was that dear, did you say you're having some piglets?' Eddie grinned, and then elaborately mouthed the words again, raising his voice to make himself heard above the overpowering whistle of her hearing aid. 'No grandma, we're - having - triplets.' This time she heard him, and flopped back in her chair, immediately dissolving into tears of joy, mopping her cheeks with her delicately embroidered cotton handkerchief. 'Ooh my dears, how on earth are you going to cope?' That was a question we had no answer for, as we had no idea either. Then she looked thoughtful. 'Of course my brother George was a twin, but his twin died at birth, he was your great uncle.' She looked at Eddie - we in turn looked at one another. Suddenly from out of the woodwork appeared yet another bit of family history, which may or may not have had some relevance to our situation. I had read in a magazine that the father's genes could influence the splitting of an egg, so if our triplets, or even two of our triplets, were to be identical, this definitely would have contributed to our situation. Suddenly a picture was beginning to take shape, quite clearly we were a lethal cocktail of genes, and now the mixing of them had turned us into an extremely efficient multiple baby making machine. One thing was sure, it was simply amazing that another set of triplets were to be born into a family twice within living memory.

***

We travelled around on our cloud of euphoria and stardom for another couple of days until thump, we hit the ground with a huge bump, reality hitting us fair and square in the face. How were we going to cope? I think the enormity of the situation really began to sink in when a few days after the scan, I felt what could only be the first movements from the little lives growing inside me. I was just fifteen weeks into the pregnancy. At first I thought it was a bad case of wind brewing, but then as the day progressed I kept on being aware of what felt like a large moth, fluttering around inside my stomach. It was early to feel this - the first signs of life - or so my pregnancy book told me. Eighteen to twenty weeks was generally normal for a first baby. But suddenly these little kidney beans with budding arms and legs were real, as day by day their kicks became stronger. With this growing reality my thoughts began to spiral. Were the triplets all going to be OK? What would their relationship be with one another? Would they fight with and resent one another, or would they be so close they wouldn't be able to cope with any kind of separation? Would Eddie and I have our favourites, making one feel left out and un-loved. Even more of a worry was would we even have enough love to go around? In fact just how difficult would it be to form an individual relationship with each child? The questions just went round and around my head until it ached.

At the age of twenty-nine Eddie was working as company accountant for a garage group, mainly based in Market Harborough, but travelling to Kidderminster twice a week. My career, on the other hand, was of the slightly less challenging variety. We had a small equine livery yard, at the pretty rose and ivy covered sandstone Northamptonshire farm house, which belonged to my parents–in-law. We had just enough of other people's horses to look after in order to pay for our two horses and to give me a small wage. My job would have to be put on hold, well certainly for the foreseeable future, but Eddie's was far too important to be affected by our impending full time family. Our home was not large, although we probably had just about enough space for three cots in the second bedroom, but we did have a lovely big garden, almost an acre which is why we had bought the little bungalow. We were half a mile out of the village, next to a stone masonry business, and also beside a redundant stone quarry which had strangely attractive qualities. There were large lagoons that attracted wildlife, and mountains of spoil and rock which, in winter time with snow and frost upon them, looked almost alpine. We were reluctant to leave there so we decided to see how we could manage with the space we had, before leaping to any rapid decisions. It had been the home of our dreams and we had taken quite a risk to buy it, taking on a mortgage that was far bigger than we had planned to have at this stage in our lives. But it was too good to miss, with its huge garden and open aspect, it was everything we had hoped for, so our readymade family would have to squeeze in for the foreseeable future.

MODULE 2:
PREGNANCY AND PRE-NATAL
EDUCATION

The phone was ringing again, probably another call to congratulate us on our news I thought, but to my surprise it was my midwife on the phone. 'Hello Gill, how are you?' She continued, not waiting for my answer. 'Now then, Doctor Taylor and I've been talking, and we think it would be a very good idea for you to start your ante-natal classes before you get too uncomfortable; after all we want you to have the full benefit from them.' She told me that there was a group starting on Friday if I would like go along.

The first class consisted of some exercises, and then a talk by Libby from the La Leche league. These were a group of women who were committed to promoting breast feeding. Libby sat on a chair in front of the semi-circle of trainee mothers, looking every bit as you would imagine she would. A mop of red curly hair, rosy cheeks and a velvet patchwork skirt. Her jumper was hand knitted, hanging loosely as it generously covered her rather round body. I sat quietly listening, and then concentration left me as I drifted into my own thoughts. What were we going to have for supper, should we have the steak that was in the fridge, or the remnants of the chicken we had had the night before? I know I should have been listening, but it really wasn't very relevant to me as I felt there was no way I could breast feed three. Suddenly something she said made me prick my ears up. 'It's such a rewarding experience ladies, I don't want it to ever end, so much so that I'm thinking of having another child. My five year old has just started school this year, and he has more or less weaned himself, well apart from a little feed at bed time. But my seven year old daughter still comes home from school every day, and has a feed before going to watch the TV.' I shifted uncomfortably in my chair, feeling a little embarrassed by Libby's revelation.

I carefully looked around to see if anyone else shared my discomfort. Just at that moment I caught the eye of another trainee mother sitting almost opposite me. She slowly raised her eyebrows - I raised mine back, in silent acknowledgement of the fact that we both thought, HOW BLOODY WEIRD IS THAT? We grinned, and then looked away, laughter not far from the surface. Just as I began to settle back into my daydreaming, the focus turned upon me. 'So Gill, what are you planning to do about feeding your three little bundles?' Never one to like the limelight I blushed at the sudden attention. 'Well, I was planning to bottle feed them actually, anatomy and all that not really lending itself to feeding three.' She looked shocked as if I'd just spoken in a foreign tongue. 'You mean you're not going to give it a go? It's not impossible you know, don't be put off by the anatomy thing. We've had loads of mothers who've fed twins.' 'Yes, but I'm having triplets,' I said. 'Oh don't worry about that, we can lend you a book written by a mother of triplets who fed them for eighteen months. That'll tell you just how it can be done, so don't let the numbers thing put you off. Oh do give it a try, it's so rewarding, you won't regret a moment of it,' Libby pleaded with me. 'I'll get your phone number and give you a ring in a few weeks when you've had time to read the book.' I thanked Libby profusely for her interest and gave her my number, 'accidentally' changing one of the digits - that should stop her getting hold of me, I thought. Although I realised she was being kind, I also realised she was a woman who was completely obsessed. Don't get me wrong, I wholeheartedly agreed with the thought that breast is best, and still do, but only if it's the best thing for all concerned, and the mother really wants to do it. In my case, it was not that I didn't want to do it, but I had to be realistic about what was humanly possible, and I did want a little bit of life outside mothering.

On reading the book it further confirmed that I'd made the right decision. This wonderful and giving mother had spent eighteen months of her life prone on a bed, while two nannies fed and watered her - delivering the children to her as and when they needed feeding, and if she wasn't feeding them she was attached to the pump, expressing milk for the nannies to feed to the odd one out. They had a large Victorian house that had a bedroom big enough for three cots, a bed for the mother, and room for a make-shift kitchen to be installed within its four walls. We, on the other hand, had a tiny room with hardly enough room to swing a cat; well certainly once the three cots were installed with a chest of drawers and a wardrobe. I finished reading the book, hoping to gain a little insight into being a mother of triplets, concluding that as their lives were so completely different to ours there was no real comparison at all. I packaged the book and sent it back to Libby with a letter of thanks, telling her that it had given me food for thought, and I would be sure to consider it.

A few days later my phone rang, 'Hi Gill, its Libby here. I phoned the midwife at the ante-natal classes to get your number. Silly old me, I must have written it down wrong. I've been trying to ring you for days until I realised

I'd made a mistake with the number.' I took a sharp intake of breath as I heard her voice, feeling quite terrible for being so mean. I feared she was going to stalk me, making me sign a contract promising to breast feed my triplets until they were at least eight years old. 'I'm so delighted that you've read the book, and that you're going to try to breast feed.' I frowned. Did I say that, I thought. 'Oh, um, yes well maybe, well we'll just have to see how it all goes, they may be very premature and not able to feed at all without the help of a tube.' The moment I'd said it I regretted it - she was off again. 'Oh that's no problem Gill, don't let it worry you as expressing is so easy. We do an electric breast pump loan, so just give me a ring and I can get one to you within a day. In fact, thinking about it, you'll need one anyway with three of them to feed. It'll be jolly handy to be able to express, and you'll probably have to top up when one's gone short. Breast milk freezes brilliantly, so you'll be able to express in between feeds and freeze some for the days when one of them is feeling extra hungry.' She had such enormous enthusiasm and I felt really mean not sharing it with her. 'Oh, that's a great comfort,' I lied. 'Well thank you so much for all your advice Libby, I'll give you a call if I need to borrow the pump when they're born, but I'll probably just buy one anyway - as you say it'll be very useful.' Once again I thanked her profusely and hung up, exhaling loudly, wondering if I had fobbed her off, or whether this was just the start of a long and very trying relationship. She clearly had my life as a dairy cow mapped out.

***

Not long after my first ante-natal class, a lady who I used to baby-sit for contacted me. She had heard through the hospital grapevine about our news. She was married to a doctor, and still lived in the house a few doors away from our old house, which I had spent my teenage years living in with my parents. The two children that I used to baby-sit for were teenagers themselves by now. But fate delivered Sandra and her husband a bit of a blow, when in their mid-forties they found they were to become parents again to twins. By now they were two years old, and clearly quite a handful for her. In-spite of this she was very keen for me to go over for the day. The plan was for us to go to the twins club coffee morning, so I could meet the other 'super mums' and then back to her house for a bit of lunch. She wanted to hand me down some outgrown equipment and as much helpful advice as she could give.

I arrived not long after 9.30 in order to help her get the sweet, impish, little identical boys organised and into the car, before setting off on the ten mile trip to the meeting. I have to admit I wasn't really a 'clubby' sort of person, and I wasn't at all sure that I would go to any more of the meetings, but it was very kind of Sandra to take me along. It would also be quite nice to meet some people who had been in the same situation as me.

We entered the large old rectory, as the two little boys ran confidently ahead of us towards the sound of children playing. This was home to the chairman of the local branch of the twins club, otherwise known as TAMBA, the Twins And Multiple Births Association. Jenny was a small lady, with mouse coloured hair cut into a short bob and a healthy rose blush to her cheeks. She was a lovely person, and quickly took me through to introduce me to the other women. 'Are there some mothers with triplets here?' I asked her, very much hoping to be able to get some advice, and maybe a little insight into what was just around the corner. 'Sadly we don't have any triplet members at the moment,' said Jenny. 'There was a set in Corby a few years back, but as far as I know there haven't been any born around here for some time. So you're very much the celebrity guest today, we're all in awe of you.' Oh dear, I thought. I was actually coming here to get some advice and have my worried mind put to rest, instead I was being put up on a pedestal as something to be in awe of. Jenny gave me a quick introduction to all the mothers and their small offspring. There were twins that looked the same but different, like Sandra's, as she chose to dress them in completely different clothes, which was our plan too. Then there were twins who looked exactly the same down to the last pink ribbon holding their pigtails in place. There were twins that didn't even look like siblings, let alone twins, one being a head taller than the other and with completely different coloured hair and eyes. Finally non identical twins, who were dressed identically along with their slightly older sister; all looking neat in their red cardigans, white polo shirts and little tartan kilts. It was quite interesting to observe the combinations, but it didn't take long for me to become the centre of attention. Then the inevitable questions began - of course one of the first being 'were you on the fertility drug?' and, 'did you have IVF?' I couldn't help but feel it wasn't really the sort of thing you should ask somebody you barely knew. I suppose in this particular company it wasn't quite so bad, as it was fairly likely that some of them may well have had either of the treatments. But when I was asked the same questions by the nosey manager in the village shop, I couldn't believe my ears; just how cheeky could someone be? Mind you I should have been forewarned, as he'd previously asked me if I my hair was naturally blonde!

However, the twins club group was generally populated by a pleasant bunch of women, and they made me feel very welcome. I sat quietly watching their children all interacting with one another, and I was keen to ask the collective of mothers whether they felt that the relationship between their twins was closer because they were twins, and did they have any spooky incidences. They were happy to regale me with tales. Some of the twins had their own language and I learnt how when one twin was away, the other showed signs of agitation. One mother told me that when one of her twins was in hospital, the other twin went completely off his food and appeared totally depressed, until his sibling returned home safe and sound.

***

Over the next few months we speculated about what our children might look like, and indeed what sex they might be. Eddie and I both had blond hair and blue eyes, so we decided our children had a pretty good chance of being blond with blue eyes too. Eddie was six feet tall and I about five foot seven, so they were likely to be of average height, with a build somewhere between skinny like me, and slightly better furnished like Eddie. But genetics work in odd ways and there could be throw backs, so nothing was certain. We were learning all the time, but something was telling me that I was about to start the most complex part of my education. I had been a poor student, failing again and again to impress my teachers, so how was I going to cope at this most advanced level of study? Would I be organised enough to manage the immense task that was before me? I was dizzy, I was chaotic, and at times, like the colour of my hair, completely blonde. You only had to look into my fridge to see how randomly my mind worked, with many varied and interesting objects lurking there, and with no sense of order at all. But the answers to my questions I was sure, would be just around the corner.

MODULE 3:
ORNITHOLOGY, YOUTH
EMPLOYMENT.

The summer had arrived, and a heatwave that was to
follow me through the entire pregnancy began. It became
hotter as I grew larger. I'd been advised by my specialist to
rest in the afternoons, particularly if I were to avoid
spending too much time in hospital on bed rest before the
babies were born.

I was to have my bag packed in readiness by twenty-
five weeks just in case, so I spent quite a lot of time on the
sun-lounger in the shade of the large Ash tree in our back
garden. One afternoon whilst I sat quietly reading, a
magpie landed in the tree just above
me. He looked very smart, like a young man dressed in a
dinner suit, with a shiny black jacket and a gleaming white
shirt. He tipped his head from side to side, taking in
everything around him, his bright eyes glistened with
interest. Suddenly, and much to my amazement, he

alighted from his perch above to sit on the end of the lounger. He weighed me up, turning his head from side to side, as he hopped sideways along the edge of the bed, until he was right by my hand which he gently pecked as he foraged around looking for food. 'Well you're a smart chap,' I said to him as I got off the bed in order to go into the kitchen, remembering that the mince was defrosting ready for our supper. It had thawed enough for me to roll up a few little balls of meat, and return to the garden with some lunch for my visitor. As I walked into the lean-to conservatory, I was surprised to see my friend had flown in and was sitting on top of the freezer. 'Here you are, try this.' I offered him a ball of mince which he took very gently from my fingers. Of course he had to be tame, but where had he come from? Mr Magee, as I decided to name him, soon realised that we gave good board and lodgings, and was generally around the garden or in the lean-to for the next week. At the weekend our neighbour, Alf, arrived back from his holiday. He was pottering around his garden and spotted Mr Magee sitting on my shoulder. He shouted across the hedge, 'I wondered what would become of the old magpie - we thought you'd probably take him in, he jumped in me van when I was doing the grocery round in the old village. I couldn't chuck him out could I? So I bought him back up here. Of course then me and Ev, went off on our holidays. Ev said you'd take pity on him and feed him.' As Ev had predicted, I did take pity on him and I did feed him, so now I had a new best friend who sat devotedly on my shoulder when I was in the garden. If I were to lie upon a rug on the lawn, Mr Magee would also lie down, fluffing himself up and spreading his wings out.

Several weeks after Mr Magee arrived our neighbour at the stone masonry business on the other side of our property called in. 'Afternoon Gill and how are you feeling?' Derek enquired, 'Oh not too bad thank you Derek, how are you?' 'Well I'm just fine thank you Gill. But we've got a bit of a problem, your magpie was seen poking about the yard this morning, and now the van keys are missing. Have you any idea where his cache is?' I felt awful, 'Oh dear Derek, I'm really sorry but I'm afraid I don't. Do you want me to help you look for them?' 'No, no don't worry, I'm sure they'll turn up,' he said patiently. Derek was a complete gentleman, in his early sixties, he was an extremely well spoken and educated man, with a kind and gentle manner. 'Would you like a cup of tea Derek?' I asked, hoping to smooth the situation. Derek gratefully accepted my offer and we took our tea out to the metal garden seat on the patio. As we sat chatting, the tea steaming in our china mugs, Mr Magee alighted on the back of the seat next to me. He gently nibbled my ear and preened my hair. Derek laughed. 'You've really got a friend there haven't you?' Mr Magee hopped along the back of the seat towards Derek, carefully eyed him up, and then gave him a sharp peck on the ear before hopping back to my side to nibble and preen my hair again. Derek held his ear, 'Ooh you little devil.' Mr Magee had clearly hurt him, so when he hopped back along the seat ready for a second attack, Derek leapt to his feet, throated the rest of his tea and made a quick farewell. As he scuttled away, Mr Magee flew after him, dive bombing him, and grabbing at his hair with his grasping claws. 'Bugger orf you dreadful bird,' I heard him say, as he ran off looking over his shoulder in readiness for the next attack. Poor Derek decided that either wearing a hat or phoning us was the better option after this experience.

***

Time was ticking by, so my midwife Mrs. Bradbury - a small and efficient little lady, with a thin, kindly face and steel grey hair, came to see me at home just as I reached twenty eight weeks. It was in order to see that our home and equipment was as well organised as possible for the babies' arrival. She looked at our stack of fluffy white terry nappies, which had completely taken over the small airing cupboard, and she laughed at my idea for a sterilizer. Our picnic cool box fitted eighteen bottles, teats and lids, and three small water bottles perfectly. The nursery was decorated in a Laura Ashley print paper, with small yellow and blue flowers, and the three cots were all lined up and in place, just waiting for their tiny occupants to arrive. We sat having a cup of tea after Mrs. Bradbury had finished her inspection. 'I really feel that you and Eddie should seriously consider having some help with either the babies - or if you can't accept that, at least some domestic help in the house.' We had actually made some enquiries about any help that we may be entitled to, but had pretty well hit a brick wall with it, as it was all means tested and pretty difficult to get. So Eddie and I had some discussion on the matter and, eventually decided to put an advert in the local paper, as much as anything just to see who, if anyone, applied.

The first person was an older lady; she was very keen to come and see us, so we invited her along for an interview. She arrived in an enormous and elderly tank of a car, and much like her car, she too was enormous and pretty elderly. Within minutes it was very apparent that she would want to completely take over, and I could see it wouldn't be long before I would have to ask her permission to pick up, feed, or even cuddle my babies. She had very fixed and, quite frankly, old fashioned ideas. 'I think babies should be left to cry, there's nothing worse than spoiling them,' she said emphatically. Then she told us that, 'I topped all my children's bottles up with Farex, which soon got them going through the night, so I'd recommend you do that as soon as possible too. It'll save all that getting up in the early hours.' This was something we definitely wouldn't be doing, so we politely thanked her and showed her the door! After several more abortive enquiries from women aspiring to be nannies, I began to think it would be easier to manage on my own, rather than fight off some rather over bearing mother's help. Then, just as I had decided It was safer and easier to cope with the babies myself, and just have a bit of domestic help instead, we received a call from a young girl. Sue was seventeen years old and had recently completed a caring skills course. We asked her if she would like to come and have a chat with us. She was dressed in a little blue pinafore dress, white blouse, and her fine blonde hair was cut into a neat bob. She had kind eyes, a ready smile, and a lovely sense of humour - we both took to her immediately. Sue was the youngest of five siblings and clearly loved babies and children. She'd been helping a neighbour at weekends and during the college holidays with their toddling twins. I looked to the heavens and said a quick prayer of thanks - she was absolutely perfect, so we offered her the job, which thankfully she readily accepted, understanding that we would contact her as soon as the babies were born.

***

We were still enjoying our social life, aware that once the children arrived we would be confined to barracks for some time. One late summer evening, we were out enjoying a quiet drink in a pretty little country pub, with some of our long term friends. John had fairly recently taken up with a new girlfriend; although we all felt she was pretty transient, we didn't really like her, and to be honest she didn't fit in particularly well with us. She was one of those girls who always had an opinion on everything. The husbands/boyfriends were all at the bar just hanging out and being men, while all of us women sat at a table quietly discussing how much longer I could possibly hang on to the pregnancy. I was really getting pretty huge by now. Then Charlene decided to share another one of her opinions with us. 'Of course you must have realised by now that you probably won't end up with all three babies surviving haven't you?' All the others looked on in shocked horror. Sarah bristled and immediately tore her off a strip. 'I don't think Gill really needs to think about that sort of thing, do you?' Charlene was un-abashed. 'Well I just thought she ought to be aware of the fact, and then she won't feel too disappointed if she only ends up with one or even two. I mean, the chance of all three surviving is, well, really pretty unlikely isn't it?' At this point I felt it was time for me to fight my corner for myself. 'Charlene, of course it's crossed my mind. In fact all sorts of things keep crossing my mind. And yes, I am very well aware of what could be the potential outcome. Perhaps I'm just being a bit naive, but if God, or fate, or whatever it is that has decided I should have triplets, hadn't felt that I had a fair chance of being able to carry them, then I don't think I would have been gifted with them. Anyway if you don't mind I'd like to bring the conversation to an end and enjoy what may well be my last evening out for some time.' Charlene just shrugged, took a gulp of her wine, and was not in the least bit bothered that she had just been brought down by a peg or two. However, I really hoped that my blind faith did have some substance to it and that I wouldn't be terribly sad and disappointed after all this.

By now sleep was getting difficult, and I found it so hard to get comfortable. If I was able to get comfortable it only lasted for a short time before I needed to get up and have a wee. My heartburn had now reached new heights, necessitating me being joined at the hip to the bottle of Gaviscon. My meals had to be extremely small now, although I was almost permanently hungry, so the need for food was frequent. When I sat in a chair my stomach rested beyond the end of my knees. I had gone from a 24" waist to a 48" waist in a few short months, and I could feel what I can only assume were bands of muscle pinging as they stretched - although I was only three stone heavier than what I weighed at my first ante-natal appointment. At times I felt quite breathless, especially when the baby who was in the head down position decided to push its bottom right up under my ribs. Then the baby who was at the bottom of the pile seemed to have taken to using my bladder as a trampoline for its entertainment, vigorously bouncing up and down, until I was taken almost to the point of no return!! Then, as if that wasn't enough physical torture, this little person would give me an almighty kick in the backside – from the inside out. When I lay on the bed and tried to rest, all three woke up and proceeded to dance an Irish jig. When I lay on my side, the weight of my ever expanding abdomen pulled the over tight skin, making me feel as if I might tear apart. A large bolster pillow became my saviour in the last few weeks - I draped it over my shoulders, sleeping almost upright with a few pillows stuffed behind me, whilst I rested my head from side to side. But nature works in funny ways and I think the sleeplessness was preparing me for what was to come, getting my body used to less hours of deep sleep. From behind it was barely apparent that I was pregnant, but from the front I looked as if I had an enormous beach ball stuck up under my dress. The sight was enough to turn heads, and I was beginning to feel a little too conscious of my size, so I didn't want to go out much. In spite of this I could still sit on the floor, and jump up off the doctor's couch un-aided. I also managed to walk a whole equine cross country course, (which was just over a mile) and even managed to climb over some of the fences, with only minimal help, much to everyone's amazement. But I was so desperate now to be able to bend in the middle again, and to curl my back into a nice C curve. By now their arrival would be a welcome relief, just so long as I could keep them cooking until it was safe for them to be out in the big wide world.

MODULE 4:
OBSTETRIC SURGERY

In the early hours of Monday September 26th 1983, our babies decided it was time to begin their journey into the big wide world. There was no warning other than a bad case of the grumps during the day. Eddie had gone off to play cricket in the tiny village of East Langton. His parting words were 'You're not going to have them today are you?' I had been particularly snappy with him, 'How should I know, I said, 'I've never done this before.' He had left a little reluctantly as I wasn't usually like this with him. I knew there was no phone in the tiny cricket pavilion, which was situated in nothing more than a glorified sheep's field and it was long before the invention of mobile phones. 'You could phone Helen if anything happens. She's only just down the road, I'm sure she'll come and get me.' He looked guilty as he left, and I felt cross. How dare he leave me when I was feeling so dreadful I thought? But nothing happened and he was home early, having not even stopped for a quick drink, which then made me feel guilty.

We decided to have an early night as I was feeling really tired. Actually for the first time in about six weeks I had managed to get comfortable in bed and was able to lie on my side. Then suddenly, seven weeks before they were due and at precisely 2.20 am, there was an almighty gush as my waters broke. Eddie was out of the bed faster than Jiminy Cricket could jump, 'Oh good grief what do you want me to do - are you all right, shall I ring the hospital?' He looked pale and shocked. 'Ok' I said 'You go and phone the hospital, while I go and have a quick bath.' 'Shhhhhh,' Eddie sucked hard on his teeth, 'I don't think you should do that,' he said, panic exuding from his voice. 'Are you really sure you're safe to, what if you have them in the bath?' Convincing Eddie that I would literally jump in and out whilst he phoned the hospital wasn't easy, but I did so and was able to lay there for a brief time, enjoying the warm water on my aching back. I watched my stomach moving vigorously around – it looked just like a sack full of ferrets as it wriggled about. Little fists with knuckles moved back and forth, just underneath the tight skin, a little heel and then an elbow. It was fun imagining what part of them I could see moving beneath the surface. I thought how funny it was that the water always made them so lively. Except for the time when I swam in the icy cold sea on holiday in Brittany, they quickly formed a little huddle in the middle of my stomach and didn't move for about an hour. I expect they were paralysed with the shocking cold, permeating in from the outside.

'Come on Gill,' Eddie was getting agitated as he paced up and down outside the bathroom, 'They're expecting us at the hospital, hurry up.' I climbed out of the water with a mixture of feelings, half dread and half excitement. Sometime during this day I would probably meet my little family for the first time.

***

Once we were on our way to the hospital my nerves really started to escalate. The children were going to be early and, although they had a very good chance of survival, nothing was certain.

We walked into the large, grey brick building which was dimly lit, although there was still quite a buzz about the place, in spite of the fact that it was only 3.00am. We were shown to a room – The Birthing Suite, with its large ugly flowered wallpaper. I was given a floral patterned gown to change into, which clashed terribly with the walls. The idea was to make it seem friendlier, more a home from home experience, but the cloying smell of the hospital disinfectant was still there, hanging like London smog, waiting to creep into every part of you. Up your nose, in your hair and into your clothing, nowhere was sacred from the smell which I so hated. In the next door room a woman was yelling. 'Good grief, that sounds awful,' I said to my midwife. Vicky had been put in charge of us and our delivery. I liked her - she was very down to earth and pragmatic, with short dark hair, freckles, a big smile and a ready laugh - I was definitely going to get along with her. 'Oh don't take too much notice of that, the lady's Indian and I believe it's part of the culture to make a lot of noise.' 'Really' I said, frowning a little, not sure if she just saying this to make me feel better.

We settled down for the wait as, one after the other, we had visits from many and varied people. Firstly our consultant Mr. Wilkin came, a tall, slim man with a quiet, calm voice, a kind face and fine, light brown hair. Then the anaesthetist Jim came, equally as tall but bigger in stature, much more the build of a rugby player with his big bushy beard and rosy cheeks. He administered my epidural and frequently popped by to make sure it was topped up enough to keep the pain at bay. Vicky, who was with us pretty well constantly, wired me up to the baby heart monitors so she could track all three beats. Then a friend of ours, Andy, popped by - she was to be the theatre sister on duty with our consultant. We also had several visits during the day from a horsey friend of ours; Sue was also a midwife at the hospital. Then finally our GP arrived - in fact it had become quite the party room, with lots of chatter and laughter, until suddenly Vicky noticed one of the babies' heart beats was beginning to dip with every contraction. A hush fell as she hurried to summons our consultant.

I lay quietly watching the clouds scudding past the window, wondering what was going to be decided about the four of us. The long heatwave had finally broken about ten days before, and I'd enjoyed a short respite from the exhausting heat with the arrival of some cooler weather, relieved to be able to get the last few jobs done without feeling so exhausted.

My consultant arrived. They all spoke in muffled tones, discussing what our fate was to be. They finally turned and walked towards us, my obstetrician as chief spokesman. 'We think it's going to be safer to give you a Caesarean section now. The babies are beginning to show some distress, particularly the one who's in lead position, we're also not quite sure if he or she has tried to turn and is now presenting shoulder first.' He sympathetically put his hand upon mine, 'I know it's not what you want but we have to think about the babies' safety.' 'Oh' I said as I stared into the distance, deep within my thoughts. He was quite right, I wasn't keen to have a section, not because I wanted to be a wonderful earth mother and have a totally natural delivery, but because I was absolutely and completely terrified, convinced that I was sure to die. 'Do you want to have your epidural topped up, or do you want a general anaesthetic?' His voice cut through my racing thoughts. There was no decision as far as I was concerned, I was going to have the epidural topped up. Try as hard as he could, Eddie couldn't persuade me to have the general anaesthetic, 'Please Gill,' he pleaded 'Don't stay awake, you won't like it, please go to sleep.' But I had made up my mind and there was no changing it. For some reason I felt I was probably less likely to die if I were to stay awake, and if I did die, then there was a good chance that I would at least meet my babies before I faded away and met my inevitable end. Within minutes the chariots rolled, like a lamb to the slaughter I was on my way to theatre. Eddie came as far as the white line and then said an emotional farewell, as he stood and watch me and our little litter disappear to our fate.

***

The theatre was very bright and shiny and, to my surprise, extremely full of people. Three people for each baby and a team of people for me, all looking rather green in their theatre gowns, only contrasted by the little white wellies they were all wearing. As the surgeon worked, we chatted, the anaesthetist Jim, David my GP and me. It was all very convivial. We passed around photos of Jim's most recently born daughter, and laughed when another lot of waters broke. 'Oh, so that's why they've all got wellies on,' I said as the 'Team' jumped out of the way, water sloshing onto the floor. Poor Mr. Wilkin, who was also called David, seemed somewhat surprised by the joviality as he worked. Every so often he chuckled at our comments and then returned to his deep concentration, until finally one by one our babies arrived. There was no little Elizabeth, Lucy or even Victoria. But Benjamin Edward was born at 4.00pm, Christopher Philip at 4.02pm and Thomas David at 4.04pm. They were small but perfectly formed, born at thirty three weeks they were going to need special care, but God willing they should all survive. I had a quick look at them, gave them all a kiss before they were popped into an incubator and whisked away to the neo-natal intensive care unit.

Strangely enough I wasn't at all surprised to find that they were all boys. Our second scan had been performed on a new machine. The dark little scanning room was packed full of doctors and radiographers all wanting to see the new acquisition in action. One of the doctors was really excited about the clarity of the new machine's picture. He leapt towards the screen pointing out with a delighted grin on his face as he said 'This one's a boy', only then to realise that he had just broken hospital protocol, as it was policy at the time to never reveal the sex of the baby to its parents. Clasping his hand over his mouth, he then muttered an apology through his fingers. Once I knew one was a boy, something, an instinct maybe, told me that they all were boys. I knew I would get along with boys as I had been, and still was, a tomboy at heart, always preferring to play footy rather than sitting making daisy chains with the girls. I knew we would have some really fun times together.

MODULE 5:
NHS SYSTEMS, PAEDIATRIC NURSING.

Eddie was sitting outside the hospital in the car, having just lit a calming cigar. Our friend Sue was beckoning to him, her blonde, curly hair blowing in the cool wind. He emerged from the car, stamping out the cigar and throwing it in the bin as he hurried towards her. He felt sure something must be wrong, he had only just had time to walk back to the car and light up, but now there she was, urging him to be quick. His heart was beating fast and his mouth became dry as he ran toward her, 'Come on Eddie' she urged, 'Come and meet your little family, quickly, they're just going down to special care, we can go with them.' Eddie was amazed at the speed of their arrival. As they ran into the warm hospital and along the corridor, the incubator, containing his three little 'piglets,' was just coming towards them. Sue informed him, as they caught their breath, that he was the proud daddy to three perfect little boys. Once down in special care the boys were weighed in - Ben at 3lb 12oz, Thomas 3lb 14oz, and Christopher 4lb 8oz. There were a few necessary things to do - drips were put up, heart beats and breathing was monitored, and oxygen gently flowed into their incubators. But they were all doing well, and Eddie was soon able to come and give me the news, with a Polaroid picture of each little boy taken by the special care staff.

Twenty-six hours after their birth, I was wheeled down to meet my boys in the intensive care unit. Cleanliness was of utmost importance and every one entering had to wash their hands in the pink Hibiscrub solution, and then put on a large blue gown to cover their clothing. It was understandably very warm in there, as all the babies were only wearing their oversized nappies, while the machines bleeped and flashed. Some really tiny babies had little woollen hats on, and others had their eyes covered as they lay under ultra violet lights. One or two had wires all over them as their chests heaved with the effort of breathing. The machines registered their heart beats, as they went bleep, bleep, bleep in time with the small pumping organ, the line on the screen rising and falling in time with the bleeping. The boys were in a little room, together but in separate incubators. 'Here she is' one nurse said, 'A very proud mummy, come and meet your little boys, they're absolutely gorgeous.' Another nurse, dressed in a tunic with teddy bears printed on it, put the boys upon me on a large pillow which lay across my lap. I couldn't believe how tiny they were, their arms no thicker than my thumbs, heads no bigger than oranges. I sat there, feeling quite overwhelmed as I realised my masters in motherhood had well and truly begun. It was to be awarded and delivered from the 'University of Life'. I would be lectured in varying mediums, with many visiting lecturers having the desire to educate me. Experiences visual, studied and practical were to be my tools for learning. Again my poor academic record sprung to mind, as I wondered how I was to cope at this advanced level of study.

Having one baby was pretty mind blowing and a steep learning curve for every first time parent. But three all at once - this was certainly going to be a very hard earned master's degree. We did have a few definite ideas on things, but most importantly we wanted them to be brought up as individuals. Even if they had all turned out to be identical, we still wanted to encourage individuality. As it was, Ben and Thomas were identical and Christopher was not. Ben and Thomas were like two peas in a pod and Christopher slightly larger and with more hair, but they all had fair colouring and looked very much alike.

***

I sat gazing upon my little litter of 'piglets' as they snuffled, squeaked and grunted. At that moment the SCBU sister came to see me. She was a rather stern looking, middle aged woman, with a small pair of specs balanced on the end of her nose. 'Now Gill, we would like you to try and express some milk for the boys, we only have a limited supply of donated milk, so a bit of mum's milk would be very good for them.' 'Donated milk, you mean the boys are drinking someone else's milk?' Ugh, how revolting I thought. 'Ok' I said, without hesitation 'I'll do it.' They led me through to a little cramped room, which was full of old equipment. There were un-used incubators sitting empty, like waiting taxis outside a station, ready for the next train to arrive. At the back of the room was a chair next to a small table which had an electric breast pump on it, clearly ready for my arrival. 'Right my dear, let's have a look at your night dress, does it open up down the front?' 'No it doesn't,' I said 'To be perfectly honest I wasn't intending to feed them, so I didn't think it would be necessary.' The sister gave me a disapproving look, 'Oh well, I expect we can manage, you'll just have to hitch it up so we can get at your boobs.' Oh good grief I thought, this was really going to take me out of my comfort zone, but there wasn't much I could do about it now. Eddie sat beside me, 'Come on Gill, I know you don't like this sort of thing, but just think that you're doing it for the boys.' He was right, so the electric pump was attached to my extremely small bosom – it was at this point I began my career as a dairy cow. A tiny amount of milk was gathered and whisked away for the boys, to be shared between them. I felt very virtuous, pleased with my efforts, thinking Libby would be so very proud of me. Every time I went down to the special care unit I went along to the parlour - until one evening Eddie and I sat in there whilst I was being milked. To my horror another couple came in to the tiny room so they could use another milking machine. 'Evening,' they nodded across the cramped room towards us. I blushed to puce red, as I tried in vain to cover myself with my nightdress, which was again hitched up to somewhere around my ears. I'd asked Eddie to go out and find me a night dress with a front opening, but – well, men and shopping, he'd come back with one that had only three buttons at the top, and an opening that finished just about where my small and insignificant cleavage began. So with my tiny anatomy there wasn't much chance of stretching that far, hence I was still in an exposed position. This was just about the final straw as we sat opposite the other mother and her husband, smiling politely at one another. The milking machine continued to pump. I looked down at the half an inch of milk at the bottom of the receptacle, 'I'm doing a bit better today,' I whispered to Eddie. 'Ummm' he said absent-mindedly as he read the paper. I glanced over to the other couple - my eyes nearly popped out. I was astonished. The other mother had only been on the pump for a few minutes but there, attached to her boob, was nearly a full bottle of milk. I on the other hand had already done one boob and was on to my second one. Looking down again I realised that I must be an extremely poor yielder, and I may as well give up now. This was lucky, as that same evening the sister came to see us. Taking my hand gently she said, 'Now Gill, it doesn't matter if you really want to carry on, but we've totally run out of the donated milk and, well, you're just not producing enough for all of them on your own, so we're going to have to top them up with the formula milk.' She looked at me with heartfelt sympathy. I on the other hand just had heartfelt relief. 'That's absolutely fine' I replied, 'That's just what they're going to get at home so it's really not a problem.' Thus ending my milking career – I was just so thankful that I wasn't a cow, as I would have been on the way to the pie factory by now.

***

Andy, the theatre sister came to see me a few days after the boys were born, 'I've heard of ginger twins, but ginger triplets, wow! Clever old you.' 'Ginger?' I said feeling quite indignant, 'They're not ginger, they're blond.' Andy smiled as she replied 'Well they were pretty ginger the other day when I popped in, you should have seen them all lying there sunning themselves in their incubators.' She laughed at my reaction as she left the room. As soon as she had gone I quickly shuffled off down to special care for another look. I was beginning to walk a little more upright now, although I still felt the need to hold gently on to my tummy, which had been stretched to the point of no return and was now like a sad, deflated balloon days after the party was over. I viewed the boys critically from all angles; above them, from the side, with the light behind them and in front of them. No, I really couldn't see it, but then the sun came out and shone into the room, catching the back of their little heads as they slept. She was right, there it was - GINGER HAIR. The throw backs that we had pondered upon, whilst imagining what, if any, of our features they would inherit had appeared. My grandfather on my mother's side had thick sandy hair as a young man, so there it was manifesting itself in our triplets. I wondered what other genetic features would filter through in the coming months, maybe my aunt's brown eyes, or my grandmother's tiny stature, we would just have to wait and see.

***

The boys did well, and after three weeks were nearly ready to come home. So the staff suggested we should bring Sue, our new mother's help in with us. They wanted her to have some expert instruction from them before being cast loose, along with us, to fend for ourselves. The boys were still fairly difficult to feed, having to have the teat expertly guided in once their tongues had dropped down from the roof of their mouths. Winding them was also a fine art. They had to be sat really upright and the heel of our hand pressed firmly into their tummies, which seemed a failsafe way to producing a large belch. They were also really tiny to bath, so it seemed to be a very good idea to introduce Sue whilst we were all still under supervision.

Ben still had a nasal tube in, through which the nurses gave him most of his feeds, although when we were there we always fed him with a bottle. It was becoming clear that he didn't really want the tube in his tiny nostril, as he kept on pulling it out. But now his nose was becoming really sore as the nurses had to repeatedly put it back in again. I pleaded with them 'Can't he manage without it, please let me have a go at feeding him all day. Can't we just see if he's able to cope?' Although the nurses were sceptical they agreed, and Ben was determined to show us that he knew what was best. He coped admirably, taking more feed than he had ever done before. Funnily enough every time Tom took a bit more milk, Ben did the same; they really were quite identical. The tube was cast out, like a dead snake it laid coiled up, lifeless at the bottom of the bin. I was glad to see the back of it, as the tape that stuck it to his skin made his peachy soft complexion sore, and his little nose red raw. Thankfully that nasty viper was now gone for good.

***

I arranged to pick Sue up on the way in to the hospital. She was going to wait near the bus stop in her village. As I drove towards the bus shelter I looked out for the sweet little blonde girl, but she wasn't there. I drove slowly past - the only person at the bus stop was a girl with black spiky hair, a loud checked coat, black leggings and black pumps. I started to worry that Sue had changed her mind. Perhaps she had decided that helping with triplets was just too big a challenge. As I drove away, I looked in the mirror to see the girl at the bus stop peering down the road after me - she looked bemused. Suddenly the penny dropped – it was her, our sweet little mother's help, had turned into a punk! I reversed back up the road, stopping next to her- she smiled as she got in. 'I thought you'd forgotten me,' She laughed, 'I bet you didn't recognise me. D'you like my hair? I did it myself last week.' She ran her fingers through the fine black spikes, which were stiffened with gel. They sprang neatly back into place again. I muttered something about being tired and not concentrating. The truth was she looked so completely different that I really hadn't recognised her. But her lovely personality which we had been so attracted to hadn't changed, and we were soon getting along famously. She thanked me for including her, then she told me that she'd been in to the hospital to look at the boys through the SCBU window with her mother. Eddie had phoned her the evening the boys were born, letting her know that they had arrived, and he was delighted at how audibly excited she seemed to be.

***

There was one other thing that had to be tackled before the boys were allowed home, and that was Eddie. He thought it was going un-noticed, the fact that he had managed to evade changing a nappy for nearly four whole weeks. But nothing was missed by the watchful eyes of the special care nurses. The night before they were due to come home we were asked to go in and run through everything. Like making up the bottles of milk and using the sterilizer. In hindsight, it was just a bit of a ruse to get Eddie there as a pupil. We had just finished giving them their supper time bottles when I noticed two of the nurses hovering by the door. I was also aware of a bit of interest from the other parents with babies in the neighbouring rooms, as they peered through the glass windows. As Eddie put Ben back into his incubator and slowly wandered over towards Christopher, I saw the two nurses performing what can only be described as a scissor movement on him, cutting him off as he moved dreamily across the room. Taking an arm each they swiftly turned him back in the direction of Ben, 'Oh no you don't Eddie,' one of them said, 'It's time you learned to change a nappy. Poor Gill can't do them all herself.' Eddie groaned, 'Ooh do I have to, Gill's much better at it than me?' 'That's only because Gill's had a lot more practice than you - come on don't make a fuss.' The two nurses had ganged up on him as a united force, ready to fight my corner for me. So Eddie had a lesson in nappy changing that he was sure never to forget.

As Eddie got the clean nappy on and neatly pinned up, Ben turned red, strained a little and delivered a small poo right into the middle of it. 'Oh dear' said the nurses grinning, 'You'll just have to do it again.' By now all the other parents were watching through the glass windows, they too were laughing. So Eddie went through the same process again, carefully folding the nappy, cleaning Ben with cotton wool and water, drying him, powdering him and then putting the next clean nappy on. No sooner had Eddie popped the nappy pin in, turned to give a proud bow to his audience, then Ben turned red again, strained a bit more and this time filled his nappy with an even bigger poo. He was determined that the audience should have their encore. Eddie looked on in disbelief, 'Oh no, I don't believe it, the little bugger's done that on purpose.' Knowing what I know of Ben's character now, I wouldn't be at all surprised.

By the weekend they were ready to come home. For the second time in six months we found ourselves feeling like minor celebrities. We were escorted to the hospital doors by an entourage of nurses, some carrying the babies, and some just coming along to say their farewells. Other parents watched as we left the safety of the hospital. 'Bye and good luck, please bring them back to see us won't you?' called the nurses. With a promise to do so and after a few hugs for our special nurses, we departed.

As we drove out of the hospital confines I felt butterflies in my tummy. The prospect of being alone, without the safety net of the hospital and its wonderful staff, was really scary. But we'd been very organised, and had made all the day's supply of 18 bottles and three small boiled water bottles before leaving home, the nursery was warm, and the cots were ready. But were we?

MODULE 6:
FURTHER PAEDIATRIC NURSING AND
PAEDIATRIC SURGERY.

The weather had taken a rapid down-turn since the heat wave of the summer. It was unseasonably cold, with a brisk wind beginning to whip the leaves from the trees, which left them looking skeletal with their bare branches. It was as if I had been in a time warp. Although I had been out of hospital for three weeks, visiting the boys daily had been my total focus, and it was as if life had passed me by. Mr. Magee had almost given me up for lost and had taken to spending hours sitting on the neck of our pregnant horse, Polly. But now we were home things could return to normal.

Sue and I sat every day in the nursery feeding the boys,

as Mr. Magee leaped up and down outside the window, scratching and banging with his beak. He had suddenly become very interested in the hive of activity and, sadly, was beside himself with jealousy. Leaping and pecking at the glass, only quietening when I went to the window to talk to him. He was also dive bombing Sue every time she set foot outside. She was terrorised, 'Will you watch out for him Gill, I know he's going to come and get me again.' 'It's no good Gill' Eddie said 'He's got to go, you can't expect Sue to put up with this, and what if we want to put the boys outside in their pram. He might come and peck their eyes out.' I couldn't argue, he was right, but I felt really guilty as the bird was completely devoted to me. We decided that Eddie would entice Mr. Magee with something shiny. He would then try to grab hold of him and take him down to the old village where Alf had found him. He would no doubt find plenty of people around and hopefully there would be a good source of food for him there, but more importantly he would probably find himself a mate.

***

The end of our first week had arrived and we'd survived it and we felt we had every reason to feel very proud of ourselves. The bottle sizes were increasing and the boys were feeding better with every day, so we had a lot to be pleased about, although the continual lack of sleep was beginning to catch up with us. We dozed in the chairs by the open fire, with the television murmuring to itself in the background. We rarely watched it between the 8.00pm and 11.30pm feed. At this point we woke the boys for their last feed before turning in for the night. This feed always took about an hour and a half, as they were at their sleepiest. Once they had finished we fell into bed, exhausted, and slept until they woke again. As soon as we heard the first signs of murmuring we got up. It was usually Christopher, generally around 4.00am. Thomas was always stirring as well so he was fed too, leaving the sleepiest, Ben, until last. But we had established a routine very quickly, and both our midwife and health visitor were amazed and congratulatory about the speed with which we had managed to do so. I was also very relieved to note that, surprising though it might seem, we did have enough love to go around, with absolutely no feelings of favouritism towards any one of them. In fact, that over-all parental gush of love for our children had kicked in very quickly for both of us, as they had all seemed so small and vulnerable, lying there in the incubators.

The second week began and Eddie had gone back to work, having had a few days at home to help with the boys now they were back with us. Sue was completely integrated into the team, and had volunteered to get picked up in the evening an hour and a half later than we had first arranged - she felt we needed her help until later in the day. Yet again I was so thankful we had been blessed with her. On the Tuesday of the second week, whilst changing Ben's nappy, I noticed a small blood blister had formed on his almost healed tummy button. 'What do you think this is?' I asked Sue, looking closely at it for a clue as to how it had appeared. Sue bent and looked closely too, 'Don't know, do you think you ought to phone someone?' So I went and phoned my health visitor, who said she would pop by in a while, just to check it. She was a thin and rather anxious looking woman, and although she was very pleasant, she always seemed to lack self-confidence, being very hesitant about most things that I asked her. It wasn't quite what I needed as a novice first year 'Motherhood Masters student'. Later in the afternoon I decided to phone her again, as by now Ben was becoming rather grizzly, and the little possets that both he and Tom had been prone to for the last few weeks were turning into more meaningful amounts of sick. As I went to the phone by the front door, I noticed an envelope through the letter box. It contained a wodge of sterile wipes. Why on earth hadn't she come in, I thought, but then I remembered that both Sue and I had popped to the top of the garden whilst the boys were sleeping to muck out my pregnant horse Polly. I was teaching Sue the art of stable management as part of her training, which she seemed to be enjoying even though she declared she was 'terrified of 'orses.' Mrs. Cannon didn't seem to have thought to come around to the back door, the door she had always used until this day. She must have assumed we were out, or perhaps she was in a hurry and it was just more convenient to not find us. She can't have felt too worried about Ben though, I thought, so I hoped cleaning his tummy button with the sterile wipes would suffice. During the evening the blood blister burst, so I cleaned the site really well with the wipes, then with micropore tape stuck another one over it for good measure, carefully folding the nappy down to avoid touching his sore little button. But his sickness was increasing, and by the morning he seemed much quieter, sleepy even, not really waking for his bottle, in which he now seemed pretty disinterested.

By Wednesday he was worse still and at times he looked almost blue. His vomiting had been quite profuse in the night too – in fact almost as soon as he had taken a little bit of the bottle it came right back. The next morning I made an appointment to see our GP, rather hoping he would say he would come out to see us as Ben was still only just over five pounds, and not yet up to his due date. But he didn't, so I wrapped Ben up warmly, as by now the weather was foul - a cold drizzle falling through a dank fog. I carried him carefully through the town to the doctor's surgery, wrapped in a soft blue blanket that covered his tiny bonneted head. Only his little eyes and nose were exposed. As I walked quickly towards the surgery, a small and ferrety faced woman passing by said in a loud and disapproving voice, 'Fancy having a tiny baby like that out in this weather, shame on you!' I was furious, how dare she, she had no idea why I was out with him, 'Well try telling my doctor that,' I quickly retorted in an angry voice. She looked slightly embarrassed and scuttled off, but it left me feeling hurt that someone would think I would do anything that would be detrimental to my beautiful and tiny baby. As I sat in the dull, uncomfortable waiting room, people around me were sneezing and coughing. I covered Ben's face as much as I could without suffocating him, feeling even more certain that if he wasn't seriously ill now, he soon would be.

'Mrs. Arthey and Benjamin,' the intercom called. I walked into the small dimly lit room, 'Come on in' said Doctor Taylor, as he pulled the empty chair slightly closer to his desk, patting the seat, indicating he wanted me to come and sit near to him. 'So what's the problem with this little chap?' he asked. I described all the symptoms while he listened in silence. He looked concerned. 'Well we'd better strip him down to his nappy so I can have a better look, but overall I don't think anything can be too seriously wrong with him, he's a lovely colour.' It was true, most of the time he was a lovely colour, but every so often it would change, taking on this blueness, at which point he looked really poorly. Although his tummy button was almost completely healed again, there was still the vomiting. 'Oh I don't think that's anything to worry about, try throwing two ounces of milk on the floor and then tell me he's bringing up his whole bottle. It's amazing how a little fluid goes a long way.' said Doctor Taylor, 'Premmie babies often are a little sickie for a while, after all everything's a bit under developed. I'm sure once he's a few weeks older it'll all stop. Anyway just to be absolutely sure, I think we'll ask his paediatrician to come out to your home this afternoon to see him.' I felt a surge of relief. Doctor Cotton, our paediatrician, was such an experienced man and I had huge faith in him - if Ben were seriously ill then I was sure he would know.

I went back home and waited for a call from Doctor

Taylor, to tell me what time Doctor Cotton was coming. In the meantime I couldn't resist the temptation to do just as he'd suggested. I threw one of Ben's bottles of milk into the muslin nappy that I was using as a bib. The little terry towelling bibs we had were absolutely useless at containing all the milk when Ben erupted. Most of it seemed to shoot over the sides and miss the bib all together, and as there was so much volume anyway, the tiny bibs had no chance of holding it all. I held on to the muslin which was much more efficient, as the milk spilled over the edges before the excess liquid was soaked up. This just went to prove that I was right, the bottle was probably slightly less in quantity than the amount Ben was ejecting every few hours.

***

Doctor Cotton was due to arrive at 3.00pm, so I sat in the lounge nursing Ben, who, having hardly taken any bottle, was sleeping again. At just after three a car pulled into our drive - I looked up, and then looked again, doing a double take. This wasn't Doctor Cotton, it was the consultant in charge of the special care unit who had had very little to do with us. He barely knew the boys, or Eddie and I for that matter, unlike Doctor Cotton who had been in at some stage most days, to see the boys and to talk to us. He had even over-ridden the fierce Sister, who suddenly decided that Christopher was going to come home when he was just two weeks old, leaving his two slightly less advanced siblings in hospital. I had been horrified, how on earth was I going to cope with one premature baby at home, and two still in hospital. 'Don't be so ridiculous,' he had told her, 'Poor Mum doesn't want to be coming back and forth to here, whilst trying to cope with a new baby at home. No, unless we're desperate for the cots they'll stay together until they're all ready to go home.' He was quite my hero, having sorted out this rather scary and overbearing woman.

Sue answered the door and showed the Doctor through to the sitting room. 'Would you like a cup of tea?' she asked. He smiled, revealing a row of straight white teeth. 'I'd love one,' he said as he walked in. Sue was growing in confidence all the time, and there was never any need to prompt her about how to be with our guests. The Doctor, a middle aged man of African descent and an air of authority, looked seriously on as I told him about Ben's symptoms and how worried I was beginning to feel about him. Ben was stripped to his nappy again. He tried to cry, but his voice was so weak now only a tiny squeak came out. Yet again his colour was good, and his chest, heart and stomach were making healthy sounds through the stethoscope. We all sat having our tea, discussing how I was coping in general with the triplets. He had a quick check over the other two whilst he was there, as they were both awake and ready for their next feed. Although he didn't dismiss my concerns he couldn't find anything obviously wrong, 'I think maybe you're just feeling a little over anxious my dear, that's not at all surprising, mind you. Often when babies are early like this they do have days when they appear to be a little off and sleepy.' 'But what about the sickness he's experiencing?' I asked, 'Well again when they're early they do find it harder to digest the milk, particularly when it's formula milk.' Oh my goodness, I thought, perhaps Libby had been right about trying hard to breast feed them after all. After about an hour he departed, leaving me feeling sure that I must be an over anxious mother. We now had two experts telling us that there wasn't too much wrong with Ben.

Our GP phoned early that evening, to make me another appointment to go in with Ben and see him again the next morning. Having spoken to the consultant after his visit - I suspect they had discussed my over anxiety, and obviously they felt it necessary to give me more support. So the next morning I took Ben back to the pit of germs - he had further deteriorated and was now hardly feeding at all, his cry was even weaker, and he was turning blue with more frequency. If he took any milk it would re-appear very quickly, now with even more force, shooting straight out and over the muslin nappy. I reported all of this to our Doctor, who this time looked more concerned, again examining him, feeling his tummy and taking his temperature. He could see what I meant about his feeble cry, as Ben emitted a tiny weak noise whist he was being examined. 'Well, if at any stage you feel you can't cope just phone me. Any time night or day, I don't even mind if you phone me at home.' At last I felt as though he was taking me seriously, although he still hadn't witnessed what we were seeing.

As the day went on Ben got weaker still, and we spent the whole night nursing him in our room, dozing for a short while, only then to sit watching him again. If he had any milk it came straight back up, which then seemed to trigger another blue attack. Eddie got up to spend a penny at about six. He had fed the other two during the night, so he could leave me to nurse Ben. I was just trying to feed Ben again when another blue attack began. He gradually became more transparent. Then abruptly, he just stopped breathing completely. 'EDDIE' I screamed as I gave Ben a couple of gentle little pushes. He lay there, lifeless, and his eyes had rolled into the back of his head. Whether it was the movement, or my scream I don't know, but suddenly he started to breathe again. 'We have to phone Doctor Taylor right now,' I said, so Eddie ran to make the call.

We were soon on our way to the hospital. Grandma had arrived to look after the other two until Sue turned up; she had volunteered to come in for the weekend, as she felt we needed more help with Ben being so poorly. This time we were going to the children's ward and not to the special care unit. We followed Snow White and the seven dwarfs along the corridors to Timpson ward, where our GP was waiting with the ward's consultant. He was an elderly doctor who reminded me of a cuddly old teddy bear. He had a round face, a button nose with a shapely moustache underneath it, a mop of grey wavy hair and a soft kind smile. He greeted us warmly and asked us to sit down while he had a quick look at Ben, who by now had returned to his lovely peachy colour. 'I don't think there's too much wrong with this little chap' he said, 'We'll just take him down to the treatment room to take some blood, and to see if anything else becomes apparent.' I had a feeling of relief as he took him from me, leaving us to chat with Doctor Taylor in the ward office.

I sat quietly looking around the small, untidy, magnolia painted room. To be honest I was now feeling absolutely exhausted. The accumulative tiredness from looking after triplets had really started to kick in, and then with the extra lack of sleep we were really beginning to understand what having triplets was all about. Eddie and Dr. Taylor made small talk whilst my mind slowly drifted, and I only just resisted the urge to curl up in the corner and sleep. But then the door clicked as it opened, bringing me back to life; kindly doctor Teddy Bear had re-entered. He had a grave look on his face as he came to talk with us, sitting on a chair at our level. 'Having not been too concerned about Ben when you first came in, I'm afraid to say we are now extremely worried about him. He's just had an apnoeic attack, it was as you described and he also stopped breathing whilst we were taking blood. We're going to have to give him a lumbar puncture to get a really clear picture of what's happening, and to make sure we're not missing anything, but at the moment we're fairly sure that he's got some form of septicaemia.' My heart took a lurch – septicaemia, that was often fatal, I thought. How on earth would a tiny little baby fight something so serious? I was certain he was going to die, but Dr. Smith said he was cautiously optimistic, 'I think we might have caught it in time, that's if there's nothing else going on.' He disappeared again and didn't re-appear for another hour, this time to tell us we could go through to see Ben. He was back in an incubator, this time with a heart monitor, a drip in his arm and a large plaster on his back, where the lumbar puncture had been performed. 'We've got some antibiotics going into him now, and the results should soon be back, they're marked as urgent so we should know in about an hour or so.' They suggested we should go home, to do what we needed to with the other babies and, then to return after lunch. Everything was peaceful at home. But I couldn't really settle, anxiety being the overpowering emotion in my head at that moment, so after nibbling at a tiny lunch, which wouldn't go down, as I had a dry mouth and a churning stomach, we soon returned to the hospital.

Doctor Smith was waiting and quickly called us to his room. 'We've got the results and I'm pleased to tell you it's not meningitis, but he does have septicaemia. An infection has somehow got into his blood, and we're very lucky to have caught it now, in fact just in time.' I knew exactly how the infection had got in - through his tummy button. Why had no one been that worried about it? He continued, 'But there's another slight problem too, well we think there is anyway. You said earlier that he's been vomiting, so we did a test feed on him. He immediately threw the small amount we managed to get him to take straight back at us. We think he also has a pyloric stenosis.' 'A what; what on earth is that?' I asked. 'It's a condition that occurs, very often in boys, and funnily enough often in first born boys. A valve in the stomach, the pyloric valve, tightens so much that the milk can't pass through, resulting in under nourishment and what you've been experiencing - projectile vomiting. We'll have to operate to cure it, but not until we have the blood poisoning under control.' My heart sank even lower, how could something so tiny and delicate survive so much?

***

But by Monday he was deemed well enough to have the operation, and survive it he did, making good enough progress to come home a week and a day later. During this time I wondered about the chances of Tom, being Ben's identical brother, also having the same problem. He too had been posseting fairly frequently, and over the last few days he had vomited with a bit more force on several occasions, so they asked us to take him in for a test feed. 'No, this one's OK,' said the registrar. So we took him home again, feeling glad that we would soon be back to normal.

Ben had come home and I was putting him to bed after giving him his very slow and tiny feed, when I heard Eddie yelling from the lounge. 'Gill help me, quick help me.' Oh good grief, what on earth was happening, my heart was beating fast as I ran to the sitting room. There sat Eddie, in what could only be described as a pond of milk – Thomas was sitting there looking quite bemused on his daddy's knee, having just had his feed. He was also covered in the milk which he had just projected over the pair of them. So the next day we found ourselves back in the children's ward, this time with Tom, who was by now a bigger and bonnier version of Ben. They operated that afternoon and he came home a week later, still looking as bonnie as the day he was admitted. I hoped now we could get on with our lives and be a family again.

MODULE 7:
PAEDIATRIC PHYSIOTHERAPY

The winter was fading and the shoots of spring were gradually appearing in the garden. I felt as though we were like spring shoots too – we began to venture out more, whilst the weather improved daily and the boys reached more and more milestones. We went to friends and had coffee or lunch, and although it was a military operation I felt it was important for them to have the same experiences that a single child would have. Friends would often offer us their children's cot to pop the boys into. On these occasions it never ceased to amaze me that, even if we lay them separately along the length of the cot, within ten minutes they would all be in a little snuggle together.

By now they were in their sixth month. Their

'ginger' hair had worn away and the new hair was growing through much thicker and very blond; their eyes were large and deep blue. Although we were very conscious to not compare them, it was beginning to become apparent that Ben was not reaching the milestones at the same rate, or even in the same way as the other two. He still had very little head control, and his large blue eyes now had a very definite squint. First one eye would turn in, and then the next time we looked at him, the other eye would be turning in. I couldn't help but have a niggling worry that all was not as it should be. It was like a gnawing woodworm, slowly making holes in my confidence. I wondered if the health professionals were really right when they continually told me that I was worrying too much. They all had good reasons why he couldn't hold his head up and steady like the other two, or why when I picked him up he still felt floppy, instead of firm and strong. They told me his eyes weren't yet ready to focus and to take into account his prematurity and illness, as this would have held back his development. On one hand I could see what they were saying, yet on the other hand his mental progress didn't seem too delayed. So why was his physical development further behind than his mental development? If what they were saying was right surely all his development would be behind, and not just part of it?

***

After a fine start to the spring the weather had taken a down turn and had become quite chilly. The boys had all gone down with an early summer cold, which, other than giving them horrid runny noses, didn't seem to have knocked them back at all. But over the weekend Ben suddenly became really quiet, and he had completely stopped eating and drinking. His temperature was getting higher by the minute, and he had even turned a worrying shade of blue again - so we decided we needed to ring the on-call Doctor. He arrived and began to examine Ben, whilst he asked us some questions. His decision was almost instantaneous. A high temperature and the blue tinge were enough to ring alarm bells, and when he held him he asked me, 'Is he always this floppy? He doesn't seem to have much head control either, I think he needs to see a paediatrician sooner rather than later, I'm going to get him admitted now. Can I use your phone?' Although it was going to cause us more hassle, as they had just started to sleep through the night, and the feeds would all get out of sync again, I still felt a surge of relief.

The ward was a hive of activity, nurses came and went, and babies cried in little isolation units, while their parents quietly tried to comfort them. Machines were bleeping, and older children were running to and fro from the play room. Doctor Cotton came in to see us, 'Now then what's the problem with young Ben?' He bent down and gently felt his clammy forehead, 'Oh dear, you're a hot little chap, how long has he had a temperature?' I answered, 'Well he's only been like this today, although they've all had a cold for the last few days. It hasn't been too bad other than a nasty runny nose, well, that's until today when Ben suddenly seems to have taken a turn for the worse. Actually, while we're in here, I wondered if I could talk to you about his development. I've been feeling increasingly worried about it, as he now seems to be falling further and further behind the other two.' I continued, 'I've also become increasingly concerned about his eyes, and he still feels so floppy when we pick him up. I know I shouldn't compare them, but he definitely isn't progressing in the same way as the other two. Everybody tells me not to worry about his eyes and that they'll soon start to focus, but I now really don't think they will. He doesn't seem to have much head control either.' There, that was it, I had poured out all my worries, in fact I had hardly paused for breath. But Doctor Cotton hadn't stopped me or found reason to dismiss my worries, whereas everyone else always seemed to. In fact he looked quite concerned. Furrowing his brow, he pursed his lips slightly as he picked Ben up for a closer look. 'Yes you are quite right, he does have a squint, in fact it's an alternating squint - if you look closely one eye turns in, and then when he looks elsewhere the other eye turns inwards.' I felt some relief as my observations were at last being acknowledged. Doctor Cotton then held Ben over the cot. 'You see this,' he said, 'He's still got the primary walking reflex, that should have gone at six weeks - so even taking his prematurity into account it should have long gone, and you're right, he does still feel very floppy. I think that the paediatric physiotherapy and occupational therapy team from the children's treatment unit will be able to help him. I'll have a word with them. They'll come out to your home to assess him, and give you some exercises for him to do.' I thanked him profusely as finally I felt someone was taking notice. Ben's temperature went as quickly as it had come, and with nothing untoward being diagnosed we were allowed back home after twenty four hours.

***

Finally the day arrived – I was so excited about the visit from the paediatric team, and I was just so eager to get on with the exercise routine, that I was sure would get Ben up to the same physical level as his brothers. The knock on the front door sent a wave of excitement through me. Both women stood there, one with a rosy, smiley face, dark wavy hair and a friendly warm manner; she introduced herself as Linda. The other woman had a strangely feline appearance; her hair was silvery grey and her whole demeanour was completely the opposite to that of her colleague. Ice queen would have been a more apt description, with her silver hair, high cheek bones and vivid hard green eyes. Although she was silver haired I would have only put her in her late twenties, or at the most her early thirties. She was obviously self-appointed spokesperson and, I assumed, the more senior of the two.

We entered the sitting room where the boys were playing on the large tartan rug with Sue, who was entertaining her attentive little audience. I was really eager to show off Ben's new found ability to roll in any direction he wished and his ability to roll to a chosen toy, either to the toy box, or to where the toys lay on the floor. The ice queen immediately threw water on my fire, her green eyes glistened as she said 'He's using a muscle spasm to roll, admittedly he's being quite clever with it, as he's learnt to utilise the spasm to take him any where he wants to go.' I listened in disbelief - how could this be? It looked to me as though he had complete control over his rolling, firstly lifting himself to his elbows, and then rolling off them, to go in whatever direction he fancied going. But she was supposed to be the expert, so who was I to argue? The visit went from bad to worse, as more devastating information was showered upon us. 'He'll probably have a normal intelligence. You've already noticed that his mental development seems pretty well on a par with his brothers but, sadly with the sort of brain damage Ben has, communication is often a problem, some never manage to speak at all.' My head spun as I tried to take in what she was telling me. Had I misheard her - had she just said that Ben had brain damage? This had never been mentioned before. 'Does this brain damage you say he has have a title?' I asked her. 'Yes, he's Athetoid, it's the most severe form of cerebral palsy. Because we've become involved early on in his development, we'll be able to achieve so much more.' She was really pleased with herself, as her green eyes sparkled and danced with the excitement of her diagnosis. 'You say he doesn't feed particularly well, that's actually not at all surprising, as swallowing is usually difficult with this condition, you must always say swallow to him when he has his food, or even his bottle. You've done very well to get him onto solids at all without our help.' She went on to describe how he would try to reach out for objects but, because of the damage to his brain, his hand wouldn't be able to go directly to it, instead his arm would sway around, jerking its way towards the elusive item. Only after a great deal of effort, would he be able to pick up what he wanted, or even direct a spoon of food or a beaker of drink to his mouth. I could hear what she was saying, but my brain didn't want to take it in. For everything she said, I could find an argument that would knock her theory off its perch.

Linda, the physiotherapist, had become strangely quiet, whilst Janet, the occupational therapist, continued her spiel. I glanced in Linda's direction to see that her expression had become fixed, her jaw tight with tension; she made no comment and passed no opinion. Part of my brain told me that Janet was the health professional, and she knew far more than my novice, parental intuition. But the logical part of my brain told me not to trust or believe what she was telling me. I failed to see what she seemed to be able to see. The two women went after an hour, leaving us with our rampaging thoughts. Why had he survived so much, if all the future held for him was being trapped in a body which could neither walk nor talk?' They had made us an immediate appointment to attend the children's treatment unit; this was at the general hospital. The appointment was for the following morning, and every Wednesday afterwards. It was to be a group therapy session, then there was to be the hydro therapy - the one-to-one session and the speech therapy session. In fact I began to wonder when we would have any time to do anything else, or in fact do anything with the other two boys either.

***

The garden was a lovely peaceful place to sit as the sun broke through the leaves of the huge Ash tree beside the paddock which enclosed my mare and foal whilst they contentedly grazed. I sat and breathed deeply, gathering my confused thoughts into some semblance of order. The warmth of the sun and the smell of the freshly mown grass from the previous evening had a soothing effect, as I slowly calmed myself and looked at things in a more balanced way. Sue was in the kitchen getting the boys' lunch ready; they were now just seven months old and eating three small meals a day. She had made me a coffee and sent me to sit outside in the warm spring sunshine; for seventeen years old she was very mature and intuitive. I just needed to gather my thoughts for a while; today's consultation wasn't at all what I'd been expecting. Eddie was away for the day at a business meeting, so I was unable to talk to him, but every bit of intuition I possessed told me that this woman was wrong with her diagnosis. I finished my coffee so that I could return to help Sue with the boys' lunch. My head was a little clearer now and Sue had her thoughts too. 'For what my opinion's worth, I think that stupid woman's wrong, and I hope you don't mind but I took the liberty of phoning my mum.' Her mother was a health visitor and also mother to five adopted children. She was a wonderfully sensible parent, and had been helping us by weighing the boys, so she had a pretty good handle on how they were developing. 'Mum thinks that woman is talking rubbish too, and she also pointed out that Ben reaches straight to his toys - there's definitely no sign of his arms waving around without any control or direction is there? Mum also said that if all she says is right, he wouldn't be able to eat the slightly lumpy food we've just started him on, and look how he pushes the spoon or the bottle away when he doesn't want what we're giving him, we don't see any jerky movements then, do we?' I had pretty well come to the same conclusion myself, but as we had an appointment with Doctor Cotton that afternoon, I could ask him all the questions I had racing through my mind.

***

Children were playing, and nurses were bustling as we arrived - it was always a busy clinic, with everyone from new born babies to senior school age children. We were sent straight off to get the boys weighed. It was always the most time consuming part of our appointment, as they had to be stripped down to their nappies. There was always a pleasant atmosphere in the clinic. There were children's pictures stuck on the wall with blue tack and large, colourful, letters of the alphabet surrounded by pictures of Disney characters. There was a large book shelf full of books, from hard paged picture books to a comprehensive collection of the National Geographic magazine. Once the boys had been weighed we sat back down to wait for our consultation. My stomach turned over, as it churned with anxiety - my mind was still playing games with me as it tousled with reality and common sense, and this woman's 'professional diagnosis.'

'The Arthey boys,' called the nurse in the blue uniform. She smiled at us, 'How are they doing, they've grown so much, what bonnie wee boys they are?' She gently rubbed the back of Christopher's hand as we walked by. He, in turn, grinned a toothless smile towards her.

Doctor Cotton's registrar sat behind the desk - my heart sank, I was really hoping that we would see Doctor Cotton himself. But here sat an enthusiastic young man, probably not much older than my 25 years. He listened intently as I related our shocking morning to him; his curly hair and youthful complexion took on a more mature look now. He furrowed his brow with concern as he walked around from the back of his desk to take a closer look at Ben, who was beginning to get grizzly and irritable. He was getting very fed up with all the attention he had generated during the day, and he really needed a nap. 'Well I can't see any signs of Athetosis, but he does feel rather floppy. I think Doctor

Cotton had better come through and have a look at him, and also have a chat with you - you've clearly had a rather upsetting morning.'

He disappeared through the adjoining door, gently closing it behind him. I could hear muffled voices and then Doctor Cotton appeared, with the young registrar in his wake. 'What's all this I've been hearing, let me have a look at the little chap, you've had a visit from the paediatric treatment team this morning, I hear. Tell me exactly what they said to you?' I again repeated everything the woman had said. He listened, occasionally asking a question, and then frowning from time to time. 'You talk as if it was only one of them that made the diagnosis, or was it both?' I told him it was the occupational therapist and not the physiotherapist who did the talking. 'How do you know she was the occupational therapist?' he asked. So I told him that I had had a job as an O.T helper at the geriatric hospital and that was how I was so familiar with the uniforms. 'Ok, well that's pretty conclusive then isn't it? Well as far as I'm concerned, Ben has no sign of Athetosis, so you can rest easy from that point of view. However, he does have quite a significant level of floppy muscle tone, or to give it its correct title, hypotonic muscle tone. It can be severe enough to affect walking and gross motor movement, and children with this problem are always prone to being clumsy. Their physical development is often quite delayed. It can manifest itself by the child being a bit clumsy – to them having to wear callipers in order to aid walking, which often leads to having special educational needs.'

I felt I should feel relieved, but was this prognosis any better? I asked Doctor Cotton, 'So where do you see Ben falling in this category?' He shrugged his shoulders and turned the corners of his mouth downwards before answering. 'At this stage it's impossible to guess, but my gut feeling is that he'll not be too bad. An awful lot depends on how determined he is to get himself up and moving, and he'll certainly benefit from lots of physiotherapy and O.T.'

My heart and face fell; I would have to have more involvement with this dreadful woman. Doctor Cotton continued, probably having read my thoughts, 'But you'll be able to do a lot yourself at home. Having two brothers the same age will also be a huge stimulus for him, and you mustn't be tempted to cosset him - put toys a little out of his reach, so he has to make the effort to move towards them. Rather than picking him up all the time, encourage him to follow you when he starts to move independently. It won't be easy, in fact it'll be far easier to give in. We'll monitor him carefully, but overall my feeling is of cautious optimism.' He smiled kindly as he left the room, telling us to make another appointment to see him in three months time.

The following day, we made our way to the children's treatment unit for our first appointment; it was the group therapy session. As we entered the old red brick building we found ourselves in a dark corridor which led to another doorway - above the door a sign was fixed. It was clearly marked 'CHILDREN'S TREATMENT UNIT.' My stomach churned as we entered. The sound of children's voices filled the air as we made our way towards the open door, which then led on into the room where the voices were coming from. I could see Linda with a group of therapists. Most of them had a small child lying over a rolled up towel. All were facing into the centre of a circle, where a small, dark haired young woman sat in the middle of them, playing percussion instruments. She was trying to encourage the children to lift their heads and watch her. There were two slightly older children standing strapped into frames, and another was lying over a giant beach ball, whilst a therapist held her gently and rolled the ball slowly to and fro. Linda smiled towards us as we stood in the doorway, 'Come on in, Anne Marie will take Ben from you, she's going to be his therapist today. You can leave

him with us and go through to the room at the end of the corridor, there's a mirror window so you can watch everything we're doing.' She smiled again, 'You'll find some toys in there for the other two boys to play with.' It was a small room with a toy box in the corner, but the mirror
window stretched from one end of the room to the other, giving a plentiful viewing area for all the parents to see their offspring performing the exercises. We watched the ice queen as she popped in and out of the session, generally being bossy as she insisted on constantly correcting the other therapists. It made me even more determined to confront her about her misdiagnosis. In the meantime Ben was not enjoying his first session; his sobs racked his tiny body, whilst his head hung in despair. Anne Marie tried to encourage him to lift his head and to join in with the musical and visual session, but he was having nothing to do with it; the session was a complete waste of time. As I watched it was very clear that many of the children were seriously damaged, some already with twisted bodies as they fought the muscle spasms. It made me feel so very sad for them and their parents, but it plainly illustrated to me that Ben's problems were of a very minor nature in comparison.

Eventually the session ended and we all filed out of the little viewing gallery. I had got on well with the other mothers and generally picked up the feeling that Janet was none too popular amongst the parents. She was clearly viewed as being hard and uncompromising, and no-one really wanted to stand up to her.

Although I didn't find confrontation easy, I felt so strongly about her outspoken and high handed diagnosis, that I waited to see her after the session. I began to speak to her but the moment she realised I was daring to question her diagnosis and her right to make it, her eyes and face changed, instantly hardening as her jaw tightened. 'Doctor Cotton doesn't agree with you. He feels you've made a mistake - he says he can't see any signs of Athetosis, and he thinks Ben's problem is hypotonic muscle tone.' She glared at me, disbelieving that anyone would dare to confront her. 'Well Doctor Cotton may not be able to see the symptoms; he doesn't see what we see every day. I feel I'm far more experienced than him at spotting this sort of brain damage. We're treating children like this every day. Take my word for it, I'm right, and you would be wise to do as we tell you if you want Ben to make any progress, and to have a future.' With an icy glare she turned on her heals and marched off.

There was a small voice of insecurity in my head niggling away. Could it be that she was right and the doctor was wrong? But then common sense took over; I realised that having seen the other children, Ben was nowhere near as poorly. What had also become very clear from this confrontation was that there was never going to be a working relationship between Janet and me. As Sue and I were getting ready to leave, Linda came over. 'Why don't I come out to your house for the next session? Ben really didn't settle at all into the group, so it won't have done him much good. Perhaps it would help if he got used to me on a one-to-one basis. Once he does then we can begin to think about the group sessions? She smiled warmly again, and I had the feeling she was very much on our side.

MODULE 8:
GENEROSITY AND GIVING

Throughout the pregnancy and then the subsequent arrival
of the boys, I never stopped marvelling at the generosity of
friends, acquaintances and even complete strangers. On
one shopping trip to our local town, a woman was so taken
with the boys that she insisted on pressing three pounds
into my hand for their piggy banks. Eddie's work
colleagues sent us carry cots, maternity clothes for me and
clothes and equipment for the babies. Friends and family
handed on cots, sterilizers, more clothing and equipment;
in fact we only had to purchase a few small items and a
cupboard full of nappies. But there was one person who

particularly stood out and bowled me over with her interest.

The first memory I have of this lady was when I was about six. She came to stay with us on one of her trips back to England from working in Africa. Having studied at Oxford, reading English, the young Maureen O'Toole went out to Africa to teach English to African students. After a while she started to teach Christianity as well. This then led her onwards to working with the publishing company for whom my father was with - The Society for Promoting Christian Knowledge, known as SPCK. Whilst working for the company out in Africa she met my dad on one of his overseas management trips. They had quickly become friends.

I remember her arriving at our home in my sixth summer - her disproportionately loud voice boomed around the house. She was a funny little lady, probably only about 4'10", with dark brown hair showing the odd streak of grey, which had been cut into a short, boyish style. Her skin was brown and slightly wrinkled. She had a round face and shining rosy cheeks; she reminded me of an over-ripe apple - her loud laugh was far bigger than her small stature. Within hours of arriving at our house she decided to wash her smalls, or to describe them more accurately her large smalls, out in the kitchen sink. Mum offered to run them through the washing machine, but she insisted that she was happy to do them by hand. She then strung the big blue gym knickers out on the line to drip-dry. Dad always had a childish, lavatorial sense of humour, so we giggled together at the line full of her big blue bloomers. Maureen found my father most amusing, and constantly laughed at his jokes, clearly enjoying his company. She also had a liking for playing practical jokes, and was frequently thinking up new pranks to tease my dad with. I really wasn't too sure about this lady. If I'm honest I was slightly jealous of her friendship with my beloved daddy. She openly admired him and told my mother that if she got fed up with him, she would be there to snap him up - she also openly admitted to disliking children unless they were African. As far as I was concerned she was someone from whom to keep my distance. However, in spite of the fact that she claimed to dislike children, she played games with me, taught me words in Swahili, in which she was fluent, and told me stories.

One particular day my dad had thought up a practical joke to play on her, and when she realised she had been caught out, her loud cackling laugh boomed around the house. She then flew across the room to pummel my father with her small brown fists. I was incensed, how dare this woman, who didn't like children, and who was obviously trying to steal my daddy from me and my mum, have the bare faced cheek to start hitting him. I flew like a charging bull across the room, and with a well aimed kick I felt my foot make contact; I had hit her fair and square on the shins. Maureen hopped around holding her throbbing leg, as dad swept me off my feet, 'You mustn't kick Maureen, that's really naughty to kick people, now say you're sorry.' He chastised me and rightly so, but Maureen was quick to defend me, 'She's only trying to protect you, Peter, don't be cross with her, it's my fault entirely.' Through the following years we came across one another many times, including when mum, dad and I house and cat-sat for her in Africa when she went on a three week trip along the West African coast for a holiday. Although I was always polite, I was still very wary of her.

By the time we moved to Northamptonshire when I was thirteen, Maureen had returned from Africa and was teaching English to foreign and British students at Kettering technical college, also in Northamptonshire. She shared a cottage in a village just outside Kettering with a friend. They had been at Oxford together but the friend, Deirdre, was now a widow. Needless to say we saw slightly more of her now she was back in England, and coincidentally living nearby. When I went to the Tech to re-sit my English GCSE, you can imagine my horror and indeed hers, when I found myself in one of her classes. She was by now very eccentric, dressing in badly matched clothes, thickly knitted and brightly coloured tights, with flat brown, brogue lace-up shoes - they were a fashion disaster and I was totally embarrassed to admit that I knew her, and that she was in fact a family friend. It was just so un-cool!!! Luckily, one of the other English teachers needed a few more students to make up his numbers, so I was the first to jump ship and change class.

My parents then moved down to Sussex when I was nineteen and Maureen had by now retired. Although she came to our wedding when I was twenty, I didn't see her again until I had the boys, which was four years later. Immediately she heard we were expecting triplets she sent us a cheque, which was money I knew she couldn't really afford. When they were born she sent us another cheque, telling us she knew it would come in handy. By the time the boys had been home for a few weeks, we had our first visit from her. Even though she proclaimed she disliked children unless they were African, she became a frequent visitor, often bringing Deidre with her, and always telling us it was Deirdre who really wanted to see them. Funnily enough, every visitor she had she brought over to see us, as they all 'really wanted to see the boys,' of course it wasn't for her pleasure at all!! As soon as she heard that Ben was having developmental problems, she sent us a book on child development - it was such a useful book having the extreme boundaries of what was considered normal. I frequently referred to it, and always found it would put my mind to rest. On one of her visits we walked across our paddock to see the new foal. I was carrying Christopher, who was the only one of the boys who was awake. The boys by now were about ten months old, and Christopher was in a particularly smiley frame of mind, having just acquired his first four teeth. 'Ooh this one's just like his Grandpa', she said, 'He's got a real twinkle in those big blue eyes, and such a charming smile.' I laughed out loud at her; even in her late sixties she still wore her heart on her sleeve for my dad.

She continued to send useful books for either us or the boys, and a cheque at Christmas, until the boys started school. By then she had moved up to live near her family in Yorkshire, as Deirdre had passed away. She still continued to speak to mum regularly for updates on their progress, until old age finally took over and she ended up in a home. Last time mum phoned her she was unwell, and soon afterwards she passed away. Such generosity was quite humbling, and it made me realise that I must never judge a book by its cover.

MODULE 9:
REACHING MILESTONES AND
ARTIFICIAL AIDS

Time was passing by and the boys were now sixteen months old. Linda and I sat crossed legged on the floor opposite one another, Linda trying to encourage Ben towards her as she held out a toy. He hovered for a few seconds on his hands and knees, before the inevitable collapse. We had been making a concerted effort to get Ben up from commando crawling and into a proper crawling stance for several weeks now. The trouble was he could move so quickly and effortlessly. Like a little worm he wiggled his way across the floor, keeping up with his brothers who by now were both toddling.

It was always hot in the treatment room, and the effort

of holding Ben up was producing little beads of sweat across my brow. Linda and I both sat up and dropped our heads into our hands; again we had failed to succeed in our campaign. 'What are we going to do Linda?' I asked, 'We're never going to get him crawling at this rate.' My face must have been the picture of despair. 'Don't worry,' said Linda 'He'll just suddenly get it, but I must admit it would be better for his progress if he did it sooner rather than later.' I knew Linda was beginning to feel a little anxious too, as so much of his ultimate progress hinged on crawling. In fact, if I'm honest his progress had pretty well ground to a halt.

Suddenly a thought came to me, 'You know those things that little Timmy has on his legs when he's in the standing frame? Well, would it be possible to make something like them for Ben's arms?' They were a boned, corset type of device, which the department made for some children in order to aid in the support of a limb or limbs. I had only seen them used on legs, but logic told me that there was no reason why they shouldn't be used on arms too. 'Well there's no reason why we can't make some, it's certainly worth a try,' said Linda. 'In fact we'll measure him now; I could have them ready in a couple of days.' It was certainly better than doing nothing, and anything had to be better than the progress we weren't making at the moment.

***

I set off for the treatment unit with bubbles of excitement welling inside my tummy; oh how desperately I wanted these gaiters to work. Linda had phoned to say they were ready. 'They're tiny', she said laughing. Then she told me to come into the unit the next morning so we could give them a try. Of course Ben was still tiny, so they were bound to be small as he only weighed 15lbs. Although Ben and Thomas' features were very identical, there was an ever increasing gap in their weight which showed a marked difference between them, particularly in height and body size. They both still had their straight blond hair and very petite features. Christopher was bigger again, with tumbling blond curls, and a very mischievous grin. He was like a male Shirley Temple. Their eyes were still large and deep blue - even though I say so, they were very cute.

Linda was waiting for us to arrive at the ugly red brick unit; she was clearly as excited as me. 'Come on, I can't wait to try these,' she said as she beckoned to us with the tiny white gators. She looked over her shoulder and was already walking in the direction of one of the treatment rooms. I took Ben's coat off as I followed her, propping him on my hip to stop him from sliding through my hands – he still felt a bit floppy in my arms, and his head still wobbled, although things were slowly improving. But crawling would definitely make a difference to his overall strength.

We took up our familiar positions on the floor, down at Ben's level. Linda sat opposite me, while I held Ben's arms out for her to apply the tiny white corsets. First one arm then the next, she carefully adjusted the Velcro tapes, twisting the devices gently to line up with the contours of Ben's arms. He sat quietly, leaning back against me between my legs, whilst Linda wiggled and adjusted – Ben watched her, taking everything in. Finally the last Velcro strap was in place. He looked down at his arms, now fixed with his tiny hands poking out from the end of the white gaiters, resembling the stiff, unbending arms of a toy doll. Slowly the realisation that he could no longer fold his arms at the elbow dawned on him. His bottom lip drooped, his eyes screwed up and his head dropped to his chest, as he let out a desperate wail, the forerunner to the sobs that shook his small frame. I turned him around and held him to me, trying to comfort him, explaining that his new gaiters were to help him to learn to crawl. As he gradually calmed down we were able to return him to the floor, playing with the toys to distract him. Finally we put him into the crawling position, with the hope of moving his arms and legs in a crawling sequence. Again his head dropped as he fell back into desperate sobs; any hope of him moving quickly went out of the window. I don't quite know what Linda and I were expecting, but whatever it was, it wasn't going to happen then, or even in the next hour. It was clear this was going to take a lot more time and patience. We decided that we had done enough for one session, so I ran through the fitting of the shackles again with Linda, then I put Ben's little navy blue anorak on and we set off for home. I felt positively deflated and I knew Linda did too; we had both been convinced that we had found an easy answer to our prayers. But nothing comes without effort, and I had a feeling a lot more effort was about to go into this rather small person.

***

Sue greeted us eagerly as we arrived home, 'How did you get on, is he crawling yet?' I explained what had happened. 'Oh' she said, her smile fell and she clearly felt as deflated as Linda and me - we all had such high expectations. 'I think we're going to have our work cut out,' I said, 'But I'm not going to give up yet.' We gave the boys their lunch and then put them in their cots for a sleep. I decided that we would have our crawling sessions when Ben was fresh - so first thing in the morning, after his morning nap and again after the afternoon nap. There was no time like the present, so after his lunch time sleep, and once he'd woken up enough, I applied the gaiters with the help of Sue. She was keen to learn how they fitted so she could help with his programme. He sat quietly on Sue's knee whilst I put them on, then I took him and knelt on the floor, putting him into the crawling position. Once again his face contorted, as his head dropped and his little body shook with sobs. I hardened myself, shutting it out, and got onto my hands and knees behind him. Sue positioned herself in front holding a toy for him to crawl towards. First I moved one arm forwards, and then with my knee I pushed his diagonal leg, then the other arm and leg. We slowly progressed across the room, Ben sobbing, me re-assuring him. This process was repeated the next day and the next. Slowly but surely the crying ceased - although he wasn't making any movements himself. But at least he wasn't sobbing anymore, and we could now manage without Sue holding a toy out for encouragement.

It was Friday morning and five days after we had started our campaign. I shackled Ben's arms ready for our morning session. He was quiet this morning and somehow resigned to our new daily routine as I popped him down on the floor ready for his lesson. His head seemed a little stronger this morning; he was able to hold it up far better than ever before, and there wasn't even a murmur of complaint from him. So with a feeling of hopeful anticipation, I got down behind him to start our crawling sequence across the sitting room. I took my hand toward his arm, but before I could get there he began to pick it up himself, putting it down a little in front of himself. I then moved my knee to push his diagonal leg, but before I could get there he had moved it himself. Then the other arm and leg, until all his limbs were moving on their own without my help - before we knew it we were half way across the room. I shouted to Sue, 'Quick, come and look, Ben's crawling on his own.' I picked him up and turned him around. By now Sue was in the room and kneeling on the floor so he could crawl back across the room to her. 'Hooray Ben, look at you, you're so clever, come on, crawl to me,' she said, as she encouraged him. Ben grinned and chuckled to himself as he set off across the room - this time completely alone, leaving me sitting there feeling quite overwhelmed with the relief and emotion of it all. I hugged my knees and rested my chin on them, watching Ben chuckling and gurgling until he finally reached Sue.

Both of us had tears rolling down our cheeks, it was such an amazing feeling of achievement. I put my tissue back in my pocket and rested my chin back on to my knees, only then to realised that my precious grey cord trousers, my most favourite trousers in the whole world, were now so threadbare that my knees were about to burst through. All the crawling had taken its toll on them, but it was absolutely worth it, and only a small price to pay for Ben reaching this huge and important milestone.

Ben continued to progress over the next few days. Even when the gaiters were off, he was trying to hold himself up with the new found ability to keep his arms straight. At first he collapsed after a small movement, but the next time he managed to move a little further, then a little further still, until eventually he was crawling all the time. By the time we had our next session with Linda, which was the following Monday, he could crawl alone and we were able to give her a lovely surprise. He had now become adept at crawling until he was tired and then swivelling around onto his bottom, just to sit for a moment before moving on.

Linda was ecstatic, 'You clever little boy,' she said, as he sat back on to his bottom and grinned up at her. She too had tears rolling down her cheeks as she swept him up and danced him around the treatment unit. 'How did you manage it? To be honest when you left last Monday, I was convinced we were going to have to go back to the drawing board. I'm just over the moon, he can now start moving on to the next stages. You wait it won't be long before he starts pulling himself up on the furniture.' She was right, and within the next week he did just that, but it was still going to be a long time before he could walk unaided. What was slowly becoming clear was that once Ben had made up his mind to do something, nothing would stop him in his determination to succeed.

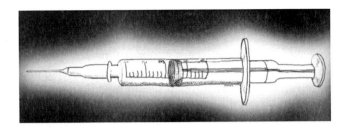

MODULE 10:
INCOMPETENCIES IN THE MEDICAL PROFESSION

Children's voices were quietly murmuring in the background as they played in the toy corner, while some parents read snippets from books to amuse their children. Sue and I were struggling to keep the boys entertained, as we played with toys and read books whilst waiting for our call. We were back at Doctor Cotton's paediatric clinic again, and the boys had just turned twenty one months. Spring had turned to summer and it was a particularly warm day, which had made all the boys fractious. Because of the clinic they had to miss their afternoon nap, which just made matters worse. They were now, of course, very active. Christopher was desperate to make a break for freedom and had twice slipped from Sue's grasp and run off down the corridor, once entering the open door of a consulting room. Inside a group of doctors and nurses were all talking in hushed and serious tones, having what looked like a case conference. Sue grabbed him and rapidly backed out, apologising as she turned bright red, then scuttled back to me. I was trying in vain to hang onto Ben, who wriggling on my lap, as was Thomas who was also desperate to pursue his sibling in a break for freedom. He arched his back and let out what can only be described as a growl as I gripped his shorts in an effort to stop his escape.

At last we were called and not before time - we were all hot and sweaty, having wrestled with and cajoled the boys in our attempts to keep them happy for the best part of an hour. They were all extremely grumpy, having been stripped to their nappies for weighing, and then re-dressed again. We entered the room and sat down at the consulting desk waiting for the doctor to appear, as always hoping it would be Doctor Cotton himself. The adjoining door opened and we looked up. Our faces must have been a picture as our mouths dropped open with shock – there in a white doctor's smock was the very needy woman from our cookery class. Fay Jolly, who was actually the last person you could describe as jolly, had secretly been the source of our amusement when we enrolled in a cookery class, just around the time of the boys' first birthday. We only enrolled for half a term, from September to December, as suddenly time became so very precious again. I began to realise that it was best to do Ben's therapy and exercise after the other two had gone to bed, so evening classes really became untenable. He never slept quite as well as the others two, so some physical exercise and then a warm drink, before putting him to bed, seemed to help him to settle quicker.

But here she was, this woman whom we had labelled as 'the pain in the arse!' was behind the desk, surprisingly in this position of responsibility as the doctor. She was a pale, mouse-like little woman, probably in her late twenties. Her eyes had large, dark bags hanging beneath them and her jowls were rather heavy; in short she resembled a small, female Clement Freud. She had nearly driven the cookery teacher mad and, for that matter, the rest of the class, as she constantly asked for comments on, and for approval of, her work. She analysed everything she did and how she did it, and talked to herself as she worked. To be quite honest she was a complete nuisance. If she recognised us now she didn't show any sign of doing so as she leant across the desk and held her hand out to shake mine, introducing herself to us. 'Hello, I'm Doctor Jolly. Doctor Cotton's on holiday, I'm his registrar so I'm taking his clinic today.' She smiled at us, obviously feeling rather smug about the fact that she had been left in charge. She showed absolutely no sign that she recognised us, and that was how I was happy to leave it. 'Now how's everything going?' she asked, barely pausing for breath and certainly not for the answer as she continued. 'I notice that Christopher and Thomas seem to be doing well, but looking at Ben's weight chart I'm rather concerned. He's significantly below the third percentile line, so I really think we need to investigate this further.' 'Oh,' I said, feeling rather surprised. Ben was still smaller than his brothers, but he ate well enough and he was definitely growing. The only thing that was really concerning me was the tendency he had to make progress for a couple of weeks, then, just as we thought he was getting on really well, he would regress. Clearly he felt very unwell at times. When he was like this, he would lie on the floor moaning, whilst banging his head up and down on the carpet. It was at times like this I couldn't help but wonder whether he was going to achieve as much as we hoped, and the niggling doubts would start to flood back into my head again.

I frowned, 'So what do you think is wrong with him?' I asked. 'Oh, well it could be a number of things, but I think we need to run some tests to find out exactly why he's failing to thrive so badly. Some X-Rays of his abdomen, a urine sample taken directly from his bladder to test for infection, blood tests before and after food throughout the course of a day - you'll have to be in early for that one, then finally an IVP so we can send some dye through his veins and around his kidneys, then we can see if they're working properly.' She looked very pleased with herself, as if she'd just discovered penicillin. I couldn't help but feel as if she were talking about giving a car a thorough service, not tests for my little boy, and I have to say I didn't much like the sound of what she wanted to do to him. He didn't exactly look to me as if he was failing to thrive anyway.

I began to wonder if we were just slotting into another little niche, which had been created by our history and initial early problems. To be honest I was just beginning to get a little fed up with it all. I started to wonder if people wanted to make our lives as difficult as they possibly could. Did they not fully comprehend just how difficult it was, trying to raise triplets with the least amount of hassle possible? We had the speech therapist that arrived at our home to assess Ben when he was only eight months old. She promptly told us that we had to stop him from using the teat that he particularly liked; in fact it was the only way we could get any fluids into him at all. But because she decided he had to get used to feeling different shapes in his mouth, we did as we were told. From that day on he refused to have any teats at all, including the one that he had originally liked. For weeks I had to spoon fluids into him, until eventually he began to use a feeder cup. We even had to make sugar-free jellies for days on end, just in order to increase his fluid intake. Then Doctor Fox, the developmental specialist came, also when he was just eight months old. He was very dismissive about everything Ben could do that didn't have a test score to fit into his charts. He returned to do his next assessment when Ben was about fourteen months old. I proudly showed him how Ben could identify every named part of his body. He could now also commando crawl to the toy box and bring us any toy we asked him to find. But this sadly had no score either, so nothing could mark his intelligence or physical ability. In the regulated tests he only scored seventy percent to normal, which meant he fell into the special educational needs category. Doctor Fox subsequently wrote to our GP and to Linda to say that he felt Ben's parents were having difficulty accepting his limitations and special needs. He told them that he felt we needed some help to adjust and to come to terms with Ben's limited future. Linda wrote straight back to say that, to the contrary, she felt we had fully accepted his problems and we were doing everything we could to encourage him to reach his full potential. Now it appeared that here was yet someone else who was just trying to upset our equilibrium.

***

The appointment for the day of blood tests came through quickly and with some instructions which told us that Ben was not to have any food from midnight onwards. We left home early, 7.00am in fact, to get to the hospital in time for Ben's first blood test. Inwardly I was dreading it as hospitals always left me feeling cold, and the blood tests made me feel even worse, but I couldn't let any of the children know how I felt. The ward sister was there to meet us. She took us to a bleak looking, sterile little side room, which was to be our base for the day.

Not long after we had arrived Doctor Jolly came in, looking every bit as pale and miserable as ever. She nervously wrung her hands as she explained to me about the blood testing routine for the day, both before and after Ben had eaten food. We stripped Ben to his vest ready for his blood test and then she dropped the bomb shell, 'Right, you can go out of the room now mum, I need to get on with taking his blood. There's a relatives' sitting room at the end of the corridor, we'll call you when we're finished.' 'No' I said 'No I won't go out, I've never had to leave him before when he's had blood taken. In fact we've always been encouraged to be with him for anything like this, so why do I have to go out just for one little blood test.' 'Oh, well please yourself'. she said shrugging in an offhand way, 'I normally find that most parents don't want to see their children having to go through this sort of thing, but that's up to you.' She walked away, trying to look nonchalant, but I could detect her tension as she nervously fiddled with the equipment on the tray. The nurse in attendance looked uneasily in my direction, and I began to wonder what on earth was about to happen – this was only supposed to be a blood test after all. Doctor Jolly walked towards us in readiness to do the test. I was still holding Ben, who quietly watched her. 'Right, lie him down on the examination couch for me will you?' she asked, curtly. I frowned, why on earth did she want him lying on the examination couch, I normally had him sitting on my knee for blood tests or injections, even when he was a tiny little baby I'd held him in my arms. But feeling her mood I decided not to question her actions again, and did as I was told. Immediately Ben started to cry. This only seemed to provoke even more tension in Doctor Jolly. 'Hold his arm out for me' she barked at the nurse, 'And hold it really still.' I held Ben's other hand and stroked his head as I leant down to be nearer to him, but his cries became more desperate. I talked to him, soothing him all the time, as the tears rolled freely down his face and pooled by his ears. Come on, hurry up, I thought, but Doctor Jolly continued to prod around with the needle – it went in and out of his arm as she tried in desperation to find a vein. The more she tried the more Ben screamed, and the more he screamed the more uptight she became. Then she almost shouted at the nurse as she ordered her to lean on him to keep him still. I was absolutely horrified as she then tried to extract blood from the back of his hand, then the other arm and hand. But she still hadn't managed to gather any more than a few small drops. I began to feel hot and sick and more than a little faint as needles weren't exactly my thing. In fact I was just being brave to be there for Ben.

The nurse was by now looking horrified as she glanced nervously at me; tears were beginning to prick my eyes. Suddenly Doctor Jolly turned on me, as her inadequate techniques became very obvious, 'You'll have to go out, I'm going for the femoral vein and I need you out of the way.' She physically shoved me out of the door, as Ben's screams escalated with my disappearance. I felt awful, I'd let my little boy down; I'd promised both Ben and myself that I wouldn't leave him. I stood there with my back to the wall, just outside the room, helpless as I fought back the tears. Just at that moment a family friend came along, she was matron for both of the children's wards. 'What are you doing here, is one of the boys ill?' I was just managing to hold it all together as I listened to Ben screaming on the other side of the door, but seeing a friendly face opened the flood gates and I dissolved into tears. She put her arm around me while I told her what was happening, struggling to get the words out through my sobs. 'Oh, Doctor Jolly again,' she said, raising her eyebrows. 'Leave it with me, there's no reason why she need do any more of his blood testing today. In fact she shouldn't be doing this one either, what does she think we have a phlebotomy department for? It isn't the first time this has happened, she needs to perfect her technique before she puts children through this sort of trauma. Poor little mite.' She shook her head and rubbed my arm, 'Don't worry, I'll go in and sort this out right now.' With that she disappeared into the room - I could hear raised voices but within a couple of minutes she re-appeared holding Ben. 'Here she is,' she said to Ben, 'Look here's mummy waiting for you.' Ben held his arms out towards me, his little face all blotchy from crying. 'I've sorted everything out. From now on his bloods will be taken in the phlebotomy department. I'll call down to them and tell them what's happened so they'll be ready for you both. Don't worry, he won't have to go through anything like that again.'

After Ben had eaten some breakfast we had to go to have the next round of blood tests. A middle-aged lady who clearly had years of experience in taking blood sat us down. She had a look at Ben's little arms, already bruised from his earlier trauma. 'Ooh' she said, 'Why on earth didn't that wretched doctor let us do this, look at the mess she's made. We take blood from children and babies all the time so we're far more experienced than her. Anyway, let him sit quietly on your knee and it'll be over and done with before he knows what's going on.' She quickly and efficiently popped the needle in and the phials filled with blood. Ben didn't murmur or even flinch, and the rest of the day went by without any more traumas. Doctor Jolly kept her distance, clearly smarting, having had a severe telling off by Matron. Finally we could go home and not a minute too soon, as it had been a long and traumatic day for us both.

I walked back into the house, which wafted lovely, homely smells. Sue had been baking cookies and was now just hand washing a few items of the boys' clothes. She always rinsed with sweet smelling fabric conditioner, so the clothes were soft against their skin. I took Ben through to the sitting room where the other two were playing. Sue followed me through, 'Shall I put the kettle on? I bet you're dying for a cup of tea.' I nodded, 'Oh yes please Sue, you just wouldn't believe the day we've had, and now I've got a pounding head ache.' I took Ben's coat off and stood him on the floor propped against the settee. The other two boys immediately got to their feet, but rather than running to greet me as I expected, they both ran to their brother and put their arms over his shoulders. Sue and I watched, fascinated by this open show of affection. Thomas leant his head against Ben's and said 'Aaah' sympathetically. Could they possibly know that Ben had been having a horrible day? Sue and I looked at one another. Could this be some kind of telepathy, or perhaps it was Triplepathy!! Thomas put his other hand down on to the seat of the settee. There on the back of his hand was a large and very definite bruise, matching the bruising on the back of Ben's hand from the bungled blood tests. 'How did he get that?' I asked Sue. She shrugged, 'No idea,' and then simultaneously we both looked to the back of his other hand. There, just like stigmata, was another bruise to match.

To this day I have no explanation for what we saw, but one thing was sure, there was a force we would probably never understand that flowed between them. We both shuddered and looked at one another, silently acknowledging the unaccountable phenomena we had just witnessed.

But all the horror of the day had left its scars and Ben wasn't himself afterwards, he was withdrawn and found strangers coming to the house worrying. He would climb up my legs and cling to me, moaning and crying. His sleep was also more disturbed and he had been waking every night, then it was very difficult to get him back to sleep. We still had the spectre of the IVP hanging over us, which was also to be performed by Doctor Jolly herself. Soon an appointment came for us to go to Doctor Cotton's clinic to get the results from the blood tests and x-rays.

We didn't have to wait long and almost as soon as I sat down, Ben put on an Oscar-winning performance for Doctor Cotton. First he started to moan as he clung to me, then he began the latest new thing which was to turn my face towards him and away from whomever I was talking to. 'How long has he been doing this?' asked Doctor Cotton, looking concerned. I explained that the day of tests had started badly, and that he had been like this ever since. 'Humm' he said in a knowing way, 'Well we need to sort things out for you, he can't carry on like this, it's no fun for anyone and it's certainly not behaviour we can allow to continue. I'll get you an appointment with the child psychiatrist, he'll give you some good advice, this definitely needs nipping in the bud.' I was really relieved as things had been getting increasingly difficult. Then Doctor Cotton began, 'Any way, back to the main reason you're here, I'm very pleased to tell you that there is nothing wrong with Ben, other than a bit of constipation which shows up on his abdominal x-ray. We can soon give you some medicine to alleviate that. But all his other tests were fine; in fact it appears that Doctor Jolly hadn't taken his prematurity into account when she worked out his charts. Although he's on the bottom percentile line with his weight, it's still within the range of normal.'

I couldn't believe my ears; this incompetent woman had not only made an awful mess of the tests, but she had put him through all this for nothing. I asked Doctor Cotton if Ben still needed the IVP which was scheduled for next week. 'No, I don't think there's anything to indicate problems with his kidneys so you can cancel the appointment. I think he's been through enough for the moment don't you?' 'Oh yes' I said 'I certainly don't want him to have to go through anything else that he doesn't need.' I so wished I was of a bolder nature as I wanted to say what I really thought - that his registrar was the most incompetent ninny I'd ever come across, and he should really keep a very watchful eye on her. She was certainly not safe to be let loose on the unsuspecting public.

MODULE 11:
CHILD PSYCHOLOGY AND COPING STRATEGIES

Doctor Jim Lord, child psychologist and general all round wise person arrived at our house one sunny, early August morning. Eddie had taken the morning off work as we both needed to be involved with Ben's behavioural rehabilitation. He was a tall, sunny man with a laid back attitude to life - he had fine brown hair and a straight cut fringe, a clear complexion and a very boyish face. He was probably ten years older than Eddie, but could have passed for ten years his junior; in fact he could very easily have passed himself off as a student.

Sue showed Doctor Jim into the sitting room where Eddie and I were playing with the boys - she came in and shut the door behind her. Ben was on the rug with his brothers, but the minute he saw Doctor Jim he crawled straight over to me and climbed up my legs, moaning and looking uneasily over his shoulder at this stranger. We all sat down and I put Ben on my knee while the other two carried on playing in the middle of the room. On cue Ben started his odd behaviour, turning my face towards him, not letting me talk to Doctor Jim. Without thinking I picked up a toy to distract Ben so I could tell Jim the sequence of events, and how soon after all the trauma of the awful day Ben's odd behaviour began. Whilst we talked Ben slowly stopped moaning and gradually started to play with his toy, until eventually I was able to stand him on the floor while he leaned against my legs, still distracted by the colourful, chunky Duplo toy.

To be perfectly honest, things had just started to improve, but it was good to hear what Doctor Jim thought. He told us that we were doing all the right things as he had watched me pick up the toy to distract Ben which he was congratulatory about. He told us we were definitely helping Ben on his slow path to behavioural recovery, by distracting him from his worries and reassuring him. Whilst we chatted I told him about my concerns over his general progress and then the sudden regressions he experienced from time to time. I told him that it always seemed to be associated with him feeling quite unwell. I described how Ben would lie on the floor banging his head and how his physical progress would fall back. His colour often looked poor, he was pale - almost grey at times. Doctor Jim looked thoughtful, 'Hmm, you said he has just started on medication for constipation didn't you? I just wonder if he could be milk intolerant - it can make children really quite poorly as toxins build up in their body, almost poisoning them until it can be excreted and cleared from the system. Then the same process starts all over again. Constipation or diarrhoea, even sickness is often a symptom. That would explain the pattern of progression and regression, as the toxins rise and fall in his body.'

Doctor Jim asked us if we knew any one with goats, as their milk would be much better for Ben and he felt it would be well worth a try; we would then get a conclusive answer if the milk alleviated the problem. Funnily enough we did know someone, so we were able to get him some goat's milk almost immediately. The change in him was phenomenal. His constipation was cured and the bad behaviour improved straight away. His regressions becoming a thing of the past as did the horrid, yellowish-grey skin colouring. Doctor Jim Lord was a miracle maker. He also revealed during our first meeting that he had twin girls of five and a little boy the same age as our boys. We arranged a get together for tea, a play, and a temporary toy swap just to ring the changes.

***

But things were about to rapidly change in our lives. We were coming up to the two year point when we had always said that we would have to manage without help. Sue had been half-heartedly looking for a job, all too aware that the boys were nearing that crucial age. Suddenly, out of the blue, she was asked to go as a full time nanny to a seven month old boy, as his mother was returning to work. This was a wonderful job for her but it was the moment I had been dreading, burying my head in the sand and rather hoping it would never happen. They wanted her to start immediately. The boys were twenty two and a half months, so of course we gave her our blessing to go. It was such a sad day and although Sue was still going to be very involved in our lives, it was obviously going to be a big change for all of us.

Sue's leaving also coincided with Christopher deciding it was time he was out of nappies, something I had hoped to delay for a while. He probably was about ready as he was fairly consistently dry, but Thomas definitely wasn't. Tom, having seen Christopher without a nappy on, announced 'nappnee off,' reached into his dungarees, and pulled out the soggy, wet one and threw it on to the floor at my feet. I began to sink in the never ending pile of dirty wet washing. Just as I thought I was going to drown in dirty washing, Eddie came home and told me he had booked us a few days away in a hotel with the boys. He had managed to book a large room which could accommodate three cots. There was children's tea and a baby listening service, so we could have an evening meal in the hotel restaurant on our own. We were going for five days and it was booked for the following week. This somehow helped to soften the blow as Sue left, but we were all missing her very much.

It was to be the first time we had taken the boys anywhere further than the privacy of our friend's static caravan on the North Norfolk coast, so I was a little nervous about being in a public place. I packed the car to the roof with all our equipment, especially the triple pushchair that Sue's dad had very cleverly built for us. It was made from a large, old fashioned double pushchair, which had been given to me by one of the mothers from the twins club, (yes I did venture back again), and a cheap, single pushchair that I had purchased from Mothercare. He very cleverly dismantled the front wheels from the single pushchair and put them on to a detachable bar. Then he made a clip device so the single chair could clip onto the front bar of the double chair, with the child in the single seat facing the two in the double seat. On the occasions when there were two of us to push, or one needed to go elsewhere, they could be separated and the single chair could have its front wheels re-attached. On the other hand I could now go out alone, confident in the knowledge that I could fit through doors and into lifts, without two of us having to physically manhandle the blue and white striped triple buggy sideways through openings, as inevitably they were never wide enough.

Funnily enough, when the boys were about ten months old, we had been asked by the hospital to get in touch with a family who were imminently expecting triplets. We went over to meet them, to give them some comfort or otherwise, and to prove to them that there was a life after having triplets. When we entered their large old Victorian house with its spacious and ornately tiled hallway and beautifully polished mahogany stair banister, I spotted standing in the corner under a plastic cover, the most amazing triple pushchair. I had instant and overwhelming triplet pushchair envy, to the point that I just couldn't take my eyes off it, until eventually I asked if I may have a proper look. It was beautiful - a Rolls Royce, no, a Bentley of the pushchair world, with its plush, padded seats that tipped and tilted into all sorts of positions. It was designed to be used from newborn upwards. There were beautiful canopies to cover each baby from the sun and the most wonderful rain covers for bad weather. Each seat had a plush-padded sleeping bag that could be fitted for the cold weather. With its large, white wheels and huge springs to make even the bumpiest road smooth. It was an object of my complete and utter desire and I yearned for it, I drooled over it and I coveted it. The pushchair was produced by a Swedish manufacturer; they were the only suppliers of triplet wheels which could pass Britain's rigorous safety standards. To say that I wanted this object of absolute desire was an understatement. But at an enormous cost of £700, which today would be about £1,800, it was way out of our price bracket, and to be quite honest a complete waste when what we had was adequate. But my little blue and white striped, second hand, width-ways buggy, with its broken handle and no proper rain cover, only little blue plastic cagoule things, with peaked hoods to cover each baby from the rain, came in a very poor second best and I'm afraid to say I felt very much like the poor relation. I'm also very ashamed to admit that

I gave Eddie a fair bit of grief over the possibility of us having one ourselves and to sod the expense!! But Bill, Sue's dad, did us proud with his invention and it more than sufficed for our needs, being built with the same layout as the Swedish one. In fact ours was much more practical really, as we could divide it up, and it was about half the size, and not nearly so un-wieldy.

The car was packed with several bags of nappies as Christopher and Thomas had been persuaded to wear them again just for the holiday - thankfully Ben was still quite happy wearing his. Then we had the little plastic bags of goats' milk, frozen solid and covered in cold packs in the cool box ready to transfer to the hotel's freezer, which we had okayed with them before our stay. Then, of course, there were the cases full of clothes for five days. I looked at our car as it stood on the driveway fully loaded; the back seemed to be sinking under the enormous weight. We were travelling down in my car which was an elderly, pale blue Ford Escort estate - it was fitted with the boys' car seats. Eddie's company car was far too smart for small babies and the potential of puke, potties and poo!

We arrived and made our way into the plush Victorian hotel entrance hall, where we were greeted by a sweet little receptionist who seemed very excited about our arrival. She wanted to know all about the boys and what they were called. 'I'm going to remember all their names' she announced. 'We've been really looking forward to you coming; we've never had triplets staying here before.' While we were checking in I noticed a tall, slim, and rather stern looking man with greying hair, watching us from the dining room. He was obviously a member of staff and at first I thought he was just glancing in our direction, but when I looked back he was still staring, with a rather serious look on his face. It was a bit disconcerting, as he had such piercing ice blue eyes. But I soon forgot about it as we checked in and the pretty, dark haired receptionist prepared to take us to our room. The hotel was very old fashioned, but also rather lovely in its chic vintage sort of way. There were large chandeliers that hung from the high ceilinged dining room, and the deep plush carpets were a regal red in colour, and the doors had stained glass panels in them. There was that lovely smell that all old fashioned hotels seemed to have - a mixture of cooking and cleaning products clung to the curtains and carpets. We followed the receptionist up the huge staircase, with its dark polished wooden banisters to our room. She unlocked the door for us and proudly showed us inside. There were the three cots as promised, lined up across one side of the room, with three matching little duvets, and our king sized bed was across the other side of the room. In the bathroom, (which was quite as big as our bedroom at home) was a huge cast iron bath - the boys were certainly going to enjoy bath time in this. There were lovely Victorian sash windows on two sides of the room - one looked out towards the quaint harbour and the other on to the busy pedestrian shopping street. But most of all it was a complete luxury for us to come away and have someone else do the cooking and cleaning for a few days. It was only as we sat in our room, after Eddie had brought the luggage upstairs which included the specially packed holiday toy box, and the boys were quietly playing on the floor, that I realised how desperately we were in need of a proper break. It was good to be just the five of us as a family, which was something we very rarely experienced. Don't get me wrong, it was lovely that we had such a lot of help, and so many of our friends and family wanted to be a part of our lives, but we rarely had some just 'us' time.

***

Children's tea was at five thirty so we made our way down to the dining room with the boys. There were three high chairs waiting for us and the high tea consisted of boiled eggs and soldiers, toast and a selection of spreads, or fish fingers, chips and beans. There was milk, tea, hot chocolate or juice to drink, and cake and biscuits. What more could three little boys want? They tucked in heartily so when it came to bath and bed time, they were full and sleepy. They all snuggled down into their cots like seasoned little travellers, giggling at one another as they peeped through the strange new cot sides. But their eyelids were soon closing, like the shutters shutting down on a shop doorway at the end of a day. Thomas gently sucked on his dummy, Christopher had his thumb firmly plugged in and Ben twiddled his teddy 'Sat Sing's' (that thing) ear. We waited for them to be soundly asleep before we went down for our dinner; the sweet little receptionist had the baby listener right by her side, 'I won't come and get you unless I really need to, if you like I'll have your key and go up to them if they cry' She looked eagerly at me, obviously hoping I would take her up on her offer. I thanked her profusely but declined, saying that perhaps the next evening I would take her up on her offer. I think we must have kept them so busy during the days that they never once stirred for the whole five nights.

Eddie and I sat having our evening meal, but out of the corner of my eye I could see the frosty looking man I had seen earlier, he was obviously the maître d', and he had positioned himself against the wall near to our table. I frequently caught sight of him as he looked sternly on, seemingly watching our every move, until in the end I suggested we should go and have our coffee in the sitting room. I smiled politely and thanked him as we left the dining room. 'I don't like the way that man keeps looking at us,' I said to Eddie, but he had been oblivious to it; he was just enjoying the first taste of luxury we had experienced for some time.

Eddie had booked the holiday through a voucher scheme they were running at work, as an incentive to encourage people to buy cars. Robert, his boss, had given us the vouchers as he felt we could really do with a proper holiday, telling Eddie he thought we both looked tired. The deal was the room came free, but breakfast and the evening meal had to be taken in the hotel, obviously at a cost. To be quite honest this was stretching our budget even to be able to do that. 'I think that maitre'd chap disapproves of our arrangement, maybe he thinks we're being cheap-scapes, after all it's quite a posh hotel. Perhaps that's why he keeps on staring at us,' I theorised as we drank our coffee. 'Oh I don't think so,' said Eddie, 'They're probably quite pleased to just fill the rooms; after all British holidays aren't as popular as they used to be. Ignore it, you're just being paranoid.' He laughed and patted my hand.

The next morning we arrived in the dining room for breakfast. Our table was all set up with the high chairs, and a jug of Ben's goat's milk was placed on our table. We helped ourselves to breakfast cereals and settled down to encourage the boys to eat; we had taken their own little bowls and plastic beakers with us. I filled the Tommy Tippee cups with milk and put the lids on – Tom's was red, Ben's yellow and Christopher's blue, all matching the colour of their bowls. The dining room was surprisingly busy. On the next table sat an elderly lady with a younger man who had a strong resemblance to her – I felt sure he must be her son. She smiled kindly at us as we sat down, and she seemed quite fascinated with the boys as she watched their every move. Thomas glanced in her direction, and being quite a shy boy he began to shift uncomfortably in his high chair, looking anxiously between her and then back to me. I chatted to him and distracted him, until he eventually forgot he was being watched and continued to eat his breakfast.

Early that evening I went for a walk, just to do a bit of window shopping, and have a breath of fresh air, whilst Eddie sat with the boys as they ate their tea. It was nice to have a bit of quiet time on my own, but when I got back to the hotel the stern maitre'd was standing by the hotel entrance door. My stomach did a lurch - oh no I thought, I've got to walk right past him. As I scuttled by he looked directly at me, giving what looked like a forced but polite smile. I uttering a quick 'hello' and shot off into the dining room, where the boys were eating their beans on toast which Eddie had cut up into little squares for them. 'That man really gives me the creeps,' I said in a whisper as I sat down at the table next to Eddie, 'He's always staring at us.' 'Oh he's alright' said Eddie, 'He probably knows he's rattling your cage; that'll make him do it all the more, just ignore him.' I supposed he was right but that evening at supper he stood in the same position by the wall near to our table, again he watched our every move. Eddie ordered a bottle of wine with our meal and Mr. Frosty made a big drama of showing Eddie the bottle and opening it at the table, pouring a little drop for Eddie to taste, then standing back almost as if he were standing to attention. It was as if he were acting out a scene in a play, completely over dramatising the situation. He even rushed to fill our glasses the minute we emptied them. 'I can't help it Eddie, that man really does gives me the creeps' I said, 'It's not normal behaviour. He's completely over doing things, I'm sure he's got a problem with these vouchers.'

The next morning, and the subsequent mornings, our table was set up for us with a small jug of goat's milk and another bigger jug filled with cow's milk. On the three high chairs, the three little cups and bowls had been set out, and now even the cereals the boys were eating had appeared on the table. The hotel staff were so kind and helpful to us, and every morning the sweet little old lady took up her position on the next table to watch us, completely transfixed by the boys as she smiled kindly towards them. But Thomas was becoming more conscious of her watching them, and had begun to frown, clearly not comfortable with having an audience.

Finally our last morning arrived and everything had been set up as usual. We popped the boys into their chairs and poured milk into the mugs, and filled their bowls with cereal. They all looked on eagerly, waiting for their bowls to be set in front of them; the sea air had given them very healthy appetites. But Ben was having one of his more wilful mornings and a battle had just begun. We had been struggling to get him to feed himself, and just because we were on holiday I didn't want to let things slip too much. But this morning he was trying to throw the spoon, and then he pushed the bowl towards me, desperately trying to get me to feed him. He saw absolutely no reason why this particular morning he should feed himself, so consequently I was busy concentrating on Ben. I didn't want the bowl of cereal emptied on to the lovely plush red carpet. With all this going on I hadn't noticed Thomas becoming more agitated about his audience. Suddenly, a movement, or something made me look up - there was Thomas, his arm raised high above his shoulder, with the Tommie Tippee mug full of milk. In slow motion he threw the little red mug with all his strength. I tried to intercept the missile as it left his hand and it slowly rotated in the air as it went on its journey toward the target, splattering milk on its travels. I began to leave my seat, knowing in reality that it was all too late. 'Duuff,' the missile had reached its target, hitting the little old lady smack in the middle of her forehead - milk squirting everywhere with the impact. All over her face, in her hair and down her jumper. 'Oh my goodness,' I said, leaping across the carpet to her table, 'I'm so sorry, I can't believe he just did that. Are you alright?' There was already the sign of a bruise beginning to show where the heavy cup had landed. She was full of apologies, telling me it was all her own fault, 'I shouldn't have been staring,' she said, 'But I'm just so taken with them. It's brought back so many fond memories for me. I had twin boys forty-nine years ago, this is one of them.' She gestured towards her son who was mopping the milk from his mother's cardigan. He was apologising, when in reality he had every right to think that we had very badly behaved children. They were so good natured about it, and we ended up laughing with them over the incident while we all finished our breakfast. As they left, the little lady came over to speak to the boys and to make her peace with Thomas, who by then had forgotten all about being self-conscious and was busy driving his tractor around the high chair table. He was happy to show it off to his one-time enemy, who was really sweet with him as they made friends.

We finally came down to the reception ready to check out. Eddie had eventually loaded the car with our enormous pile of luggage. The lovely receptionist was waiting for us, coming out from behind the desk to say her goodbyes to the boys. 'Oh,' she said, 'I mustn't forget to tell you that it's Mr. Marchant's day off, but he asked me to say goodbye to you, and to tell you how much he hopes you will come back and stay again next year with the boys.' 'Really' I said, struggling to hide the shock in my voice. 'Oh, I know he seems a bit fierce at times, but he's a big old softie really. He's been very taken with your boys and he thinks you two deserve a medal. D'you know he's been into the dining room early every morning to set your table up. He wouldn't let anyone else do it in case they forgot your goat's milk, or muddled up the boy's bowls and mugs. He even came down this morning to do it before he went off for the day.' 'Oh' I said, feeling quite ashamed of myself. I hoped with all my heart that he had no idea I was so wary of him.

Yet again I had just had a big lesson in not judging a book by its cover. He had seemed so disapproving, but all the time he was just trying to help us by making our stay more enjoyable. Fortunately we had brought the staff a huge box of chocolates to thank them for all their kindness as we had believed that it was the rest of the staff doing the nice helpful little touches, and not Mr. Marchant at all. We didn't go back with the boys again as life moves on, but Eddie and I returned to the resort in 1999. We stood looking at the old hotel, having a trip down memory lane. It looked rather old and tired, somehow a shadow of its former glory. I couldn't help but wonder if Mr. Marchant was still there, or if he had moved on, not being able to cope with the hotel dropping its high standards. I suspected he probably would have gone, and it made me feel quite sad as I looked upon the now rather shabby old hotel.

MODULE 12:
PLANNING A NEW BUSINESS

We enjoyed a lovely Christmas, made extra special by the return of Sue to the fold. I felt very lucky as we had recently been awarded the attendance allowance for Ben, so there was a little bit of extra money to make our life a bit easier. Then, just as we were awarded the allowance, the nanny job that Sue was doing suddenly ended - the young mother she was working for decided that being parted from her first born was just too much to cope with. So she decided to give up work for the foreseeable future, which obviously made Sue redundant. It couldn't have worked out any better for us, and I think Sue felt the same; there was much excitement in the household upon her return.

Eddie had been thinking for quite some time that he would like to start his own business, and he realised if he didn't do it soon, he probably never would. One of his colleagues was also very keen to go into business with him, so they began to make a few plans. It was decided that they were best to stay within a field they knew well, so the motor trade was the obvious choice. Eddie had the accountancy knowledge on his side and John was sales manager at the garage where they both worked. John, too had a young family, although his girls were a little older, having both now started school. The search began for premises to buy or lease, hopefully somewhere not too far out of the area, as neither of us really wanted to move far away from our family and friends. I didn't think anything nearby would turn up in the imminent future, if ever, so I had pretty well put it out of my mind. And as we were so busy anyway, not much else other than the boys' daily existence entered my head. Then one evening Eddie came home from work bursting with excitement, his face glowed and as I looked into his eyes they were sparkling. 'Look at this' he said, plonking an open page of a magazine in front of me. 'What is it?' I asked as I began to read the advert with the red pen circling it.

SMALL GARAGE, WORKSHOP AND FORECOURT IN
A POPULAR MARKET TOWN IN
NORTHAMPTONSHIRE.

I looked up, 'Where is it?' Eddie's eyes shone 'You just won't believe it, it's in Oundle. It's the old Oundle motors, they're selling up as the father has retired and the son doesn't want to carry on with the business. They had the Ford franchise until a couple of years ago, so I don't suppose it'll be too hard to get it back again. It's just too good to be true.' I had to agree it was too good to be true. Oundle was only about seven miles from our house, and although it was probably twenty miles from John, it was still commutable. John was happy to travel until he could find somewhere a bit closer to work, and not too far from their friends and family.

So the business of raising the funds began, which proved harder than could be believed at times. They went to bank after bank to try and secure a business loan in order to buy the premises and the stock. The more the banks turned them down the more despondent they became – until the day they met Mr. Frazer. He was the manager of one of our local banks. He was a short, stocky man with a large greying beard, a red face and twinkling eyes. Being a kind, and it appears, a wise man, he told them, 'I like to buy into people, as much as the business itself. You two have a great business plan and more importantly, I like you. You both have all the relevant experience and I believe young people should be encouraged to get a start.' It was an amazing chance he had given them, and with the money under their belts the process of negotiating with Ford to reinstate the franchise began. Luckily they both had such good knowledge and experience of the product, making an agreement was straight forward and the reinstatement was quickly signed. In April, when the boys were only two and a half, the garage became ours. So Eddie went from being a very hands-on dad, to a very absent dad.

He was working from dawn till dusk seven days a week. He and John were so determined to get the business up and running and to turn it into a success. I often took the boys over to the garage so they could see Eddie, and on Sundays I cooked the roast, put it in the cool box to keep it hot, and we all ate together on an old pasting table in the service reception. It was an unsettling time for the boys and I know they missed him dreadfully, especially at bed times, as I was a very poor second best when it came to telling the bed time story.

One day Sue and I watched with fascination as the boys busied themselves, going back and forth with their little yellow rucksacks on their backs. Ben was using the blue and white wooden trolley that dad had made him to help him with his walking, which apart from a few steps between the furniture, he wasn't quite able to do unaided. It was nice and heavy, and it gave him a good firm base to hold onto. He was waiting at the door as Tom and

Christopher ran inside to fetch more and more toys. Some were deposited into the trolley and some were carried in the rucksacks, as they disappeared time after time to the top of the garden and into the empty stables. Their blond heads bobbed up and down as they went on their way. Thomas's little duck-tail curl rolled over the top of his collar, Christopher with his bubbling blond curls, and Ben with his little head wobbling characteristically from side to side as he walked with his trolley. They were clearly on a mission. Eventually our curiosity got the better of us, 'What are you doing boys, you're very busy. Are you going on an adventure?' They barely stopped to answer as they started off on their next journey to the top of the garden in the direction of the stables, but then paused, casually turned to answer us, and said, 'We're going to see our new dad Vincent and our best friend Bommie.' Sue and I looked at one another in disbelief. They were clearly missing Eddie, but quite where had they dreamt up these names from? We had no idea and as for the imaginary friend, surely imaginary friends were exclusively for lonely children and only children, weren't they? Bommie and New Dad Vincent lasted for only a few weeks and then became consigned exclusively to our memories.

***

We were beginning to notice that there was never any evidence of conversation or planning when they started a new venture. Whatever it was they were doing just seemed to evolve, almost as if there was no need for communication. There was the time when they were still too young to be really talking, other than the few odd words. We had just been given a large quantity of jigsaws, all aimed at a slightly older age group than the boy's eighteen months. They ranged from larger pieced puzzles for pre-school children, to 500 piece puzzles for adults and older children. I had carefully stacked them onto the top of their wardrobe ready for another day. Although I was able to reach the top without standing on anything, as the wardrobe wasn't very tall, the boys definitely couldn't. Of course the thought never crossed my mind that they would be able to get up that high and reach them. But only hours after the jigsaws had been placed there, the boys had evolved one of their unspoken plans. They manoeuvred the little red cosy-coupe car into a suitable position, climbed on top of the high yellow domed roof and then pulled the whole lot down. Sue and I suddenly became aware of giggling behind the door of their bedroom, which was slightly ajar. This wasn't altogether unusual as they often laughed to the point of giggle tears at one another's antics. A particular favourite was peeping at one another through the hole in the bottom of a large cardboard box. But today we had walked in to be greeted by the most unbelievable mess. They were all sitting on the floor surrounded by a sea of puzzle pieces, which had been mixed into a jumble. They were throwing the conglomeration of bits up into the air with both hands, and then giggling hysterically, as the pieces rained down on top of their heads. Perhaps they were just so in tune with one another there was never any need for discussion. Or was this just another example of the powers of 'Triplepathy?'

***

Ben's language skills had suddenly started to develop just as everything else started to fall into place when he began to walk with the aid of his little blue and white trolley; by now he was two and a half. This all tied in with him feeling better as he started to have goat's milk. He began to talk, and talk and talk, until my head spun with the extra concentration, as he asked me question after question and experimented with his new found linguistic skill. But it was a language that was only understood by a handful of people. In fact his pronunciation made the words sound more like a foreign language. Daddy was 'gassie,' Postman Pat sounded like boatman bat, Thomas was 'gomas,' Christopher 'fiffa' and a fox was a socks. This all coincided with Doctor Fox, the developmental specialist, coming to assess him again. I was hoping he would be quite astounded by Ben's progress. The last time he came Ben could neither stand nor really even support his own weight – well not for more than a few moments. He was also unable to say very much either. We knew he felt that Ben's potential was very limited so thus began an interesting afternoon.

Doctor Fox was a tall, slim, mild mannered man, with dark curly hair and an olive complexion. He was very sweet really, but he was totally obsessed with his charts and scores which I found awfully frustrating. I felt they didn't always give an accurate reading of Ben's real ability, particularly as his behaviour could often be difficult in forced situations.

We had set up the little wooden coffee table in the sitting room; it was a perfect height, falling just between Ben's waist and chest. He could stand quite comfortably against it, for hours at a time if something really interested him. The other two would quite often run back and forth, bringing him new toys to play with and different books to look at, stopping for a time to play there themselves, before setting off on their quest to keep Ben entertained.

'Ben, this is Doctor Fox,' I said as we entered the room, 'He's come to play some special games with you.' Sue was busy rugby tackling the other two boys as she tried to stop them in their tracks - they were desperate to join in with what looked like being an afternoon of fun. Doctor Fox had entered the house armed with a couple of red plastic boxes full of exciting looking toys. Ben looked up at me and repeated 'octor socks.' 'What did he say?' asked Doctor Fox. 'He was just saying your name, but he can't pronounce all his letters properly yet.' Ben was smiling shyly at him, his head slightly tilting to one side and his squint just showing itself as his left eye drifted inwards. Doctor Fox seemed most impressed that Ben was talking at all. 'Now then Ben, I'd like you to try and do this little puzzle for me,' said Doctor Fox. Oh no, not puzzles I thought. Ben hated doing puzzles, so Doctor Fox couldn't have started with a more onerous task. This was sure to get the afternoon off to a bad start, and once Ben had made up his mind he didn't want to do something, there was very little anyone could do to change it. 'I garnt goo at, I goo boorly,' Ben said, hanging his head as he did a very good impression of feeling poorly. 'What did he say,' asked Doctor Fox again, as he turned to me and looked enquiringly. 'He said he can't do that as he's too poorly.' Doctor Fox laughed, 'Oh well Ben, we'd better find you something else to do then.' He continued to chuckle as he reached into the red plastic box and fished out a laminated picture. 'What gooin octor socks, are gon be boat man bat?' Doctor Fox asked me to interpret. 'He asked you what you're doing and are you going to be postman pat.' Doctor Fox laughed again, 'No Ben, not today, but I want you to have a look at this picture, then I'd like you to tell me all about the things you can see in it.'

This was much more up Ben's street, so I was hopeful he might score well on this test. I acted as interpreter as he told Doctor Fox about the mummy in the garden hanging up the washing, the dog or 'gos' playing with the ball. The children playing in the 'and bit' (sand pit) and gassie (daddy) mowing the lawn, he could see the sun and clouds in the sky, and he identified every single item of clothing that was hanging on the washing line. Until finally Doctor Fox had to stop him as he had a list as long as his arm. 'At his age I only needed him to identify five things, but he's well exceeded that.' Doctor Fox sounded very surprised and somewhat impressed. The afternoon continued in the same vein, with Doctor Fox continuing to be surprised by Ben's answers to his questions and by Ben's lively sense of humour. 'I can't believe the change in him since I last assessed him.' I really wanted to say, stop looking quite so much at your charts and numbers, and instead just watch and listen to the child and his parents. But I resisted the temptation, as by now he was back into his charts again totting up the scores. 'This is unbelievable,' he said, 'I must have mis- calculated, bear with me while I check my adding up again.' I sat quietly playing with Ben as Doctor Fox took a gulp of tea, before re- calculating the scores. 'Well it appears I was right the first time - he's got a pretty amazing result. We know his physical side is still significantly lower than it should be, so this brings the overall mark down a bit, but his verbal ability is incredible. He's scored four years and ten months, with his chronological age at two years and six months. I think you can safely say from this that he'll be able to cope with main stream education, even if he needs some help physically.' I smiled and thanked him for his time and patience. As he left he shook my hand and said goodbye to Ben, 'Bye bye octor socks,' was Bens' reply as he grinned at him, this time the shyness had gone. Doctor Fox chuckled to himself again as he left, shaking his head whilst he walked down the garden path, in complete disbelief at the afternoon he had just had, and at what he had seen.

MODULE 13:
FURTHER OBSTETRICS, PROPERTY MARKETING AND EARLY EDUCATION

Shards of burning sunlight glimmered through the gaps in the leaves of the shady ash tree. We were in the garden under the huge tree, keeping out of the powerful sun during the second week of a heatwave. The boys were playing in the paddling pool. I sat on a garden chair watching them whilst I scraped the new potatoes for our salad supper. Ben, now aged two and three quarters, was just walking although he was still rather unsteady on his feet. I seemed to spend a lot of time running to stand him up again, as he was still unable to get up from the floor without some help. The other two were really sweet with him and often ran to his assistance, or held him by the hand to steady him. But now the end of the most exhausting fortnight was in sight, as thankfully Sue was due back from her holiday. I couldn't believe how much it had taken out of me looking after the boys on my own, and I had spent most afternoons desperately trying to not fall asleep. But only another day to go and she would be back.

Sue returned home looking very blonde and bronzed. She was clearly as excited to see the boys as they were to see her. On her first day back we went into town as I had some photos to pick up from the chemist. They had been in there for a fortnight as it was always such a struggle to take the boys in to the shops on my own. We were on our way out for lunch and playtime with some friends, so Sue stayed in the car while I ran in to the chemist for the photos. There was a queue, and the woman in front of me was having a problem getting the film out of her camera. The plump, red-faced lady behind the counter struggled with it, screwing up her face with the effort, wriggling and pulling at the camera as she held it in a black velvet bag, to stop the light getting in and ruining the film. Her face was almost puce as she struggled; she looked as if she was fighting with a cat in a sack. It was really hot again and I was seemingly feeling the heat more than ever today. As I stood waiting, I started to feel sick, and then my head began to swim. If I didn't get out of this hot shop soon I was going to be on the floor. Someone once told me if you clench and unclench your buttocks rapidly when you feel faint, it sends blood to your brain to recover the situation. So I tightened and released my buttocks, working them like a pair of pistons until they began to ache. But it wasn't working and I was getting ever nearer to fainting. 'Oh do hurry up pleeeease' I muttered under my breath. Then I started frantically looking around for something to sit on. Just at that moment the woman in front of me turned around, 'Are you OK? You look terrible.' 'No, no actually I think I am going to faint if I don't sit down, I think this heat's getting to me.' The plump, red-faced woman behind the counter rushed round to assist me, and before I knew what was happening they were almost carrying me to the dispensing area to sit me on a chair. The customer fanned me with a pamphlet about childhood vaccinations, and the plump, red-faced shop assistant rushed off to get me a glass of water. I was so embarrassed, I wished a large hole would open up so I could just slip into it and disappear. People were staring; one rather large, sweaty child didn't take his gaze off me, as he watched with his sullen, piggy little eyes. In fact all I could think about was getting out of there as quickly as possible. Bugger the photos, they could wait for another day.

Sue was sitting in the car playing spotting colours with the boys, 'I was getting worried about you,' she said as I got in, 'Oh my goodness, you look terrible, what's happened?' So I told Sue all about it, 'This heat is really getting to me, I can't bear it much longer, it's making me feel really ill and so tired.' Sue looked at me, 'You don't think you could be pregnant do you?' I laughed, 'No, of course not, why do you ask that?' Sue looked across the car towards me in a knowing sort of way. 'Well, you've just nearly passed out and you said you've been really tired while I've been away. I also seem to remember you telling me that the heat was making you feel really sick.' She raised her eyebrows in a 'I know something you don't' sort of way. I laughed a nervous laugh, as I racked my brains and frantically thought - oh good grief, when did I last have my monthly friend? A few quick calculations revealed that it was seven weeks ago, in fact thinking about it everything fitted perfectly with Eddie's birthday celebrations. A pit opened up in my stomach, at the realisation that Sue was probably right. I really did feel sick now, sick with absolute horror. We didn't have enough room in the house for another baby, and the garage was only just up and running so we were financially still under masses of pressure too. Sue ran back into the chemist for the photos and to buy me a pregnancy testing kit. I didn't know how I was going to break the news to Eddie if it were to prove positive. It wasn't something that we'd discounted forever, but we had definitely decided that it would be wise to wait until the boys had gone to school, and certainly until we knew the garage was going to be a viable business. So I decided that I'd better forewarn him before I did the test, then he could mentally prepare himself if it were to prove positive. I cooked a nice meal that evening and opened a bottle of wine, in the hopes of softening the blow as by now I was quite convinced that Sue was right.

I did the test the next morning and the little thin blue line appeared - all I could hope was that it wasn't going to be another litter. By my calculations I was just coming up to eight weeks, so we decided not to announce it until we knew more, and as so much can go wrong in the early stages it was best to wait for a few more weeks. However, we did go to the doctor swiftly, as we wanted to make sure we weren't expecting another small brood – thankfully the scan revealed just one little alien this time. In a funny way, although we hadn't anticipated extending our family just yet, I felt quite excited about the prospect of having one little baby to enjoy.

***

After getting used to the shock, we started to investigate the options open to us for extending the house versus moving. We spoke at length to a builder friend of ours who, to our surprise, flatly refused to extend for us anyway. 'You'd be really silly to waste money extending a semi-detached building,' he said. 'The extension would cost more than it would increase the value of the bungalow.' So after this exercise we decided it was going to be more sensible to try and move. We were sad, as it had been a very happy home and a good house to us, but we had to be sensible about things.

The next house we were looking for had to be as near to perfection as we could possibly find and, of course, afford. Not that we were fussy or anything - but it had to fill certain important criteria. First and foremost it had to have at least as much land as we already had. Then it needed to have five bedrooms, or if any less they needed to be very large. It mustn't be too far from the garage, Eddie's parents or my parents, and we wanted it to be in a rural spot, preferably with some nice riding nearby should we ever have time to ride a horse again. In short it had to be at least as nice as what we already had, or even nicer if that could be possible. I'm afraid I felt we were asking for too much - but the search began.

***

In the meantime, with everything going on around us, the garage and then the pregnancy, I hadn't given even a moment's thought about the fact that the boys were soon going to need to attend play-school; that was until Maggie from the village play group phoned us one mid-August evening. A rather bossy voice was at the other end of the phone, 'Hi I'm Maggie Smith from the village play group and I was just running through our list for September. I couldn't help but notice that you're not on it. Most parents want to get their children's names down as soon as possible, we're a very popular group here you know. But maybe you've made other arrangements for your boys. I thought I'd better phone and tell you because if you don't get their names down soon, there won't be any places left.' I just had a feeling I was being rather ticked off, so I apologised for not being more on the ball. I did just as I was told and put the boys' names down on the list, only then to realise that we were going to be away on holiday for the start date. Maggie sounded mildly irritated, 'Oh well, never mind you'll just have to miss the first week and start the following Monday. If you and your helper want to come and stay with them, at least for the first morning, I think that would be a good idea, but after that they should be OK. We usually advise parents to just creep away as soon as their child is playing happily, but I suppose that might be a little hard with three of them keeping an eye on you.' I didn't feel very comfortable about that idea at all, but I supposed this must be how it was done. I went on to explain about Ben's difficulties, and how he was still a little clingy, and more than a little clumsy as he was still very wobbly, but she brushed the information aside as if I were the novice mother that I was - she was absolutely sure they would settle without any bother at all.

So we went off on our week's holiday which we spent in Devon, near to Dartmoor. This time in a very child friendly farm house, with a playroom and freshly cooked children's evening meals, and a child listening service so parents could eat later, once the children were settled. It was beautiful, with views from one side across to the moors and from the other across to the sea. During the week we had many trips to see the Dartmoor ponies as the boys became completely obsessed with them - or we visited the Farm Park nearby that did pony rides. Eddie crawled around on our large bedroom floor with the boys all lined up on his back, endlessly being a 'horsey', and when he tried to have a snooze on the beach they all piled onto his back, jigging up and down clicking their tongues to emulate the clopping of hooves. So when we returned from our holiday, not only was Eddie now completely exhausted, but we also had a phone call from some friends to tell us that a small first pony had our name on her, so we relented and went to have a look. She was a funny little thing. Shetland/Welsh - she had the rather large head typical to the Shetland breed, but the tiny ears of the Welsh pony. She had big brown eyes, a wild mass of white mane and an equally wild bushy tail at the back end of a round fluffy white body. Her legs were short and she was slightly knock-kneed – in truth she was pretty ugly, but she had a beautiful temperament and the boys adored her. She clearly loved their attempts to groom her, and when they tried to pick up her tiny hooves she obliged by holding them up one by one for them to scrape away the mud with the hoof pick. The family were delighted that Sparkie was going to come to us and have a lovely long term home; they kindly sent her with all her wardrobe of equipment too. We were very lucky to be given her and she was the beginning of many fun times we spent with the boys and their equine interests.

***

But the day I had secretly been dreading arrived - the first morning of play-school. I don't know why I was dreading it so much, probably because we'd been cocooned in our happy little world for nearly three years, but I guess there was also the fact that I wasn't quite ready to hand my precious little brood into a complete stranger's care. I had a mixture of feelings really, in some ways it would be nice to have a bit more time to do other jobs, particularly in the house. But in another way it was the start of the next phase in their lives; it was an inevitable passage and the sooner I got used to it the better.

It was a cool, grey day so rather than walk with them in the buggy to the village we decided to take them in the car. Christopher was very excited about the prospect of gaining more friends and going to more parties, Thomas thought it 'might be nice,' and Ben just said in a very serious voice, 'gon't ont go pay gool,' which translated was he didn't want to go to play-school. They all sat in their car seats quietly as we drove down to the village, past the haunted house on the hill, then past the funny shaped three-storey house on the corner, and finally round the village green to park outside the old orange coloured iron stone ex–school room.

There was a little group of mothers chatting, having just dropped their children off. Sue and I got the now rather quiet boys out of the car. One mother came gushing over to us and the other four slowly followed, 'Ooh are these the triplets, we've heard all about them coming. How do you cope? I struggle just coping with one,' she rolled her eyes back then continued, 'But three, oh my goodness! Well I must say you look remarkably sane on it.' Her eyes drifted down to my small but obvious bump, 'You're having another one, oh my God you're brave, it isn't another three is it? How on earth will you cope?' She didn't wait for an answer and barely paused for breath as she rolled her eyes dramatically, 'I couldn't have another one, not with Robert around.' She paused for a second and looked thoughtful. 'Yes, in fact he'd probably kill it.' I raised my eyebrows, wondering what kind of a monster Robert must be. 'Anyway must dash,' she said, 'I've got loads to get done before Robert comes home.' With that she was off, her legs almost a blur as she ran in the direction of the main street. Sue and I grinned at one another. 'She's like that Disney character, Road Runner,' I said to Sue, who was unpicking Thomas from her leg – he had suddenly become very shy, even Christopher had taken hold of my jogging bottoms, whilst Ben sat aloof in my arms as I carried him, comfortably sitting just above my bump. 'Yes she was a bit full on wasn't she?' said Sue, as we made our way slowly down the path towards the school gate.

As we walked through the passage and into the school yard, I noticed a flat-roofed shed with an open door. A few toys lay untidily inside, but the majority were outside in the playground, scattered randomly around waiting for play time. As we walked in I couldn't help but noticed how unkempt it all was. Large cracks had appeared in the tarmac allowing invasive clumps of weeds to grow, and the paint was peeling from the rotting wooden window frames. Nowhere was there any grass to play on, and all I could visualise was Ben trying to play in the playground and falling on the uneven tarmac. His head control, although better, still wasn't good enough to stop him from bashing his head on the ground most times he fell, so we did everything we could to avoid him falling on anything too hard. Poor little chap almost constantly had bruises on his forehead. As we made our way inside, there was an overpowering noise coming from the room that lay behind the closed door. There was a big notice, PLAY GROUP, and underneath it said PLEASE SHUT THE DOOR BEHIND YOU.

We entered as a bunch, by now the boys were clinging on very tightly, having somehow joined Sue and I together with their gripping little hands, worry written all over their faces. Now the source of the noise had become obvious – a small boy with a blade-two hair cut was running around the room, eyes fixed in concentration, a frown on his face as spittle flew from his lips which expelled this dreadful noise. His arms were spread out wide as he flew around the room, back and forth, in and out of the chairs and tables and around the other children who, unbelievably, seemed oblivious to him. The boys looked horrified. 'Oh hello, come on in and find some toys,' said a dark, curly haired woman. She walked towards me as I held out my hand to shake hers in recognition of the fact that she must be Maggie. 'Hi I'm Maggie, you must be Gill.' 'Yes' I said 'And this is Sue with Thomas. I have Ben here and this is Christopher beside me.' She gave a cursory glance in their direction and then led us off to a table in the corner, where she told us we could sit until the boys settled. 'Help yourself to some toys, they'll soon be fine.' But I had my doubts. Ben clung on to me, his knuckles white with the effort of holding tight, Tom climbed onto Sue's knee and Christopher stood quietly watching what was going on, one hand on my knee, and the other on Sue's, as we sat on the small chairs. We tried to encourage them to play with the few toys we had gathered on the table in front of us, but the terrible noise continued as the plane flew round the room, although Christopher was slowly letting go as he started to make his way very tentatively towards the sand pit. Then Thomas cautiously followed him, but Ben wasn't going any further than where he was now standing on the floor between Sue and I, half heartedly clip-clopping a toy horse around the table in front of us. Suddenly there was a loud cry. Christopher was holding his hands over his eyes. Thomas started to run back to us. 'That bloody child's just chucked sand in Christopher's face,' said Sue as she leapt to her feet to rescue him. The aeroplane had flicked sand up as he flew past the sand pit and it had gone straight into Christopher's face. Maggie stopped the plane for a second, 'Now then Robert, we don't throw sand do we. Do you remember I told you not to do that last week? Off you go and play quietly somewhere or there will be no outdoor play time for you if you're naughty again.' Sue and I looked at one another. Robert - so this was Robert. I could now see why his mother thought he might kill a small sibling. Ryan Air Robert flew off again, having taken absolutely no notice of Maggie at all. She came over to see if Christopher was alright, 'We'll be having drinks and biscuits in a moment, that'll cheer him up,' she said, not even offering us a tissue or a wet towel to help us in our effort to wash the sand from every facial orifice that Christopher possessed.

We had the drinks and biscuits and then it was outdoor playtime, which was every bit as dangerous as indoor playtime. Ryan Air Robert's flying escalated to new levels once he was outside. He raced around the playground, pushing and shoving other children and kicking toys out of his way as he flew, with little or no discipline he left a trail of destruction behind him. Finally it was time to leave. Sue and I breathed a sigh of relief as we loaded the boys into the car. I looked across at Mrs. Road Runner leaving with Ryan Air Robert; poor woman looked quite exhausted, which wasn't at all surprising, as we felt exhausted from just watching him for a morning.

When we got home I did something that was very out

of character - I phoned a local private nursery that I knew some of our friends' children went to. I was sure it would be far too expensive for three of them, but I might as well ask the question and see if they had any places left. A well spoken voice answered the phone. 'Hello, Linda Saunders speaking,' I was taken aback by the speed and efficiency with which she answered the phone. 'Oh, um, hello you don't know me but my name's Gill Arthey, I'm just phoning to make an enquiry - I wondered if you had any places left for this term or even next term, and how much you charge. The problem is I will need three places.' 'Oh hello Gill, actually I do know you and I know your parents-in-law very well. Do you remember you came and played tennis here one evening before you were even married?' Of course, I did remember; how stupid I was not to have put two and two together. At the time I had wondered why there was so much outdoor play equipment all over the lawn, but not being particularly interested in having children at that moment I didn't even enquire.

I went on to explain to Mrs. Saunders about our horrendous morning and Ben's troubles, telling her that I couldn't possibly leave my 'precious brood' there and feel they were safe. She was really lovely, and told us to come over on Friday for a trial hour. She was certain she could make some room for them every Monday. She couldn't offer us anything more at that moment, but she was sure some places would become available as the year went on. 'We always get some natural wastage as families move away from the area,' she told me, 'But Mondays are fairly quiet so we have enough spaces for you to have at least one day a week.' I thanked her profusely and rang off. Sue had been hovering. 'So can they go?' 'Yes,' I said 'And even better, it's only fifty pence per child more than the other playgroup. I think it's worth every penny to know that they'll be safe. They have a drink, either milk or fruit juice, and a fruit snack at break times. She suggests we stay until break time on Monday, but to tell them even before we arrive that we'll only be staying until then, and that we'll be back by lunch time to pick them up. It seems a whole lot more honest and sensible to me, rather than this sneaking off thing at the other group.' Sue agreed with me. I then did the bit I was dreading and phoned the other play group to tell them we wouldn't be going back. I had the reception I was expecting, but I had to do what I felt was right for the boys. I wanted to say to her to tell Robert's mother to investigate Ritalin, but I resisted the temptation, after all who was I as a trainee mother to give anyone advice?

The boys started Canham House Nursery on Monday, joining Edward, Sam and James who were their regular playmates. We left at morning break without them even murmuring. They just about had time to look up and wave as we went.

MODULE 14:
BREAKING AND ENTERING, AND THE FACTS OF LIFE

There was a small knock at the back door. It was Larna, the young girl from the village who had been coming to ride Sparkie and generally help with her care. She wanted to know if there was anything else I wanted her to do before she cycled back to the village, as it was beginning to get dark. The boys had been in the bath after their tea and they were all hair washed, scrubbed to a shine, and in their pyjamas and dressing gowns ready for a story and bedtime. Larna was the love of our three little boys' lives; at just fourteen she was fun and had endless time and energy for them. They fought to get out of the door, like a litter of small, eager puppies, waiting to escape from the pen. I struggled to talk to Larna and at the same time hold the three of them back. There was a cool, early autumnal wind this October evening so I was keen to keep them in the warm. Finally I managed to extricate myself and close the back door momentarily behind me, keeping them in the kitchen whilst I made further arrangements with Larna in readiness for the coming weekend. I held on to the door handle as Christopher pulled it up and down in his anxiety to get out. He shouted out, 'Open the door naughty mummy, want to see Larna. NAUGHTY MUMMY.' Everything went quiet for a second – and then disaster. I heard the click of the key as it turned in the lock. 'Huh' I gasped, 'Oh no, he's locked the door on us.' Larna and I ran round to look through the kitchen window. 'Christopher, be a good boy and turn the key the other way please, you must open the door for mummy.' He looked back at me. A large and cheeky grin appeared on his face as he shook his head, his fair curls bobbing back and forth. With that he took the key from the lock and popped it into his pocket as he ran off laughing. He disappeared from the kitchen and into the depths of the house. Thomas, obviously realising that some excitement was on the cards, shot off in hot pursuit of his brother.

Ben had been happily playing with the Fisher-Price Zoo, but he too was just beginning to crawl over to a chair to pull himself up in readiness for walking. I turned to Larna, 'You stay here and keep an eye on Ben, if the other two come back into the kitchen, try to persuade Christopher to un-lock the door. I'm going round to the front of the house to see if our bedroom fan-light window is open.' As I ran around the corner, I passed the front door. Through the small panes of glass, I could see along to the bathroom. To my horror the sink was overflowing onto the floor and Thomas and Christopher were dancing and stamped their feet in the ever growing puddle. I ran on to the outside of our bedroom to see if by any chance one of the windows had been left even slightly open. My heart sank as I remembered closing the fan light only an hour earlier, so I ran back to the front door to see how flooded the bathroom was.

By now the terrible two had the potties. They were tipping water over one another's heads; at least Ben didn't seem to have joined in with the fun though. There wasn't much I could do other than knock on the window, waggle my finger and threaten, which had absolutely no effect at all. I ran back round to Larna who was still at the kitchen window. She had a look of complete horror on her face, 'No Ben,' she said, 'No don't get up there, you might fall.' Ben had got himself on to his feet with the assistance of the chair and, realising there were no adults around to control affairs, had pushed it across the slippery lino floor to the work surface. He was suspended across the chair when I arrived at the window, wriggling and heaving himself onto the seat, grunting with the effort as he pulled himself up. He wobbled precariously whilst holding onto the surface, and then grinned with delight as he saw us peering through the window.

We stood watching with bated breath as he spotted the small cottage pie waiting on the work surface for Eddie's supper. Then his eyes drifted towards to the dog's dinner cooling at the other end of the surface. Ben leant over to pull the two bowls towards him, getting them nicely positioned. He looked back through the window with a smug expression on his face. 'Ben you're not to touch them, you'll be in big trouble if you do,' I threatened. He grinned, knowing that we were helpless to do anything. The temptation was just too much, he dipped both hands into the bowls, squeezing the mixture between his dainty little fingers, carefully mixed the two meals together. 'Oh for goodness sake,' I said, 'I just have to get in somehow.'

By now I was desperate, so I went and found a hammer and chisel in the shed and started to chip away at the putty, hoping to be able to lift the pane of glass out. Not a very practical idea, but what other options were there? Larna was running to and fro keeping an eye on all the mischief while I chiselled away. At that moment my neighbour Evelyn appeared. 'Have you got a problem?' she said.

'The boys have locked me out of the house,' I told her. 'Ooh the young buggers,' she said in her broad Northamptonshire accent. 'What can I do, shall I go and find Alf for you?' 'Oh would you?' I said feeling relieved. She disappeared off, then just as I was beginning to wonder where she had got to, my parents walked round the corner with a key. We rushed in to find the boys who by now were bored with their activities, and were in the lounge playing quietly with tomorrow's toy box. I was so relieved and my whole body was now shaking. I turned to my parents to ask, 'How on earth did you know to bring a key, and where did you get a key from anyway?' Mum looked rather pleased with herself as she answered the mystery. 'When you went on holiday in the summer and left the key for dad so he could decorate the hall, I went and had a key cut so that we always had a spare. Evelyn phoned to tell us you were in trouble and that she couldn't find Alf. Unfortunately, he was out exercising his greyhounds so she wondered whether we had a key to let you back in. She said you were desperate.' I was so relieved that Evelyn had the sense to phone mum, and was even more grateful that my mum had had the sense to think ahead to this kind of eventuality. They say mum knows best and I would never need proof of this ever again. The boys were none the worse for their moment of being 'home alone' and seemed oblivious to the horror it had caused.

The only one to lose out was poor Eddie, who had to have fish fingers and oven chips for his supper. Basil the dog had a lovely dinner, as his boring dog meal was now mixed with prime beef cottage pie. This small incident made me realised that my three little piglets were certainly a force to be reckoned with. With triplepathy and the ability to work so well as a team, this meant that they could cause as much devastation as the iceberg did to the Titanic.

***

Not long after this incident we decided to breed with the boys' pretty little black Netherland dwarf rabbit. Larna's dwarf white male rabbit Lulu (named as a baby when they believed him to be female) was getting older, so she desperately wanted to have some of his babies, as he had such a lovely nature. I decided it would be a good exercise to teach the boys the early rudiments of the birds and the bees, so we agreed that she could bring her rabbit up to our house on Saturday morning. We told the boys that their rabbit was going to meet Larna's daddy rabbit, so that they could make some babies together. Christopher and Ben seemed to have only a passing interest, but Thomas was fascinated by the whole procedure, even getting himself a stool to stand on so he could get a better view into the raised indoor run, which had at one time housed our predecessor's budgerigars. Unfortunately, Lulu had very little idea in the arts of wooing a bride, or indeed how to carry out his marital duties. After much sniffing and several abortive attempts to get on with the job, he decided that her head must be the end that babies were procreated from. Thomas looked on until eventually other things took his interest and he moved away to play elsewhere. I hoped that he wouldn't remember too much about the way the rabbits had gone about things, after all I would hate him to have got the wrong idea on the matter. Fortunately it all seemed to be quickly forgotten and Lulu returned to Larna none the wiser that he'd got things dreadfully wrong.

A month later my cousin and his wife came to visit my parents. Having got married earlier in the year, they were expecting their first baby and, being a bit ahead of me, their baby was due within the next few weeks. We were all in the sitting room and Louise was playing with the boys on the floor. As she knelt to stand up Thomas looked with wide blue eyes at her expanded abdomen. 'You got a baby in your tummy?' he asked. 'Yes I have Thomas,' replied Louise. 'Hmm' said Thomas in a knowing way. 'My rabbits having babies too.' 'Oh is she, that's nice' said Louise. Thomas continued in his matter of fact way. 'Yes, Larna's daddy rabbit gave my mummy rabbit babies up her nose.' Louise's mouth dropped open and my cousin George nearly choked on the mouthful of tea he had just taken before exploding into convulsive laughter. All I could hope was that Thomas would forget about his early lesson in the birds and the bees, which had seemed like a good idea at the time.

MODULE 15:
THE PROPERTY MARKET, THE
FORTH TRIPLET

With our pending delivery getting ever closer we still weren't any nearer to finding our next home. A cold and snowy winter was now upon us and, although we had been to view several properties, nothing was coming in even a near second best to the home we already had, with the exception of one which was too far out of our price range - so much so we hadn't even been to view it. However the estate agents all seemed to feel it was the only one that fitted our requirements so, consequently, the details kept on falling through our letter box with repetitive regularity and had been doing so since late summer. I was desperate to see it, as it was just what we were looking for. But Eddie was adamant that at £98,000 it wasn't even a consideration and at least thirty thousand above our budget. Now, it seems such a small price for a five bedroom house, but in 1986/87 it was a lot of money. We had had three different agents to value our home and they all valued it at between £43,000 and £47,000 - a long way off what we needed to be able to buy our dream home. But I really couldn't believe that our house was only worth what they were telling us and I was convinced that all the agents were valuing it as a village semi-detached bungalow, rather than the individual property that it was. It was set away from the village, had amazing views and three quarters of an acre garden surrounding it. We had been prepared to lay down our life savings and were very happy to be really frugal in order to buy it, so I really couldn't believe someone else wouldn't feel the same as us.

Then one evening Eddie came home from work looking thoughtful, and as we sat having supper he said 'Perhaps we'll just go and have a quick look at that place you like the look of.' I raised my eyebrows. 'Why the change of mind?' 'Well, the tenant in the flat above the garage came in to give his notice today. He's moving into a house that he's buying nearer to his work and he's taking on a mortgage of forty thousand. It set me thinking that if he could afford that amount, then perhaps we could too. Maybe I'm just being too cautious. I'm not promising anything, but it's worth a look; they'll have to move a lot on the price for us to afford it, though.'

So we made an appointment to see the property the following day. It was everything we could have asked for and more. There were five bedrooms, four smaller ones down stairs and one bigger room in the roof. There was a large L-shaped lounge/diner, and a decent size kitchen. Along the hallway, by the bedrooms, was a separate shower room and a family bathroom – all be it with a dreadful sunken bath. The property needed some work, although it was mainly decorating and nothing that time and energy couldn't put right. But it was certainly somewhere we could move into immediately without a need to do anything. Attached to the house was a large garage big enough for three cars, with an inspection pit which was boarded over, and a loo in the corner. This would be a wonderful playroom, big enough for outdoor toys, but with a connecting door into the house. Outside there were about two acres of land, three wooden stables and a four-bay lean to barn. Its position was amazing, being surrounded on three sides by a conifer forest and on the other side parkland belonging to a large country house. There was a mown riding leading straight out from the side of the property and into the woods. In front was a clear area of about an acre with a small, wild pond that belonged to the Forestry Commission. The access was off a bypass road and up a bridle path track through the woods. The road continued over a cattle grid, into the park and through an avenue of trees. It was at least a mile from the nearest road so our animals would all be safe, so too would the boys as they grew older and were able to explore more. The parkland was the home to an internationally renowned equine event. There was also an abundance of Horse Chestnut trees in the park for our little boys to collect conkers from.

In my wildest dreams I couldn't have wanted for anything better for our family to grow up in. BUT, although we both loved it there was the issue of the money. The people who were selling it were unwilling to budge an inch on the price because they had only just reduced it by seven thousand, so it was just out of the question. Eddie, by now was also getting a distinct case of cold feet. 'I know you love it Gill and I do too, but we'll just have to go back to the drawing board and find something a bit cheaper. I'm afraid it's just a step too far for us. After all it's not that long since we've taken on the expense of buying the garage. No, I'm sorry but it's just too risky.' He shook his head and walked off looking dejected. I felt so disappointed but it wasn't fair to put more financial pressure on him so I started to trawl around the estate agents again.

We looked at house after house but nothing even remotely came up to the mark. 'Perhaps we'd better think again about extending our house,' I said one evening. Eddie answered me. 'Well you heard Andrew, he said he wouldn't do it because the house wouldn't be worth the cost of the extension. But I know what you mean, it's all beginning to look a bit hopeless.'

Our builder friend Andrew had been adamant that it would be money wasted, so what else was there to do other than to cram in and wait for goodness knows how long until the right thing came along? Then, the week before our baby was due, I was doing the weekly rounds of the estate agents looking for any new properties listed. Whilst I was looking on the smart, stainless-steel edged board in a new agency that had recently opened in the town centre, I became engaged in conversation with the manager. It was a smaller agency and one we hadn't actually used for a valuation. 'Can I be of any assistance to you, madam?' the rather large gentleman asked. Perhaps he was sensing my despair. I told him about our requirements and how impossible it was proving to find anything. 'I've got the perfect one for you, the vendor has just asked us to market it and I know they're getting pretty desperate to sell. In fact we've only just been given the instruction so there are no printed details yet.' My ears pricked up. 'Really, where is it and, more importantly, how much is it?' 'It's actually been on the market for quite some time, but with several other agents. It's a bit off the beaten track so it's not everyone's cup of tea.' I halted him in mid-sentence. 'Before you go any further is it just outside the village of Brigstock? Because if it is, we've been to see it and it's too far out of our price range, but yes it's our dream property and nothing else even begins to match up to it.'

He confirmed that it was the property, but that he thought they may now be open to a lower offer as they were becoming pretty desperate to sell. 'What's the property like that you're selling?' Jim asked. I told him about our lovely position and the three quarters of an acre garden, and how I felt it was being undervalued. 'Yes' he said, much to my surprise. 'Yes I agree with you, it's being valued as a village house, and they're certainly not valuing it as a house with the sort of land you have around you. I'll come and have a look at it this afternoon if you like, but at a guess I would say it's worth ten to fifteen thousand more than the current valuation. In fact I have at least three people looking for something just like it.'

I positively skipped out of the shop in my eagerness to get home and phone Eddie. That afternoon Jim valued our house at £60,000, and we had the first people around to see it that same evening. Before the other interested parties could come and view, the first people offered us the asking price, which needless to say we didn't hesitate to accept. Just to make absolutely sure we were still as enamoured with it, we had another visit to the dream house. There had been a shower of rain, but the sun was now shining again - as I stood outside I could smell the fresh scent of the pine wood and I listened to the soft munching of the cattle out in the park, but more than anything I listened to the peace and quiet that surrounded the property. How could anything be better than this I thought? It was simply perfect.

***

Eddie agreed the final deal with the vendors on Sunday the 8th of March 1987, two days after our baby was due. In the early hours of March 9th my labour started and Michael Robert was born at 10.20am, eight hours after I first awoke with a few small twinges in my stomach. The labour was a little drawn out as Michael wriggled and kicked his way into the world, but one last big push did the trick and he arrived with a flourish, slithering rapidly into the hands of the rather surprised, and only half gowned midwife. Eddie and I both gazed down at our new little son as he lay upon my stomach. 'Huh,' I gasped, 'What's wrong with his nose?' We both looked at the screwed up, red-faced, angry little boy. With his tiny fists tightly clenched and, his white knuckles tucked up under his chin, he looked as if he'd just been ten rounds with Mike Tyson and was ready for more. 'Poor little chap' said Eddie, 'He'll have to have plastic surgery, he can't go out into the world with a snozz on him like that.' The midwife laughed at our complete horror. 'Don't worry, it's only got squashed. He had his head back throughout the labour. It'll soon look perfect. You wait and see, he'll be absolutely beautiful in a couple of days.' I couldn't help but register that this new little baby of ours had had his head tipped back; so that would explain why I had just experienced what I can only describe as a task nothing short of trying to push a watermelon down a drainpipe. We both looked back down at our little boy, feeling extremely doubtful that he would ever look beautiful!

Later on in the day Eddie brought the boys in to meet their baby brother, who was just three and a half years their junior. Thomas burst into tears of joy, it was love at first sight as far as he was concerned. Christopher peered into the clear Perspex crib. 'Urgh, baby Michael's got a really funny nose, it's all flat.' Ben couldn't quite bring himself to even look. In his mind Michael was the biggest threat so far to his position of supremacy. When Eddie's sister told our two year old niece Jane that she had a new baby cousin called Michael Robert, she went and told her big brother William that their new baby cousin was called Michael Rabbit. Michael, being the youngest of the six grandchildren, was sure to be cherished, particularly by Jane, his rather motherly and only female cousin. We gave the boys a doll each so they too had a little one to change and bath, and 'Michael' gave them all their first proper knife, fork and spoon set.

But the old niggling worries crept into my mind as I lay

in the hospital bed after his delivery: would the triplets accept another person into their cosy little gang of three? Would little Michael have an unhappy childhood, feeling left out and ostracised? On the other hand, perhaps they would totally accept him into their gang, even allowing him to become a member of the exclusive triplepathy club. Only time would answer this for us, and he wouldn't be going back to where he had come from, that was for sure!

***

Michael's arrival coincided with a late, cold snap which was the finale to what had been a very cold winter. There was even snow on the ground the day he was born, so in order to keep the house nice and warm we kept a coal fire burning in the grate, which was safely contained behind a child-safe fire guard. When Eddie made up the fire and sorted out the ash he put the fire guard against the far wall and encouraged the boys to stand behind it to play lions in a cage. Maybe it was just fatigue, or some reason known only to Eddie, but he cleared out the hot ash underneath the grate into a plastic bucket. It doesn't take much to guess that the glowing ashes took only seconds to burn through the bottom of the bucket, spilling hot ash and molten plastic onto the relatively new carpet. 'Oh bollocks,' shouted Eddie, realising his error. Ben, who was still enjoying experimenting with his new found linguistic skills, tried out the new words. 'Oh bowocks', he grinned, feeling very pleased with himself. ' Ben, that's a word only daddy can use,' said Eddie. Ben continued to quietly try it out. 'Just ignore him,' I said, 'He'll soon forget if you don't make an issue of it.'

It was soon forgotten about as I predicted, or so we thought. The following week Ben had his therapy session. Linda was getting Ben to stack the bricks up one upon the other. The pile of bricks grew until he got to four in height, then they all tumbled down. 'Oh bowocks,' he said. I took a sharp intake of breath, trying not to catch Linda's eye, hoping she wouldn't understand what he was saying. The same process was repeated, the bricks finally tumbling to the floor. 'Oh bowocks,' said Ben again, this time putting even more intonation and feeling into it. 'Is he saying what I think he's saying?' asked Linda frowning in puzzlement. 'I'm afraid so,' I answered looking suitably embarrassed. She grinned. 'Oops, oh well never mind it happens, don't worry, he'll soon forget it.' Then Linda had an idea. 'Ben, when the bricks fall over you have to say oh wow wee - ok?' Ben continued to stack the bricks, his pink little tongue poking between his rosebud lips, he was deep in concentration. Down the bricks tumbled again. A cheeky grin appeared on Ben's face as he said, 'Oh wow wee,' then swiftly followed by ' Bowocks.' So what could we say to that? It was all we could do to stifle our laughter, but I really did hope he would soon forget his newly acquired word - somehow I had my doubts.

MODULE 16:
REMOVAL LOGISTICS

The boxes were piled high in various rooms; we had nearly finished the packing ready for our move. On returning home from hospital with Michael and in between feeding the troops, Sue and I spent the next eight weeks packing and getting everything ready. The solicitors had all been instructed and with no upward chain we were on schedule to move in another week's time.

The day in early May arrived, with the sun shining on us to help the move go smoothly. All the boys had been despatched to a friend's and Michael's bottles had all been made. The excitement of the day had ensured we were all up early and the boys were in a particularly helpful mood, packing their little rucksacks with some spare clothes themselves. Eddie then went to fetch the horse box lorry we were borrowing from our friends, David and Pam, to use for the move.

Eddie soon arrived back, whilst Sue and I had been stacking boxes into relevant piles ready to be loaded. As the new house was only ten minutes from the old, we were happy to do several trips in the lorry in order to shuttle all our worldly goods from one home to the other. Sue, the two grandmothers and I were the cleaning team, and Eddie and the two grandfathers were the moving team, helped with voluntary man power for the heavier things by two of the boys' godfathers, Billy and Thomas. The day went unbelievably smoothly, and we were loading the final things by 2pm. There was a small space at the back of the lorry for Sparkie, the rabbit and the two hens. Eddie was just closing the ramp whilst I had a final cast around the house for anything we had missed. Just as I came out into the lean-to conservatory I spotted Eddie's slippers in the corner. 'Wait' I shouted, 'Here, pop your slippers into the back.' Eddie poked them through the nearly closed ramp, just under where Sparkie's head was tied. With one last sentimental look back at the house of so many happy times, I got into the car and shot off in front of the lorry to get to the new house first. By now mum and dad had gone off to fetch the boys for me. I knew they would be so excited when they arrived, as they hadn't yet seen their new home. It was going to be a dream location for them, with all the space and freedom they could ever want for their future, as they grew from boys to young men.

I walked through the front door and in to our new house for the first time since Eddie and I had become its joint owners. I felt as if I were the luckiest person alive. Boxes were strewn all over the kitchen floor and the living room was the same. All the boxes that Sue and I had so carefully labelled with the relevant locations on them had been placed accordingly. Michael's equipment - bottles, formula milk, sterilizers, changing mats and nappies had all been loaded into my car, as we would need them instantly.

Soon the lorry rumbled into the drive, chug chug chug as the ageing engine ticked over. At the same moment mum and dad rolled into the drive with the boys. We quickly undid their seat belts, leaving Michael in his baby seat for a moment to sleep. We watched their little faces as they took in the openness of their new surroundings. 'Is this our new garden?', asked Christopher, looking around at the huge area with his large questioning eyes. 'Can we go in to that wood?', asked Thomas, pointing towards the trees. I was quick to answer that question. 'Never on your own, but we can go for lots of walks and take Sparkie for rides in there.' The mention of Sparkie drew their attention away from the new house. 'Huh, where Barkie gone?' asked Ben, looking alarmed, wondering whether she had been forgotten. 'Well let's see who's in here, shall we,' said Eddie, as he undid the clips on the lorry ramp. Slowly he pulled it down, the boys' eager little faces waiting to see who was there. Sparkie, who had by now managed to untie herself, was facing in the opposite direction. The boys' toilet humour was developing at a healthy rate and as the ramp opened further it revealed that she had just delivered a steaming poo straight into Eddie's slippers, which were situated right underneath her rear end. The boys laughed and laughed at the sight of the poo and at Eddie's reaction of complete disgust over the fate of his beloved slippers.

***

Only two weeks after the move we went on holiday to France. It had been booked months before, and well before we knew we were going to be moving. So cancelling wasn't an option as we were going with some friends to a large 'gite' in Brittany. Eddie decided it would be a good opportunity to have some carpet laid along the hallway, which had a horrible red lino on it, and some carpets in the bedrooms. It was also a good time to have a bit of gloss paint on the doors and a coat of emulsion paint on the walls, just to clean and brighten the place up.

Packing the car and cases for the holiday tested every bit of energy I possessed, as I was without any help the day before we were due to go. Whilst Michael was asleep and the boys were at nursery I made a pretty good start on loading the roof rack, so some of the work had been done. But after lunch we had to go into Oundle to get Thomas some new shoes; he had just had a sudden growth spurt and I was aware his old shoes were now getting rather tight. The new ones were little emerald green and white ankle boots, which he had been particularly taken with, so we also bought some emerald green shoe cream to clean them with. We arrived back home just as Michael was due for his feed. He was such a good baby and rarely grizzled, but he was just starting to get a bit fractious so it was priority to feed him before I did any more packing. Although Eddie had said to me, 'Just do what you can, and what you can't we'll do tonight,' I desperately wanted to get it finished - after all we were going to have an early start and a long drive the next day. I sat quietly in the toy strewn kitchen feeding Michael, while the boys played just outside the open kitchen door on the front lawn. Suddenly I became aware of an ominous silence. I felt a lurch in my stomach as this was always the pre-curser to mischief, so I got up carefully and walked to the window, trying hard to not disturb Michael as he fed. The boys were no longer on the lawn. My eyes darted frantically to and fro, trying to see where they had gone. Suddenly my eyes fell upon a horrendous sight - the car windows were now all coloured green, the same green as the shoe cream we had just purchased. My heart sank as I burst into tears of exhaustion and frustration. Now I would also have to find time to clean the car as well as finish packing it. They really were a force to be reckoned with when they all put their heads together. It always seemed to happen so quickly. Although I was slowly learning that I needed to be a step ahead of them, I still wasn't quite up to speed. One day I hoped I would learn how to master this art of being a mother.

The holiday had actually come at a good time as I had a pending operation, so it did me good to get away and forget about it for a fortnight. Michael really was such a well behaved and easy baby, with a ready smile for everyone. He watched the boys constantly and Thomas absolutely adored him, helping with him at every opportunity. Ben was now accepting him and would have the occasional cuddle, and Christopher loved and cuddled him as long as it didn't interfere too much with quality playtime. As predicted by our midwife in the hospital, his nose was now completely normal and even if I say so myself, at ten weeks old he was beginning to look quite pretty. So much so he attracted rather a lot of attention from baby admirers during our holiday. With his fair hair, large and focused blue eyes, framed with long dark eyelashes, dimples in his cheeks and a huge smile, he was always having his cheek tickled, or being told that he was gorgeous by people who peered into his pushchair.

***

Our holiday was a change, but not really a rest. We were, however, very excited about returning to our new home, especially to see the smartly decorated walls and doors, and the fresh new carpets in the hallway and bedrooms. As we pulled into the property early that evening, we were a little surprised to see mum and dad's car on the drive. I had phoned them the day before while we were still in France, to tell them our estimated arrival time. But I hadn't expected them to come up until we phoned to say we were home. To our surprise there was no overpowering smell of fresh new paint, only the overwhelming smell of bleach and cleaning products. There was no sign of mum and dad and no sign of painted walls either, although the new carpet had been laid in the hall. 'Mum, dad' I shouted,

'We're back.' They appeared at the top of the stairs from the spare and biggest bedroom. 'What are you doing up there?' I asked, laughing at the oddity of seeing them appear at the top of the staircase. 'We're just coming down,' they said, as they descended the rather steep, narrow wooden staircase. I was still puzzled as to what was going on.

The boys had rushed into the large garage to play with their toys, having missed them during the holiday. Michael was still asleep in his baby car seat on the kitchen floor. Mum and dad came through whilst I put the kettle on for a cup of tea. 'So what's going on?' I asked. Dad looked fraught. 'You don't want to know,' he said. 'Where did you get that dreadful painter from, Eddie? You've got no idea what a state he's left this house in, and as for the painting, well the only paint to leave a tin in the last fortnight was yesterday, and that went all over the new carpet.' Eddie and I listened in shock as mum and dad went on to describe the chapter of events. Eddie had found him by word of mouth; apparently he was trying to set up on his own as a painter and decorator and was very keen to get some local business. As he had a tenuous link, having once purchased a car from the garage, and also being a friend of a friend, Eddie decided he could be trusted with our door key as obviously he needed to have daily access to the house. It was arranged that he would decorate throughout the fortnight while we were away, and then the carpet could be laid at the end when the painting had been done. Dad continued. 'We came up yesterday morning just before lunch to check everything was finished and in order, ready for you coming home, only to find the house in a horrendous mess. The sink was piled high with dirty plates, at least a fortnight's worth. The hob was thick with grease and burnt matter and your best saucepan had chip oil in it. There were bits of burnt chip lying in a cruddy mess at the bottom of it. And finally, all the work surfaces needed bleaching where the remnants of their Indian take away had left yellow stains everywhere.'

We listened, hardly able to believe our ears. Mum took over. 'All of this would have been just about acceptable if he'd done the job he'd been employed to do, but he only opened the first tin of paint yesterday when he suddenly panicked, realising you were on your way home. As we walked in he was scraping paint off the new carpet. The stupid man had opened the pot of paint, propped it on the step ladder and, not surprisingly, it had fallen off spilling all over your new carpet. You can't believe what a state it was all in. I thought your father was going to hit him, I had to physically restrain him he was so angry. Well, needless to say, dad told him to sling his hook and wait until he was contacted by you on your return.' It appears he had moved himself and his girlfriend into the spare room and, imagination would tell you what he'd been up to for two weeks, and it certainly wasn't painting. To add insult to injury, when I went up to the spare room, there under the bed were her ghastly, pink fluffy slippers. I had a ceremonial burning the next day. There wasn't even a slightest chance he would get any recommendations from us as a painter and decorator. We heard later in the year that he had taken a position as a chef in a local pub - not a pub we'd be eating in, judging by the state of our kitchen. It was a good lesson to us in trust, and we wouldn't be making that mistake again.

***

But we were still very pleased with our new home and not long after returning from holiday something happened to confirm just how lucky we were to have found it. The boys had been in the garden all day with us, so bed time was rather later than normal. With the increasing day light as spring had rolled in to summer, it was becoming harder to get them to bed. They had been in the bath and were just sitting in the lounge having a drink of milk and a story before bedtime. A light mist was just rising around the dew pond as dusk fell, probably heralding another fine day tomorrow. Thomas suddenly sat upright on the settee, staring out of the French windows and down towards the water. 'Look' he said, 'There's Father Christmas's reindeer by the pond.' We all looked up. There grazing in the mist on the area of open grass were five fallow deer, their little tails flicking as they swished the midges away. We were all so amazed to see such a sight right on our door step, and again Eddie and I realised this was going to be the most wonderful place for our children to grow up. We definitely were the luckiest little family.

MODULE 17:
SURGICAL PROCEDURES, EMULATING BEHAVIOUR AND THE PITFALLS OF EMPLOYMENT

Only a few weeks after returning from our holiday I had to go into hospital for a small operation to drain an ovarian cyst, which was spotted on my first scan. Hospitals were never my favourite places and to be perfectly honest I was again truly terrified. Somehow having the children was a means to an end, and at least I came out with something after all the terror. But this was something else and I became convinced I would die, much the same as when I convinced myself I would die if I had a general anaesthetic whilst having the boys. Then there was the issue of the needles, something I have had a pathological terror of since having the yellow fever injection at the 'hospital for tropical diseases' when I was seven.

Mum and I had travelled up to London for the day so we could have our injections in preparation for our year long trip to Africa. It was one of the few places that did the yellow fever vaccination in those days. We queued like cattle in the stiflingly hot room waiting for our turn. As we drew near I pushed mum in front of me, not much fancying the look of the brown liquid that was about to be infused into my arm. The injection itself didn't really hurt much at all, but as we went over to the woman at the desk for our certificates I began to feel a bit peculiar. She handed me two jellies, as was customary with children, which I normally would have gobbled down in seconds. But by now I was feeling decidedly sick, and as mum was rushing off ahead of me I could do nothing but clutch the sticky jellies in my hot sweaty little fist and trot after her. As we flew down the corridor and into another room to join yet another queue the room started to look very weird. In fact everything had turned black and white and I felt as if I was disappearing down a tunnel. A stranger grabbed me and sat me on a chair next to her. Then she tapped mum on the arm and alerted her to the fact that I was feeling pretty unwell. Mum was mortified, she had been so anxious to get everything signed and dealt with in order for us to get back to dad's office. In her hurry she hadn't noticed me fighting to survive my experience.

Although I can be totally rational about the fact that I was only about to faint and nothing more, it left me with a complete phobia of needles and indeed hospitals. In fact it's something of a miracle that we have children at all as I had to deal with some terrible gremlins to become a mother. Now here I was in another terrifying situation. It's probably a good job I didn't know what was round the corner as the tiny operation turned into a big one. Once they had a look inside it was decided to remove the whole ovary, rendering me a patient for not just one night as we'd expected, but five nights instead.

Sue had recently been asked by some friends to go to Torquay with them as they were setting up a T-shirt business on the beach front for the summer. We were very sad to see her go, but Larna was just breaking up from school so she was happy to come and help us through the holidays. She was going to stay in the upstairs bedroom, and we were going to give her some money for her efforts so she could earn herself some holiday pay. It would give us a bit of time to decide what help we needed for the future, as Sue wasn't sure if the job in Torquay would be ongoing. But obviously we hadn't anticipated my being so indisposed, so Eddie had to take some time off work to help. With a four month old baby and three and three quarter year old triplets, there was just so much to do. Mum and mother in law were really great, helping with the meals and Michael's bottles. Larna had been babysitting for us on the odd occasion when our parents couldn't, although we never went very far away. But we hadn't left her totally on her own with them when they were awake, so we worked out a rota to make sure she always had someone with her in the daytime.

One afternoon, a couple of days after my operation, Eddie arrived at the hospital to visit me. He looked fraught and pale, with dark bags under his eyes. His thinning blond hair was all over the place, probably from dragging his fingers through it with exasperation. 'Whatever's the matter?' I asked him, as I lay back on my hospital bed, just beginning to enjoy the rest. He rubbed his brow and shook his head. 'You just won't believe what the little buggers have done today. I really don't know how you cope with them. You need eyes not only at the front of your head, but at the back and the sides too.' I couldn't imagine what they possibly could have done that had been the cause of all this stress. 'Go on,' I said, 'You'd better break it to me.' Eddie began, clearly traumatised. 'Well you know we've just had the sitting room painted?' 'Yehhs' I said hesitantly, feeling that creeping feeling of dread. 'And you know the powder paints Lucie gave them for Christmas?' 'Yehhs, but they can't get at that, I put it up on the high shelf in the toy room, there's no way they could reach it up there.' Eddie shook his head and looked back at me with tired eyes. 'Well they can. They only brought the Cosy Coupé in from the garage, climbed up onto the roof to give them some height, and reached up to the shelf.'

Lucie was soon to become Michael's godmother, and had been involved with the boys since they were tiny. Our friendship with Lucie was quite unique in as far as we were as friendly with Lucie as we were with her parents. I was almost exactly as many years older than Lucie, as her parents were older than Eddie. Soon after the boys were born she arranged for her parents, David and Pam, to bring her to our house every Sunday morning so she could help us with the boys' care. This carried on until university necessitated her leaving the area, when the boys were almost two. But, as soon as the holidays arrived, she took on the role of general playmate and fun person again. The boys loved Lucie coming to visit as much as they also loved her ability to buy great presents. We, on the other hand, began to nervously anticipate what she would think of next. The finger painting set, the plaster foot moulding kit and a pot of slime with rubber bugs in it. Then came the noisiest percussion band set and the latest were the industrial sized pots of powder paints which had been involved in this recent escapade!

I could just imagine the scene. Ben would have been the driver, Tom would have held it steady and Christopher, being the biggest, would have climbed on to the roof to reach the paint. Of course this had all been performed before and had been honed into a fine art. So with the height of the domed roof on the little car, their team effort and the inevitable triplepathy at work, they would have easily reached the high shelf. Hum, I thought, the Cosy Coupé again. It had been an accomplice in a crime before, and now it had been involved in yet another crime. This innocent looking, little red and yellow car might just have to mysteriously disappear for the foreseeable future. Eddie continued. 'Once they'd got it down, they took the pot of red paint into the bathroom and mixed the whole thing up with water. Then they armed themselves with a paint brush each, and painted all the lower part of the wall next to the fireplace. Then, as if that wasn't enough, just to colour co-ordinate things, they painted the back of the settee too.' Eddie buried his head in his hands in despair. 'You've got no idea how much of a mess it all is. I've got the worst off, but the new paint's going to have to be re-done. And as for the settee, that's never going to recover. It's a good job it's only a hand me down and we were going to replace it when we had some spare money. Well now we might just have to find that spare money, because it's going to have to be replaced sooner rather than later.'

He looked so miserable, and I did feel really sorry for him. But on the other hand, it didn't do him any harm to see at first hand how quickly and easily their triplepathy worked, and just how big a handful they could be when they put their three heads together. It was quite amazing as they had shown only a passing interest in the painter's work, quickly returning to their play after only a glance. But obviously it had made more of an impression than we thought, and this emulation of the painter's handy work made us all too aware that we could never turn our backs on them. They were a united force of energy, ideas and mischief, and we could never be complacent.

***

As the summer progressed we realised we needed to get some form of more permanent help. Sue was phoning us every week, so we knew that she was expecting to be employed in Devon until at least the end of October. Then she thought there would be a chance that she might be sent to France for the winter to help the company open another

T-shirt shop. So we decided we needed to look for some permanent help. We had a girl apply for the live in post, as we now had a perfect spare room to offer for a live in position. She was a girl from the nearby town, but thought she would quite like to experience living in the countryside. We offered her a week to try us and for us to try her. Poor girl really hadn't got a chance. She was a rather large and un-fit looking girl, having been very obviously a sick note when it came to school sports. She had long, greasy looking dark hair, and a good crop of spots, although she told me that she 'couldn't understand why, as she never ate crisps or chocolate.' She lumbered after the boys as they ran rings around her and when they found out she was terrified of every kind of bug that lived (and most of them lived in our house), they collected a sample of each one and put them in her bed. Suddenly we were alerted by loud screaming coming from her room, so we both ran to find out what was causing the blood-curdling cries, only to find the poor girl quivering in the corner of her room. When it became apparent what the cause of her terror was I needed no guesses to know what had gone on and to know who had created the bug zoo that was tucked up in the bed.

This signalled the end of her time with us so we had to go back to the drawing board, but not before we found the biggest haul of empty crisp packets and chocolate wrappers left behind after her hurried departure. Then we decided that I could probably cope with the boys on my own if there was some domestic help, probably three mornings a week would suffice. The appointed person could help me to keep the house clean and also help with the washing and ironing, plus any other jobs that were necessary. There was always the solid fuel burner to keep topped up; it heated the water for the central heating and our hot water supply. Then there was the preparation of the vegetables for our evening meals. We certainly wouldn't have any problems keeping someone busy.

As soon as we advertised a lady applied from another nearby town, so we asked her if she would come over for an interview. She drove into the yard in a decrepit old rust bucket of a car, not that we had any problem with rust buckets as I had driven very similar vehicles before we owned a garage. Larna and I were in the sitting room with the boys while we waited for the woman to arrive. Her remit was to entertain the boys whilst I conducted the interview in the kitchen. But as the woman got out of her car a look of complete terror appeared on Larna's face. 'Oh my God,' she said, 'She's just like a witch.' The woman had a craggy, wrinkled face, a hunched back and a large hooked nose. She scuttled rather than walked across the drive towards our house.

Another child-hood gremlin of mine was witches. I absolutely hated witches. They terrified me when I was a child, and I used to have regular dreams about them which left me sweaty and trembling in my bed. I was usually too scared to shout for my mother in case the witch herself appeared. But here was the epitome of my fear about to arrive at my front door. Knock, knock, knock - her craggy knuckles hit the wood. I slowly opened it only to see she was every bit as scary as she had first appeared, with large, hairy moles all over her wrinkled face and a permanently hunched back, she was positively grotesque. Her head turned to look up at me from her stooped position. She held out her hand to introduce herself, smiling to expose a row of rotting teeth. I almost recoiled in horror and had to take a firm hold of my emotions. I decided that I mustn't judge the book by its cover, as her credentials seemed pretty solid from a cleaning point of view. She had worked for various families, and also as a school cleaner and dinner lady. She told me how good she was with children, and how she would like to become involved with the boys' care, being willing to babysit at any time should I ever need her to. Then, in the next breath, she told me that her son was in a special school for children with extremely disruptive behaviour. But, we weren't in a position to be too fussy as she had been our only applicant. I offered her the job and asked her to start the following Monday, which she was happy to do as Larna would be back at school by then.

In the first week she managed to shrink Christopher's lovely little blue Guernsey jumper. It was so small it wouldn't even have fitted a cabbage patch doll, let alone any of the boys. The second week she washed the boys' new chino trousers on a boil wash with a red sweat shirt. As they emerged from the washing machine I could see the sweat shirt was now fuchsia pink, having generously shared its colour with the cream chinos, which were now also fuchsia pink, rendering them un-wearable. These too were also condemned to the bin. 'I'll do all the washing Marge,' I said, not wanting a confrontation. 'I don't mind doing the washing if you can keep up with the ironing.' But sadly that was no better and Eddie frequently found burns on his shirts, and any of the boys' sweat shirts with appliquéd motives had them melted and smeared all over them.

Then she managed to break the mirror in our bedroom and nearly blew up the solid fuel boiler by overloading it. It was bubbling and banging like a stoked steam engine ready for a journey. I feared it would explode with enormous velocity, so I had to get the boys out of the house before running around to Graham next door to ask him for his help. He had to put all the radiators on and run the hot taps for half an hour to get rid of the boiling water. There wasn't a week that passed without her damaging or shrinking something, so much so I wouldn't leave Michael with her for even a moment. By November Sue had returned, conveniently coinciding with us winning a Ford sales performance trip to Florida and the Bahamas, so she volunteered to come and look after the boys for the week we were to be away. Margery continued to come in to do the house work to enable Sue to concentrate on looking after the boys.

My dad was becoming increasingly unwell again, having suffered a small heart attack the previous winter. Thankfully, they had moved to a bungalow in the village so they were only five minutes away from us. But the last thing I wanted to do was put too much pressure on my parents whilst we were away, so having Sue back was wonderful for us all. On our return from the trip Sue told us that if we wanted her to stay she would love to have her old job back. 'To be honest, Gill, although it's been a fantastic experience going down to Devon, I don't want to go to France for the winter. We were living in what I can only describe as a squat, with no real furniture and only a couple of mattresses on the floor. We had two camping gas rings to cook on, and hardly any hot water to wash with, in fact I had cold showers most of the time. It was fun for a summer but I don't want to go to France and experience the same.'

Sue then went on to reveal what Margery was up to in our absence. She told Sue that she was helping herself to the loose change in our bedroom and pinching the new packs of tights that I kept on buying, laughing in her horrible cackle about the fact that I was apparently not noticing them going missing. I had actually noticed, although at first I thought it was just me being dizzy, but then I gradually began to suspect her on both counts. Other than putting security cameras in the bedroom I didn't know how to prove it and I never liked to think badly of people. She told Sue that she sat down to watch the television for an hour whilst I took the boys to nursery, making sure that she had the ironing board up so it looked as if she was working when I arrived back. In fact she was thoroughly horrible about us and had plans to start pinching even more, encouraging Sue to do the same. I was amazed at her stupidity, confiding in someone who was so clearly a friend of ours, and who had also so clearly been through so much with us. Sue was very much more to us than an employee. 'She's really got a chip on her shoulder, she calls you the rich bitch,' said Sue, 'I know you won't have treated her as anything other than a friend.' That was the most hurtful thing about it, I had treated her very kindly in spite of her determination to destroy virtually everything that we had ever owned, including our home. Knowing all of this made it pretty easy to terminate her employment, especially now we knew what she thought of us and what she had planned for us in the future. It was horrible and we were very relieved to see the back of her.

The author at 6 months pregnant.

The author with Mr. Magee the magpie and the dog.

Holding the boys for the first time at just 24 hours old.

A spring outing into the garden in the triple buggy.

The christening with Eddie's Grandma and her great grandchildren.

Sue, Eddie with Thomas, Father Patrick with Ben, and the author with Christopher on the christening day.

Sitting in the cool shade of the big Ash tree.

A large box provided endless hours of fun. Left to right, Ben, Tom and Christopher.

Eddie spent endless hours being a 'horsey'.

Even when he tried to sleep on the beach.

Ben, Christopher and Thomas amusing one another.

All wearing the same but different Fair Isle jumpers.

Ben pushing his little wooden walker made by Grandpa.
Thomas at full tilt.

The homemade triplet pushchair made by Sue's dad,
'Uncle Bill'.

My mum with the boys in the Cozy Coupe.

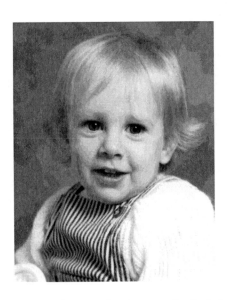

Michael aged 9 months. An angelic little boy.

Hours of fun in the mud at our new home.

Ben diligently practicing the piano.

School photo from Glapthorn. Christopher, Ben and Thomas.

The first skiing holiday. Christopher, Thomas and Ben.

Pony club camp. Ben on Misty, Michael on Taffy,
Christopher on Penny and Thomas on Whisky.

MODULE 18:
ORTHOPAEDICS AND THE EARLY
YEARS EDUCATION SYSTEM

I had watched with interest the development of the triplets'
language skills, which had developed in the order we had
grown to expect. Christopher was the first to start
experimenting with words, followed by Tom. They were
neither surprisingly early to speak nor were they late,
unlike Ben who was just on the side of late at nearly two
and a half years old. Even though his pronunciation was
poor he spoke in sentences right from the word go. Much
to my relief though, there were no signs, other than their
triplepathy, of a language all of their own, which we were
warned to be vigilant about and to nip in the bud if we got
even a hint of it beginning. Cute though it may seem at the
time, it was a dangerous road to go down and would
ultimately delay their conversational skills with the greater

general public and, of course, the family too.

Michael, however, developed at a much faster pace, having the most lovely, happy, easy going nature and language skills way in advance of anything we had seen with his brothers. By seven months old he could say 'clap', clapping his hands together to prove that he knew what he was talking about. By eight months he could say, dog, da da, mama and bye bye, waving to anyone who was leaving. And by nine months he was often found crawling down the hall following his brothers, who were busy playing Bat Man, singing 'na na bat bat, na na bat bat' as he tried to join in with their games. He constantly giggled at their antics and sat amongst them while they played. I think it was at this point that I realised he had slotted very nicely into the role of the fourth triplet. At ten months old he was spotted sitting in the dog's bed with Basil the dog, putting Eddie's 'Arthur Daley' hat on to his head and then swapping it onto Basil's head, saying 'mine 'at, dog 'at.' By the time he was a year old he was just about walking and had a string of words which we had long since lost count of. I had every reason to feel optimistic about this little chap who seemed so bright and forward with everything he did. Simple shaped jig saws had been conquered well before his first birthday, and he could identify and make the noise of every animal in his picture books. With language skills like these he was going to take to reading and writing like a duck takes to the water.

With the year flying by so fast we decided to look at the options of the primary schools in the vicinity available to the boys. The local school was lovely but fed into the worst senior school in the area. Although there were other good schools, the local authorities were tightening up all the time, particularly on children being accepted into senior schools for which their junior school was not a feeder for. Then it was suggested by an acquaintance of Eddie's that we should go and have a look at a small Church of England primary school in Glapthorn, a village a couple of miles from the garage. It was rumoured that they were having a particularly low intake and were keen to recruit pupils from out of the area. It was wonderful news as it fed into the three-tiered system that was particular to the catchment area. Both the middle school and the senior school were extremely well thought of, so it seemed to be a very good option. It would at least be sensible for us to go and have a look.

We arranged an appointment one afternoon towards the end of the pre-Christmas term to take the boys to meet the headmaster and for us to see the school. The head suggested we should go along at the end of the school day in time to coincide with the last lesson, but also in order for the boys to have a bit of time with him and the reception class teacher on their own, once all the children had gone home. We arrived in time to peep through the class room doors to see happy, attentive little faces concentrating on their teachers' every word, as lessons were just coming to a close. We were also able to establish that there was a happy atmosphere in each class. Once the school was empty the secretary, Heather, made cups of tea for us and plastic beakers of orange for the boys.

The headmaster was a willowy man of relatively small stature. He wore thick rimmed glasses and had a head of dense wavy greying hair, with a friendly boyish smile and a very warm attitude towards both us and the boys. I had a really good feeling about this school. 'Would you like to do a nice drawing for me, boys?' he asked. They all nodded enthusiastically, as tins of crayons were placed in front of them on the miniature round table. Each boy was given a large sheet of cream coloured sugar paper. We chatted with Mr. Palmer and the sweet, elderly, little reception class teacher Mrs. Green who, with her round eyes, peered like a little bird over the top of her metal, half rimmed, spectacles. We discussed Ben's needs and how all the boys interacted with one another, whilst they continued to draw their pictures for Mr. Palmer. I felt so happy when

Mr. Palmer said he was pleased to offer the boys a place at the school which, of course, we accepted.

As we stood discussing things, the boys announced that they had finished their pictures. 'Oh well done, boys,' said Mr. Palmer, immediately turning his attention to them. 'Are you going to tell me all about your drawings?' Christopher, in his role as head spokesman started. 'This is a farmer and this is his tractor in the field with a trailer full of yellow corn.' There on the paper was an impressively drawn and coloured tractor and trailer, something Christopher had been quite proficient at for some time. Thomas then described his picture which illustrated our house and his pony Sparkie on the front lawn. Slightly less mature with his drawing skills than Christopher, he had still made a very good effort to produce something that looked remarkably like a pony and a house.

Then we came to Ben who was still adding a few final touches to his art work. It was mainly coloured in black and blue wax crayon. A scribble here and a squiggle there, it didn't really resemble much at all, so Mr. Palmer asked him to describe his picture. 'Iss 'ere is a car at gassies (daddies) gawarge, and iss 'ere is the gawarge.' He pointed to the large black and blue scribbles on the page. He continued, 'iss is Gassy, and iss 'ere is a pun'er.' Eddie and I blushed, casting looks at one another, knowing just what he had said. Gordon, Eddie's Cockney service receptionist and, to a certain extent Eddie, had fallen into the habit of calling the customers punters. As Ben was particularly keen to go with Eddie to work on a Sunday morning so he could 'help' Gordon, he had obviously picked up the 'car salesman's' lingo. Eddie and I hoped Mr. Palmer wouldn't ask us to interpret, but inevitably he did so we rather unfairly blamed too much time spent in cockney Gordon's company. He grinned, seeing the funny side of the things that children say, and indeed at our apparent embarrassment. From this exercise he also had a fair idea that although the other two showed a budding flare for art,

Ben had absolutely none.

***

However, the winter had taken its toll on my Dad, who had now had three heart attacks. He was weak and visibly losing weight, complaining that he felt sick most of the time. Mum contacted our GP who was rather dismissive about the situation, until a chance visit to her dentist revealed what was possibly the problem. He asked after my father and mum found herself telling him about dad's feelings of nausea and his three heart attacks. 'Well that'll be the Vegas nerve causing the sickness. You must get him to see a heart specialist as soon as possible.' My aunt and cousin had been convinced for a while that our GP was being too blasé about dad's condition, and being London based had made enquiries about who dad should see in the city regarding his heart. They had the name of a cardiologist who was prepared to see dad, so after an angiogram it became apparent that he had at least three blocked arteries to his heart, plus significant damage from the three heart attacks. The consultant was very keen to get dad into hospital as soon as possible, so he was moved to the top of the list for an urgent heart bypass operation. By now it was early June, but we were all too worried about dad to notice the weather or indeed anything much else that was going on around us. Nursery carried on much as usual, and the boys still had plenty of friends to play, but with dad's operation to concentrate on our life had to be put on hold.

The operation was carried out in the middle of June but dad was just too weak to survive, and after several weeks in intensive care on life support he passed away, leaving mum a widow at the age of 65. She was so thankful to have us close by, and no one could be completely miserable for very long with the children around. Eddie was put in charge of the boys whilst I stayed the night with mum in her home after we returned from London. Eddie phoned us first thing in the morning, just to see how we both were, and to tell us that Ben and Christopher had been bouncing on the beds in their room before nursery. Ben had fallen off and looked rather pale, but he was still going to take him as his colour had come back and he said he felt OK. He thought it was probably just a bit of bruising and shock.

When Eddie went to pick up the boys, Mrs. Saunders told him that Ben had been uncharacteristically quiet, and she was concerned that he had done something more serious to his shoulder as his head seemed to be lilting towards the injured arm. By now mum and I were back at our house, so when Eddie arrived home I was able to have a closer inspection. I carefully pulled open the neck of his little yellow T-shirt only to see a large lump on his collar bone, and when he moved his arm it made an awful grating noise. 'I think he's broken it,' I said. 'What do you think we should do?' We had a quick discussion and decided the best idea was to phone Linda, who was well aware that my father had been gravely ill, and as none of us felt up to a few hours spent in casualty she was the best first port of call. Linda was very sorry to hear about our loss, and was more than happy to help. Just by coincidence, the orthopaedic surgeon was holding a paediatric clinic that afternoon at the children's treatment unit, so Ben's timing was impeccable. He quickly confirmed that Ben had indeed broken his collar bone, so Ben returned home with his wing up in a sling, as there was very little else that could be done for this particular injury.

***

With all the trouble we had been having with dad's illness and subsequent loss, we had missed the first two pre-term social sessions at Glapthorn School. These had been organised to introduce next year's intake of pupils to the other children who they were going to be starting school with. It consisted of a story with Mrs. Green and then a drink, biscuit and a play in the school's playing field with some of the games equipment. The mums were given tea or coffee by Heather and we were encouraged to stay and chat to one another. Although some mothers stayed, some didn't. Sadly, our boys only had the one session as we had been so busy, but I was relieved to find that I got along really well with the group of other mothers. They were all very kind and invited us to join in with a regular play session that they had organising between themselves and which was to continue throughout the summer. These consisted of going to one another's houses once a week. The children could then play while the mothers had a cup of tea and a chat. The idea was that by the time the first day of school arrived they would all be really excited about seeing their new friends.

Leaving Canham House was a sad occasion though, especially as Sam, Edward and James were all off to the Convent School together. They were such good friends, it seemed a shame to break up the happy little band. But with long school holidays, summer evenings and birthdays, the intention was for them to still see each other pretty regularly. Michael's name had been put very definitely on to the list to start nursery the following year, and Edward's little brother William was also going at the same time. There really wasn't that much to feel sad about as all of us mums were also such good friends we wouldn't want to go for too long without having a catch up with one another!!

MODULE 19:
PRIMARY EDUCATION AND EQUINE STUDIES

The end of the summer heralded the beginning of the next phase in our lives - full time education. I had a mixture of feelings really. In some ways it would be nice to have a bit of quality time to spend with Michael and I desperately needed to catch up with the jobs that had been put on hold for some time. But on the other hand I would miss them and particularly the fun that we enjoyed most days. We would often laugh from dawn until dusk and it was so fascinating watching the relationship they had with one another, as they developed and changed. I wondered what impact school would have on this. To be honest they hadn't been quite as triplety since starting nursery and as friends had become a bigger part of their lives. It was also becoming more noticeable that Ben and Tom seemed to have very similar interests when it came to what and how they played. They would wile away several hours arranging the box full of farm animals into lines, as they re-created the grand parade at the East of England show. And a tube of Smarties could also entertain them for hours. The Smarties represented the hunt - the red ones were the huntsmen and masters, or red coats as they called them. The brown, yellow and orange ones were the hounds, and the green and blue ones were the hunt followers. They moved them all round the loud and ugly swirling patterns on the sitting room carpet as they played their imaginary game. The swirls became ploughed fields and woods in their imaginative little world, as they galloped their little pack all around the room. Christopher would only appear at the end of the game when it was time for the Smarties to be eaten.

Christopher, on the other hand, was very good at constructing elaborate buildings with the ever growing collection of Lego, or drawing precociously advanced pictures which he would spend several hours perfecting. It wasn't that they were growing apart, as they were very quick to zone back in to one another and they frequently played happily for many hours as a trio or quartet when Michael wanted to join in. But the differences were beginning to show between their characters, and it was noticeable that the identical two were definitely more alike, both in their looks, thought processes and interests.

Actually, they had definitely become a bit more of a handful of late, as they clearly needed to have their little brains occupied more. Christopher had also developed quite a wilful independent streak and could be very difficult about what clothes he should wear, having very definite ideas about what looked good and what didn't.

There was no popping him into any old clothes to play in anymore. 'Where does he get this behaviour from?' I asked mum one day in my exasperation. I was fighting with him to get a particular jumper on that my aunt had knitted for him, whereas he wanted to wear the pretty well outgrown one that I had knitted. It had three teddy bears on sledges tobogganing down a slope, knitted onto the front of it, and very colourful Fair Isle arms which he loved. Mum grinned. 'You obviously don't remember the lovely little blue and pink smocked frock I made for you when you were about the boys' age. We were going to granny and grandpa's for tea, and granny was desperate to see you in it. But you had other ideas and we had such a job to get you to wear it. Once you were dressed, dad and I went to get changed. Whilst our backs were turned you went and climbed into the coal bunker to hide. Needless to say, the dress was in no state to take you out in, so that day you won the battle.' 'Oh' I said. 'Well I'm sorry for doing that.'

She continued. 'Then there was the time you wanted to wear those horrible stripy slacks to granny's because your cousin George was going to be there and you knew he'd be in trousers. So you got under the gate-leg table and clung on for all you were worth, while daddy and I pulled and tugged to get you out. I seem to remember you won the day that time too.' She was about to start again. 'Ok, Ok I get the picture, it's my entire fault that I have an abnormally fashion conscious son.' We both laughed, but I suppose what goes around comes around.

***

The boys had been getting bolder as the summer progressed towards their first school term, and they had just started to wander a little further away from our garden and front drive on their own. We had put the fear of God into them about the perils of wandering into the woods, or down to the dew pond as the 'dew pond monster' would gobble them up. But a couple of times I had found them with the Cosy Coupé on the bumpy roadway just into the park. It probably didn't hold too much danger for them, but I didn't like not knowing where they were.

We were well into summer and I was busy inside doing some jobs with Sue. Suddenly we became aware of the ominous silence that had once again fallen over the house. 'Where are the boys?' I asked Sue, for some reason thinking she would have more idea than me. 'I've no idea,' she said looking alarmed. We both called out to them, and when there was no reply we shot outside to look. I ran to the park and Sue ran to the back of the house, then out to the paddock where Sparkie was quietly grazing with Polly. We reconvened outside the front of the house and confirmed that there was absolutely no sign of them at all. By now my heart was pumping as we ran to look in the dew pond. It was only a muddy puddle really at this time of year, and thankfully there was no sign of them there. But now I was beginning to think that someone had come along and snatched them. So I ran breathlessly, partly from panic and partly from the fact that we had been running back and forth, to ask my neighbour if he'd seen them. Graham had a catering business so he was at home most of the time during the daytime. I ran past their window to get to the front door, but as I did I caught sight of him standing in his kitchen. There at the breakfast bar sat all four boys, their legs swinging from the bar stools. They were clearly enjoying eating something whilst they chatted in an animated way to Graham. He was laughing and obviously enjoying their company. I felt a surge of relief as I knocked on the window. 'I thought I'd lost them, how long have they been in here?' I asked. 'Oh not too long, only about ten minutes. They tell me they haven't had any breakfast because you've run out of food until you go shopping again.' I couldn't believe my ears. 'Well the little monkeys,' I said. 'They had cereals and toast for breakfast only an hour ago.' Graham laughed, turning to his small clients as they sat sheepishly eating their second breakfast.' 'Well boys, I thought you said you hadn't had any breakfast, mummy tells me you have.' The boys grinned at him, continuing to eat what had been prepared for them. They had every variety of eggs. Christopher was carefully eating his boiled egg and soldiers, Ben had a large plate with fried egg on toast and Michael, aged only seventeen months, had a bowl of scrambled egg and carefully cut up pieces of buttered toast. He was wielding a large spoon as he concentrated hard on guiding the wobbly egg on to the toast. Thomas was munching his way through a bacon roll because he didn't like eggs!

But the summer began to draw to a close and the last few weeks of August were spent getting all the school kit sorted; shorts and aertex T-shirts, plimsolls and new shoes - nothing could be forgotten about. Reading bags were carefully crafted by mum and the boys' initials embroidered on to the front. Then the big day arrived and with varying degrees of excitement the boys got into the car.

***

Everything went extremely well for the first few weeks, until one morning just after their fifth birthday. They were in the playroom, playing with some new toys before school. 'We don't want to go to school anymore,' said Christopher who, as always, was the spokesman. The other two shook their identical blond heads in agreement. 'Well I'm sorry boys,' I said, 'School is something you have to go to every day now. I'm afraid it's not negotiable, so come on up you get, we have to get into the car.' They all stood up and looked every bit as if they were going to get ready for school, then ran off in three different directions.

This was a new bit of triplet trickery that we hadn't experienced before. Michael was still in his high chair as Sue was on her college day. She had just started a nursery nurse course, so she went on a day release once a week. Fortunately Eddie hadn't left for work, so he helped me to capture the boys and bundle them into the car. As I drove the eight miles to school they screamed and kicked their feet, working themselves into a frenzy, whilst Michael sat quietly in his car seat leaning forwards to watch his brothers in a bemused way. Needless to say we were a little late getting to school and the playground was now empty. I sat contemplating how I was going to get them from the car and into school. First of all I took Michael out from his car seat and stood him on the pavement, placing him by the school fence. By the time I had returned the couple of steps back to the car they had undone their seat belts and locked the car doors. Another triplet conspiracy was in action. Fortunately I'd foreseen this being a probability and had taken the keys with me, so I unlocked the door again. It was a car developed before the central locking system, so every door had an individual lock. As fast as I was able to unlock a door, they jumped across the car, working as a team, locking door after door faster than I could unlock them.

Then, with a wave of relief, I spotted Helen and Barbara appearing on the steps as they came out from the school. They were deep in conversation as they slowly descended the steps unaware of my struggles just over the fence. But when they came through the five barred gate onto the pavement they spotted me waving to get their attention. 'Could you two give me a hand please?' I called. 'I'm having a bit of trouble.' They ran to my assistance. 'If I grab them one at a time, perhaps you two could hang on to them for me.' One by one I extricated the boys as they screamed hysterically from the depths of the car, while little Michael stood in stunned silence watching his brothers' apparent anguish. Finally with all three of them out of the car, I picked Ben up and had him on my left hip, and Michael was on my right, ready for the march into school. In the meantime Thomas and Christopher had now developed a severe case of floppy leg and were collapsing onto the pavement, completely refusing to walk with Barbara and Helen, whilst their screams were now at full volume. Barbara scooped Thomas up who promptly sunk his teeth into her arm. 'Oohh' I said. 'I'm so sorry Barbara.' She grimaced for a second and then smiled the stoic smile of an experienced and sympathetic mother. Helen had picked Christopher up, but she too was struggling with him as he threw himself backwards and kicked and screamed. We made our way noisily towards the school. Heather had heard us coming and was ready, holding the door open for us to enter. She then ran to open the reception class door so we could post the boys through it, while Mrs. Green expertly closed it on us before anyone had time to escape. The boys banged and screamed at the door and I looked totally distraught. 'Give them a couple of minutes and they'll be fine,' said Heather, with the voice of experience. So Helen asked Michael and I back to her house for a coffee so that we could phone the school after a few moments.

But before we had walked through the door, the phone was already ringing. 'They're fine now, the little monkeys stopped before you'd even driven away, and they're all playing happily in the play house,' said Heather. When I picked them up that evening there was no sign that they hadn't had anything other than a lovely day. Yet again it made me realise that with their combined efforts they could cause us the maximum amount of disruption!

We had an interim parents' evening after half term - they were all doing well and were well behaved and polite, making progress in the order that I expected them to. Christopher had taken to the reading programme well and was showing signs of being able to work out easy words and had progressed to the next level of reading books. Thomas was a little behind him, but was expected to go up a level any minute, and Ben was half way through the first level. They were all writing their names, which they had actually learnt to do at nursery, and they also recognised most letters of the alphabet and numbers one to ten. Mrs. Green confided with us that although the children weren't allowed into the orchard where she often sat and ate her lunch when the weather was nice, Ben would often creep in to sit with her. 'He really can be a most engaging little boy,' she said smiling sheepishly. 'I always feel he's probably a bit safer with me rather than having to face the rough and tumble of the playground.' I didn't like to burst her bubble of protectiveness towards him. I felt sure that if only she could see how he held his own with his brothers she would realise he wouldn't come to much harm, even if he was still a little wobbly on his feet.

Soon after they started school Doctor Fox wrote to us and copied Linda in to say that the physiotherapist from Kingsley school, which was a special school in Kettering, would be going into see Ben at Glapthorn. He wanted her to explain to Ben's teacher how she could incorporate some exercises especially for him into the PE lesson and his daily activities there. I was rather surprised by the letter, after all this woman had never seen Ben. But not long after I had opened the letter Linda phoned me. 'I'm furious,' she said. 'What good is it for someone who doesn't even know him to go in? If you don't have any objection I'm going to phone Doctor Fox and tell him I'd like to go instead.' Of course we had no objections and it made absolute sense. So after a conversation with Doctor Fox, Linda was given permission to visit the school. Ben was especially excited as he could now show Mrs. Green his exercises. He began by demonstrating bouncing a ball and turning in a circle whilst doing so, until he was dizzy, then giggled as he reeled about for a few seconds before gaining his balance again. Then he carefully demonstrated how he was learning to hop and balance on one leg. He wobbled a little and then took off across the play ground, managing several hops on one leg before overbalancing, having to put the other foot to the ground. Mrs. Green clapped her hands with delight and laughed with him as he performed exercise after exercise for her. Linda was equally delighted by Mrs. Green who was so keen to help Ben in his endeavour to gain better balance and co-ordination. It all confirmed the fact that we were having no regrets at all with our choice of this little rural school.

***

But now the other part of their education had to be attended to as well. Just after Christmas we heard of a quiet first ridden pony for sale. She was the next level on from Sparkie as she could be safely ridden off the lead rein by small children. She was surprisingly cheap, apparently because she wouldn't let small children lead her in from the field, dragging them back to the grass at the first opportunity. This was a minor problem for us, as in reality we would always be there to help them, and it certainly wasn't a big enough problem to put us off. Taffy stood tied up in the farm yard, waiting patiently for us. She was grey, or white to be more accurate, and had the prettiest little head, with enormous kind, deep brown eyes, a dished nose and tiny ears. Her legs were rather longer than Sparkie's, and of a slightly better shape. Her coat was also finer than Sparkie's thick, dense coat.

Christopher was elected to be the first to ride, as he was slightly more advanced with his riding skills than the other two. Taffy was quite angelic and, true to their word, didn't put a foot wrong. She trotted back and forth, up and down the lane with all the boys in turn and was just perfect for them, so we felt we really had been very lucky to find her.

***

Finally the end of the boys' first year at school arrived. They had been rehearsing for an end of year concert, which the boys had been very secretive about. In fact all we were allowed to know was that there were to be two shows, one in the afternoon and one in the evening. Eddie particularly wanted to go to the early afternoon concert, as his rota meant he had to work late. We decided that he should go to the early performance and then I would go and pick them up from school and take them home for their tea. The two grandmas, Michael and I would then go back for the evening performance.

But just as I was about to leave to collect the boys Eddie phoned. 'It was really good Gill,' he said. 'I won't tell you about it and spoil it for you, but I just wanted to let you know that Thomas was being very odd. In fact he had his hands over his eyes most of the time. I wondered if he's not feeling well. Maybe he's got one of those funny headaches he gets when he eats eggs. Well, anyway you'll sort it out, but I just thought I ought to warn you.' As I drove to school I wondered what I was going to find. Thomas hadn't had any eggs as far as I knew, so I was sure it couldn't be one of the funny eggie, migrainey things that he suffered with.

As I pulled up I could see Christopher and Thomas racing around the playing field with their friends. There didn't look to be anything much wrong with him now. They all ran to get into the car, excitedly telling me how well the concert had gone. 'Yes, daddy said how good it was. But please don't tell us anything because I want it to be a big surprise for Michael and I tonight.' Then I asked Thomas, 'Daddy said you were covering your eyes during the concert. He wondered if you had one of those funny headaches that make you sick, but you seem alright now.' Thomas frowned and then with a look of anguish he replied, 'Oh mummy, I was so embarrassed 'cos daddy's hair was all sticking up at the back. I just couldn't look at him, so I had to cover my eyes.' Poor Tom had such a cross to bear having a parent that caused him so much angst.

After the show, which had a Noah's ark theme, the

children who were about to leave read their essays that they had written about their years at Glapthorn School. They related tales about what the school had meant to them and what they were looking forward to in the future. I have to admit I found it all quite emotional and wondered how the parents of these children were managing to keep a dry eye. I was sure when it came to our turn I would be quite inconsolable, but with a few years to go I didn't have to worry about it yet.

MODULE 20:
TRAVEL AND TOURISM,
OPHTHALMOLOGY, FOOD BACTERIA

During the boys' second year at school Ben was called for his eye correction operation in early April. This was to be a day case procedure. But as sods law always seems to arrive just when you wished it hadn't, Thomas and Christopher both went down with conjunctivitis two days before Ben was due to go into hospital. I phoned our GP immediately who prescribed antibiotic eye ointment for the boys with the infection, and drops for Ben as a precautionary measure. I took him to the hospital in Leicester the day before he was to have his op to meet the surgeon and to have his squint measured. I was quite convinced that the operation would be cancelled due to the conjunctivitis rampaging through our family, as by now Michael had signs of it too. But the surgeon wasn't at all perturbed. 'I'm not worried,' he said. 'He's going to be on antibiotic drops for the following month anyway, so there's no way he'll pick this up from his brothers.' In some ways I was relieved as it would get the whole thing over and done with, and it was going to have to be done some time, preferably sooner rather than later. If I'm truthful there was also the tiny bit of neurotic mother in me that didn't want him to have it done at all. But the other children were beginning to ask him what was wrong with his eyes and, why did his eyes look in a different direction instead of straight. So it was a must really, before he became self-conscious of it.

The morning arrived and I'm ashamed to say that I turned into a complete jelly like wimp, making Eddie take him to the hospital on his own, leaving me feeling tearful and out of sorts at home. Since the terrible day of test a few years earlier, I had been even more edgy about hospitals, and there was something about doing things with his eyes that really turned my stomach. Also at the back of my mind was the incident when Tom had twin empathy, so I quite expected that I may have to go and rescue Tom from school, finding him struck down with mysterious eye pains.

The next few hours dragged until Eddie phoned to say it was all over and that Ben was fine. Even his eyes didn't look too bad and only a tiny bit bloodshot. He was going to have to wait until the surgeon came in to check him after lunch, but he expected to be home before tea time. Ben bounced through it without looking backwards, other than a couple of days of slightly double vision, 'I can see an extra two of my brothers,' he said when he saw them, but we had been warned this might happen, so we weren't too alarmed. Thankfully, Thomas also sailed through the day with no adverse reactions. Ben had to have his eye drops in three times a day for a month, but he hardly broke from his play. The improvement in the cosmetic look to his eyes was unbelievable, and it even seemed to have improved his sight which hadn't been expected. He no longer needed his glasses, which was probably a good thing because he never really wore them anyway. When we did manage to get him to wear them, he would drop them down to the end of his nose and tilt his head so he could look over the top. But more often than not they would be on the floor nicely positioned for someone to tread on, or left somewhere in an undisclosed location so we couldn't find them for several days at a time.

***

With all of the worry of the eye operation now in the past, we decided it would be nice to have a holiday in the sun. The May half term seemed as good a time as any, so Eddie went to the local travel agent to ask them to find us something fairly cheap, definitely cheerful, and in the sun. Nowhere too hot, but somewhere where we could have sand and sea for the boys, and a bit of R and R for us. They came up with a three star, half board hotel in Portugal, with a heated indoor pool and in a prime position only two hundred metres from the sea front. There were squash courts and tennis courts should we want to have a game, and table tennis and pool tables too. There was also a children's play room and a children's outdoor play area with swings and slides. It all sounded perfect and just what we were looking for in order to have a hassle free week of rest and relaxation. Time passed quickly and the evening before our holiday I got the boys into bed a little bit before their usual time, as we had an early start in the morning. I finished the final bit of packing, then Eddie and I also turned in early so that we would be bright and breezy for the early morning start, and what was sure to be a tiring day of travel.

At about eleven o'clock I was woken from that first deep sleep of the night. For a second I couldn't understand what had woken me so I turned over to try and get back to sleep, but then I heard the unmistakable sound of someone being sick. I leapt out of bed to find Thomas in the bathroom, having tried unsuccessfully to get to the loo in time. He had turned grey and looked really poorly. I couldn't believe that we were about to get a bug just as we were going on holiday. The night steadily got worse as Christopher and Michael then joined Thomas. So when the six o'clock alarm rang we were all exhausted and ready for sleep, having had a terrible night. We made a sorry sight as we left the house, looking like something from the Adams family, with white faces and huge grey bags under our eyes. Only Ben looked remotely human, having slept solidly throughout the whole of the terrible night.

We arrived at Faro airport on time and our transfer wasn't too long, so we were able to get into our rooms to have a little rest. The rooms were adequate, and at least they were right next to one another, although there was no adjoining door as promised. But the walls were so paper thin, even a knock or a small shout could be easily heard. We had a light supper and then went to bed for an early night. But not long after falling asleep I heard Eddie getting out of bed – the dreaded bug had landed again. I lay there wide awake listening to Eddie and wondering when Ben and I would have our turn. The morning arrived after a long night so with plenty of positive attitude, our fingers crossed, and armed with a blue sandcastle-shaped bucket just in case, we made our way to breakfast and then on to the welcome meeting.

Our tour rep was sat behind a table at the front of the rather stark, bare looking room, as we all slowly gathered. She was a pretty girl with sun-kissed skin and blonde hair tied back into a neat pony tail. She sat behind the desk sorting through the paperwork, smiling as every new family arrived, reminding people to help themselves to 'a nice fruit drink.' Soon another couple of girls appeared in the same yellow polo shirts and blue shorts. They leant their heads together busily looking through the paper work until the the head rep stood up to introduce herself and her team. She spoke in a broad Yorkshire accent. 'My name's Janet and I'm your resort rep, so if you have any problems at all you'll need to see me. I'm based at the hotel Paradisimo just down on the sea front, but I'll be here every morning from 9.00am 'til 9.30am. These are my colleagues, they're based here to run the little T club from the play room just over by the pool.' She gestured towards the pool which was on the other side of long folding glass doors. 'Sandra is on my left and Mandy on my right.' Mandy had her brown curly hair tied up into bunches; they were bundled together with blue and yellow ribbons, matching her shorts and top. She gave a little wave, and beamed a wide smile, particularly aiming it towards the children.

Sandra, on the other hand, was an amply built young woman, with huge bouncing breasts. Her fair hair was cut into a neat bob and she bounded about like an over excited puppy. 'Hi everyone,' she said, as she waved with both hands to her audience, her ample bosoms jingling up and down like a pair of cats fighting in a sack. Sandra looked fun. She took over from Janet, announcing in a loud Scottish accent that she was in charge of the little T club, and she was here to gather up all the 'wee children' to take them off to play. She called out a list of children's names that were eligible to go to the activity group which, needless to say, included our little trio. She apologised profusely when she realised this didn't include Michael, who was sitting on my knee still feeling pretty sorry for himself. I smiled and waved her apologies to one side. The other three looked horrified, their eyes pleading with us, but we felt it looked a bit churlish to not make any attempt to join in.

The boys reluctantly followed Sandra and Mandy, looking miserably over their shoulders towards us as they followed the girls out of the room. Janet continued her well practiced information spiel as we only half listened, both struggling to concentrate as we were by now feeling tired out from two nights of sleep deprivation. Michael remained on my lap, snuggling his head back into my chest, while I absently- mindedly stroked his fine blond hair. Suddenly Michael sat up and leant forwards, looking around me and towards the back of the room. I heard the small scrape of a chair moving. Eddie and I continued to try and concentrate on the various trips and activities that were on offer, but frankly we didn't much fancying any of them. It all seemed too much hassle and it really wasn't what we'd come away to do. Beach, sun and relaxation was all we wanted, interspersed with a game of tennis with the boys or a bit of swimming just to ring the changes.

Michael was still leaning forwards, suddenly looking a little bit more cheerful as he concentrated on something at the back of the room. Then he let out a little giggle. My attention slowly turned to where he was looking and to what was causing him so much amusement. I followed his gaze. There were the boys, on all fours, crawling behind the tables and chairs. I nudged Eddie, and whispered. 'Look behind you, what are they doing?' Eddie looked round, raised his eyebrows and shrugged his shoulders. 'No idea,' he whispered, 'Looks like they're making a break for freedom.' We turned again to see them making progress as they crawled along, one after the other, like a line of little ants slowly marching towards us, but still managing to keep their cover as they weaved their way through the tables and chairs. Just as they arrived by our side the meeting drew to a close. 'What are you doing boys, why aren't you in the little T club?' They whispered to us, looking furtively over their shoulders worried that someone may come to drag them back again. 'We sneaked out of the room when that fat lady was doing a silly dance, she wanted us to learn it. Christopher, as usual, was the spokesman for them, but Ben and Tom nodded enthusiastically in agreement, chipping in with their opinions from time to time. Funnily enough it appears that Tom had led the escape; he was just beginning to show some emerging leadership skills, which had otherwise been overshadowed by Christopher's apparent role as the pack leader. Eddie and I went to the little T club to explain their disappearance to which, worryingly, they all seemed completely oblivious. We told them that we didn't think the boys would be attending the club as we had so many things planned for the holiday, and they would be spending the time with us. We thanked them and quickly made ourselves scarce.

The sun was shining so we decided to take ourselves off to the beach for the day, having packed up towels, buckets and spades, sun cream and swimming kit ready for a day on the beach. It was now a beautiful morning and the sun was starting to feel really warm. We lost ourselves into the process of making sand castles on the beach, not realising the sun was slowly disappearing behind a cloud - then another cloud and another, until there was no blue sky left at all, just thick, grey, angry looking clouds. By now I was feeling quite cold and a chilly wind had started to blow. The boys, who had been busy digging a large pit, suddenly appeared complaining that they too were feeling cold. Eddie was determined we were going to stay on the beach, as the sun was sure to be only temporarily lost behind the clouds and there was nothing that a jumper and stiff British upper lip couldn't cope with.

But it continued to get colder and by now the boys had given up digging and just like a litter of puppies, had curled up under the towels together to keep warm. We decided to give up and go and find some lunch, as our stiff British upper lips were beginning to droop, and there was always the hope that this was a temporary blip and the sun would re-appear again in the afternoon. It didn't, so we went for a walk around the shops that led back towards the hotel; at least behind the buildings there was a bit of shelter.

Eddie decided now would be a good time to try out the indoor swimming pool, so we all went up to the rooms and got changed, then rushed back down to the pool, the boys all excited about the prospect of extra swimming practice. Michael had his little arm bands on, but the older boys were now able to swim so they all rushed ahead with Eddie, who had his arms loaded full of towels. They were in their swimming shorts which exposed their ever growing and rather skinny, gangly pale limbs, whilst Michael and I made a slightly slower journey down to the pool. We passed a fellow holiday maker on our way down the stairs. 'Huh, you're brave!' he said to us, as he pulled a grimace. 'Yes I suppose we are,' I said, smiling at him, assuming he was referring to us taking four little boys swimming. As Michael and I arrived at the empty poolside, Eddie was half way down the steps, getting into the water. 'Bloody hell, it's cold enough to freeze my crown jewels in here,' he exclaimed, taking short rapid little breaths.

At that moment Christopher, who was always rather too brave with water, ran and jumped in. He emerged with a gasp. A look of shock across his face as he paddled rapidly back towards the edge. 'It's horrid in here,' he said, looking as if he might burst into tears. 'It's really freezing.' I encouraged him to swim quickly to warm up, and then dipped my toe in to see what all the fuss was about. They were right, it was bitterly cold. I always thought I was pretty hardy when it came to swimming, having almost had to break the ice during school swimming lessons at my junior school. And Tom's godmother Rosanne and I used to swim in her pool as early as April when we were teenagers. But this was something else, it was nothing short of torture and I had no intention of going in, and I certainly wasn't going to take Michael in to the icy water either. Ben and Tom both ventured in for a very quick paddle up and down before all four of them admitted defeat, climbed out and ran for their towels. I rubbed and dried as quickly as I could. Their teeth chattered and they shivered violently until they were dry enough to scamper back to our rooms. I quickly ran a bath to warm them up. That was the first and last time we used the pool, and as far as I could see we were the only people to go in all week.

Monday morning arrived with a shock, as we were woken at 7.00am by a loud banging. 'What the devil's that?' I said as I got out of bed, my heart still beating hard from the fright. I rubbed my eyes sleepily as I looked over the balcony to see if there were any workmen outside. The slow realisation dawned that the noise was an internal one, and it sounded like someone was trying to break through the wall at the end of our hallway. By now the boys were knocking on our door to come in. 'What's that banging noise?' they asked looking worried. 'I don't know boys, but we'll ask the rep after breakfast,' I said, just beginning to feel a little disillusioned with our longed for holiday.

It was yet another grey day and we were the first down for breakfast, having been woken so early by the increasingly invasive noise. But it wasn't long before others rolled in too, having also been woken early. After breakfast we waited in reception for our rep, Janet to arrive. She rushed in ten minutes late, looking very harassed, and by now there was a small gathering of people waiting to see her. We were first in the queue so the inevitable question had to be asked. I got the distinct impression this was a weekly occurrence for her, as she seemed so well rehearsed. 'It's only going to be for a couple of days, they're just finishing off the squash courts which are on the other side of the wall at end of your corridor.' She brushed the fact to one side, as if it was totally unimportant. 'But even a couple of days is a bit unreasonable when they start at seven in the morning, can't they start at nine when most people are up and about?' asked Eddie. 'Hear, hear' a voice came from behind us, quickly joined by several more; in fact we all seemed to be there for the same reason. Janet promised to look in to it, and to ask if it was possible for the work to start a little later.

We then decided to hire a car so we could do a bit of exploration as the weather was still deteriorating. The hire company gave us a map with the car, so we confidently drove off into the middle of the countryside, hoping that the weather might improve a bit as we made our way inland. But it didn't, in fact it just got worse, and the rain becoming a torrent, washing water down the road in rivers, peppered with stones and small bits of rubble. As we drove further and further into rural Portugal the roads got worse, and at times we seemed to be on nothing more than a farm track. We progressed on our journey which, according to the map, should take us over the hills and ultimately end up coming down in to a little fishing village. Well, at least that was how it appeared. Then I started to notice the odd landmark that looked vaguely familiar. A tree here, or a large boulder there. I just had that deja-vu kind of feeling. 'Eddie, I'm sure we've just been past this boulder,' I observed. 'No, no we're on the right route, I'm sure.' He stopped and looked at the map. 'Yes we're fine, if we carry on this way we should be able to see the sea very shortly.'

But the journey continued as we wound our way up and down the steep hills, on nothing more than shingle tracks, and the rain continued to pour. Suddenly Eddie did a double take. 'I'm sure I saw that little shack a few minutes ago.' He looked puzzled and ground to a halt to look at the map again. It was a simple map without much detail, so in theory it should have been easy to follow with only the more major roads marked on it . But it didn't seem to have any degree of accuracy at all, and was nothing like as easy as it had first appeared. I began to wonder if we were ever going to get out. In fact, all I wanted to do was get back to some sort of normality, as I was getting that creeping feeling of panic.

By now the boys had all woken from their motion nurtured sleep and were beginning to pick up on our panic. Just as we passed the large granite boulder next to a self-set olive tree for the fourth time, we noticed a tiny little track with a sign carved into a piece of stone. 'Let's try that track' I shouted. Within ten minutes we were back into civilisation. It was so unusual for us to get lost like this; Eddie has his own built in sat nav system. With an extraordinary sense of direction he could usually navigate us into or out of anywhere and end up pretty well where we needed to be.

The next day we decided to stay closer to home and make for the beach, as the weather was slightly improved, with the sun attempting to shine even though it was still very windy. With an early start again due to the building works we were on the beach by nine so we decided to have a game of French cricket to get everyone warmed up and into the holiday spirit, as by now our mood was rather low. The swimming pool was too cold to contemplate another dip, the tennis courts promised in the brochure were a few marker pegs in the ground, and the children's play area had got some play equipment in it, but it was built on a concrete base and had chewing gum and graffiti all over it. Even worse, I think it must have been the local dog toilet as it was covered in dog poo. As for the squash courts, if I thought about them too much I would probably lose the plot completely. All in all it was turning into a pretty miserable holiday.

So we got the plastic cricket set out that we purchased on the way to the beach, in the hopes of some fun for the day. We started to play but the wind got stronger – and stronger and stronger, until it was nothing short of a gale. The sand whipped up into swirling and abrasive low flying dust clouds, as it scurried along the beach, gathering more and more sand on its way, whipping around the boys' bare legs, stinging them until they cried out. 'This is hopeless,' I said, throwing down the towel that I was trying to wrap around my legs to stop the stinging, feeling very near to tears as our holiday was turning into the holiday from hell. 'Come on everyone,' said Eddie. 'Race you to the coffee shop, pick up everything on your way and we'll have an ice cream and a drink.' We grabbed everything from the spiteful stinging sand and ran. I picked up Michael, who by now was standing stock still on the beach with his eyes tightly closed, afraid yet another sand storm would come and hit him in the face.

We sat and gathered our breath in the little beach cafe, and Eddie bought an English paper that was on a rack beside the till. 'Here you are,' he said handing me a bit of it to read. The boys were now colouring in the little books we had bought to keep them entertained. 'Well bugger me,' I said in absolute despair. There on the front page was the headline – 'BRITAIN BASKS IN FIRST HEATWAVE OF THE YEAR'. People were expected to flock to the beaches at the weekend, as the temperatures were set to soar for the bank holiday. I just couldn't believe our bad luck. Here we were stuck in Portugal's version of Fawlty Towers, with pouring rain and gales, and pretty awful food too if I was honest. The beds were uncomfortable, and the whole place smelt; drains and sewers sprung to mind. And then every single skinny, mangy, three-legged stray dog seemed to live under our balcony, making me want to set up a rescue home for all of them, which needless to say Eddie was extremely discouraging about.

Finally the last day arrived and thankfully so did the sun. It was beautiful and now really warm, so we headed for the beach armed with buckets, spades, cricket kit and the tennis rackets that we had carted all the way from the UK in anticipation of tennis courts at the hotel. We had a lovely day and at least we would go home with a little bit of holiday glow. 'Keep the boys covered,' Eddie said

'Make sure they don't get too much sun.' All day I diligently applied the sun cream and made sure any hats that were removed were soon replaced, until we walked back to the hotel, tired and sun-kissed at the end of the day. We went down to supper after having our showers, ready for the final evening. Half way through the week we had been treated to a gala dinner. It consisted of a large buffet which had chicken pieces, prawns and cold meats of one variety or another, but since then we had been finishing the buffet off in one form or another, with the food dished up and disguised as something else every night afterwards. Tonight it was some sort of paella thing with bits of chopped chicken, prawns and bits of salami in it. Michael had barely eaten a thing all week, but as he was a confirmed fussy eater I wasn't that surprised. The other three boys, however, were completely different and would give anything and everything a try, so they had eaten quite well once the sickness bug had passed. But as we sat eating our final meal, Ben began to push his food around the plate. 'I'm not very hungry tonight,' he said. His cheeks were burning hot and bright red. I felt his forehead and that was burning hot too. 'You've let him have too much sun, I told you to be careful with them,' said Eddie. 'Oh I see, it's my fault is it?' I retorted. We were both so fed up with the holiday that it was making us grumpy with one another. But as we had an early start in the morning we decided to turn in soon after supper, and Ben was by now looking decidedly peaky. So Eddie went into Ben's bed in the other room, and I had Ben in with Michael and me. Here began what I can only describe as the night of torment.

At first we all dropped into a light sleep, but then I was woken by Ben sitting up in bed shouting out, 'Get away, get away ghosts', as he flayed his arms, hitting out at his visions of horror. I leapt out of bed and tried to comfort him only to find he was absolutely burning up. So I ran to the bathroom to get a cold flannel to put on his head. Then

I ran back for the Calpol. Only moments after giving him Calpol he was sick, so then the dilemma was - should I give him any more? I came down on the side of giving him some, as it was really important to try and reduce the burning temperature. We managed to get a little more sleep and then the hallucinations began again. This time I resorted to cold flannels as he really couldn't have any more medicine. So I decided to wet the hand towel and cover his hot body with it. Then the diarrhoea started. This was far worse than the bug we had taken out with us. So when five-thirty arrived and we had to get up for our transfer to the airport, I have never felt so relieved that a holiday was coming to an end. Home seemed suddenly a very safe place to be.

But we weren't there yet. We still had to get through the trip to the airport, the time at the airport and the flight back, not to mention the car journey from the airport to our house. Once we arrived at Faro airport, Ben and I became very familiar with the filthy, dirty toilets in departures. I felt sure we were going to pick up something even worse if we spent much time in them. We had checked our luggage in on our arrival, and then had gone through security quickly, only to be told the flight was delayed by two hours. It seemed interminable as we waited to be called, until finally we boarded the plane for home. Of course, we had to explain our predicament to the lovely air hostess, who very kindly sat us at the front of the plane near to the toilet.

When we landed she let us get off first, so we could go through passport control and get to the toilets quickly. Then we could pick up our baggage as soon as it appeared on the conveyor belt from the plane. I stood waiting for the carrousel to start up, and felt a surge of relief as it started to rumble slowly round with the first few bags as they began to appear. We would soon be on our way home. At last a few more cases appeared and then one or two items of clothing. 'Hum, poor things,' I said to Eddie. 'Yes, that's bad luck isn't it, having your case break open on the conveyor. ' A tooth brush wrapped in a plastic bag sailed by followed by a pair of spotty knickers. I stood there looking on, thinking how funny it was that people often do the same things as one another, like putting tooth brushes in plastic bags. 'Aren't they the same as your knickers?' asked Eddie. I had been thinking the same thing, but M & S has a wide following, so I thought no more of it. At that moment a blue and white striped T shirt the same as Michael's sailed past, swiftly followed by another pair of knickers, also the same as mine. Slowly the penny dropped. They were my knickers, and there was the offending case spewing out dirty clothes as it travelled its way along the conveyor belt. 'Quick Eddie' I shouted. 'Grab it, it's our case, and those are my dirty knickers. Oh good grief, how embarrassing.' I ran frantically along the conveyor, dodging past the eager people all waiting for their cases to arrive, grabbing clothes as they passed by, until I had an arm full of items. The tooth brushes could jolly well stay there, I thought, as by now I just wanted to get out of the place. We shoved the offending items back into the case and did up the half open zip. 'I had a padlock on this lot' I said. 'And the tooth brushes were wrapped individually in plastic bags and put into that front zipped pouch bit, how on earth has this all come open?' 'Never mind now, let's just get to the car and go home', said Eddie, as desperate as me to get back to the safety of our house.

That night things only got worse and Eddie got to see the full extent of what I had been dealing with the night before. Not long after going to bed Ben charged into the sitting room. He looked petrified as he scaled up Eddie, just like a monkey up a palm tree. 'There's a bull coming', he shouted, as he looked in terror over his shoulder. He was so convincing we almost expected to see the bull himself charging through the door. The hallucinations continued all night, with trolls and ghosts visiting us, even though he was having four hourly Calpol and cold flannelling.

The next morning I made an emergency appointment to see the only free doctor at our practice. She sat there behind the desk, her dark, greying hair scraped back into a tight bun. She had a scowl on her face. I didn't care for her too much. She hadn't been at our practice for long, but I always felt that she must have missed the lectures on bedside manner, because she had absolutely none. She told me that the foreign food often didn't suit young children and it had probably been far too rich for him, but if we chose to take our children on holidays like these, what did we expect. If the diarrhoea continued until Friday then I was to take a sample into pathology. So I went back home and completely ignored her instructions, taking one the next time he needed to go to the loo, as by now there was blood in it. Thankfully the pathology department was open, so I was hopeful they would get a result to us pretty quickly. In fact it was quicker than expected as our own GP phoned by tea time to say Ben had Campylobacter, a serious form of food poisoning and he needed antibiotics immediately. The medication kicked in pretty quickly and with youth on his side he made a fairly rapid recovery, although he did manage to get an extra week off school.

As soon as I had time to unpack properly it became apparent that we had been robbed. The dirty washing case had been opened at Faro airport. Everything that was new had gone – they had carefully sifted out the decent new clothes from the older stuff to find the worthwhile items. Eddie's brand new trousers had gone, Tom's lovely new yellow trousers with the stripy pockets and, to my utter horror, Michael's brand new Osh Cosh blue and white striped dungarees, which were my pride and joy. The insurance company only paid out half the value of the clothes as they said they had been worn, so the dungarees were sadly never replaced. They had been bought in a sale, so the opportunity never arose to buy them again at that price.

A month after returning from the nightmare holiday, I had a call from the environmental health officer. He wanted to come and see me about Ben's food poisoning and asked if it would be convenient to come sometime during the morning, which put Sue and I into a complete panic as we felt sure it was going to involve taking swabs from the fridge and the toilet. So we set about rushing around the house with the anti-bax, cleaning everything.

The gentleman arrived. He was a short, round little man, with slightly greying hair, thickly thatched on the top of his head. 'Um, nice spot you've got here' he said. 'Yes, thank you, we're very lucky,' I replied nervously. I anticipated white overalls and a mask appearing, whilst he took swabs from all around our house. 'Can I take a seat?', he asked, gesturing towards the kitchen table and chairs, as he put his briefcase down on the table. 'Oh, of course, sorry I didn't know if you wanted to inspect anything first', I said, feeling rather embarrassed. He laughed at my obvious anxiety. 'No no not at all, I've only come to ask you some questions, so that when all the information is put into a national data base, hopefully a picture will begin to emerge as to where the poisoning has stemmed from. Unfortunately, as it's obviously come from your holiday, unless there just happens to be another couple of cases that link to where you've eaten or been staying, it probably won't be traced. Anyway, I would still like to ask you the questions, just in case.'

We chatted happily as he asked me the relevant questions, and he seemed pretty convinced that the piece of under cooked chicken that I had put to one side during the gala dinner, and which had then mysteriously disappeared, was probably the culprit. I suspected at the time it was probably Ben who had picked it up off the rubbish plate in the middle of the table, as he had been particularly partial to the barbeque flavouring they had on them. Little hands seemed to dive into everything, so it had been easily missed. He told us that the culprit was usually raw meat dripping blood onto cooked meat, often when poor fridge hygiene was the problem. I had little knowledge of the state of the kitchens, but judging by the standard of the rest of the hotel nothing would have surprised me.

As he supped his cup of tea and chatted away we got on to the subject of our life style, which was clearly very different from his own. 'Do you mind living out here in the middle of nowhere? You wouldn't find my wife living like this, it would frighten her to death, and she'd be real twitchy with all these woods around and the cows out there in the fields would really terrify her.' I laughed, 'I suppose it isn't everybody's cup of tea but we absolutely love it, and it's great for the children to have all this space.' He looked thoughtful. Just at that moment one of our red hens wandered in to the kitchen to see if there were any scraps. He grinned. 'Yes, and all these animals around them. In fact I'm really surprised that one of your children has picked anything up at all. You see, living the life they do, with all the dirt and bacteria that they have with the animals around, would give them a far bigger exposure to the bugs. But on the flip side it gives them a far greater immunity.' He admitted that since doing this job he and his family no longer had pets, even though they all liked dogs and cats, and he admitted that he had become a little bit obsessed with cleanliness. He looked thoughtful for a moment. 'Hum, I must say I think your children are having a far more natural upbringing than mine, if I'm honest. Perhaps I'll think about letting them have a dog. They're absolutely desperate for one. It's just that when you learn how people get some of these illnesses, and how many bugs can be carried by animals, it puts you off a bit.' I repeated what my grandmother used to say when I fussily picked over her home grown lettuce, just to make sure it had no greenfly or caterpillars in it. 'You have to eat a peck of dirt before you die!' He laughed as he left, 'I'll give it some thought, it doesn't seem to have done you and your children much harm, has it?' With that he got in his car and drove away. I often wondered if his children were able to enjoy the pleasures of a pet after our meeting, but that would be something I would never know.

MODULE 21:
FURTHER EARLY EDUCATION,
YOUTH ORGANISATIONS AND
MUSICALITY

Michael skipped happily along beside me, his warm little hand clutching mine. 'I'm very 'cited Mummy,' he said, as we turned into the gravel drive of Canning House. I, on the other hand, had a large pit in my stomach. It would seem really strange not having him around two mornings a week.

Sue had been child minding Linda's little boy Alistair three mornings a week, and one or two of our friends were using her on a freelance basis at our home. It was boosting her salary a little, and as there wasn't as much work with us, it helped to keep her busy. But recently Linda had changed jobs and was now working in Peterborough, so we were no longer on route for her to drop Alistair off on her way to work. Sue was now engaged to her boyfriend and imminently going to be married, and with Linda's change of circumstances this was the catalyst that made her decide to look for work nearer to her home, which she could walk to. With Michael starting nursery there was going to be even less for her to do, so the timing for both of us was perfect, other than we would all miss her terribly - she was so much part of the family by now.

Within a few days of her beginning to look for other work, a friend told her that a nursery in Corby was looking for another assistant, so she applied. With credentials as good as Sue's she was offered the job immediately. But Michael was really looking forward to starting nursery, so how could I feel sad? His friend William was going, James's little sister Jennie had been there for a year already and Thomas's godparents were sending their daughter Clare, so he would have plenty of his friends to play with. As Michael was always striving to catch up with his brothers, going to nursery, in his mind, was another step closer to doing just that.

***

As things worked out, it was all probably for the best, although Sue had become a dab hand at the mucking out and handling ponies. I was beginning to find looking after them quite a big job. As someone once said, don't worry about finding the right ponies for the children, they'll find you. How right they were. After Sparkie had 'found us,' Taffy did pretty well the same, followed by Dolly and then the most wonderful little pony called Whisky. By now we had our own two horses, Polly who had been around from the year dot, and Kelly who was a later and rather extravagant addition, so Eddie had something of his own.

Whisky had been living in the village, and belonged to some people we knew vaguely. He had been stricken with a crippling condition called laminitis the previous summer. It's a condition caused by eating too much rich grass and can be very severe, in fact life threatening, particularly if the pony isn't removed from the source of the problem. My friend Caroline had nursed him through his near death illness, when one morning she had arrived to check her pony at the field, which she shared with Whisky's owners, to find him lying flat out and in agony. He was unable to get up and continued to be unable to rise for several days. The vet predicted he would never recover from the condition as it was so severe, so he had wanted to put him to sleep there and then. But with the promise from Caroline to nurse him diligently, they gave him a few days to see which way the illness went. Thursday morning was to be the day of decision and, if he wasn't back on his feet by then, the vet was going to put him out of his misery. Caroline went back down to the field first thing on Thursday morning to see how things were looking. As she walked across the grass towards Whisky, he lifted his head and whickered to her. She knew that whatever happened he just had to get up, or else it would be the end for him. She pleaded with him, encouraging him as she pulled and pushed him. Suddenly he made an enormous effort and put both front legs out in front of him. Caroline realised this was her chance, and she mustn't miss it. She got behind him and pushed with all her strength 'Come on Whiz, you can do it. Up you get.' With one more huge shove from Caroline and an enormous effort from Whisky, he scrambled to his feet. He could only move very slowly and painfully to the stable and enclosed yard area, but now at least he couldn't eat the grass anymore. But since then Whisky had spent his time shut permanently in the yard and stable, eating just hay. The family that owned him had now lost interest, and he hadn't been ridden for over a year. So when they heard through Caroline that we would be grateful to borrow another pony for the summer, they were delighted to let us have him as they were going to Florida for three weeks. Whisky was the last of the four ponies to join us for the summer fun.

But now with two horses and four ponies to look after I

had my work cut out, especially as they had to be stabled some of the time to avoid the dreaded laminitis. Obviously stables had to be mucked out, so Sue had become a dab hand, but she drew the line at riding. So when Sue left it seemed a good idea to find someone who could help with exercising the horses. The lady we found came from the village. She was happy to ride the horses and the ponies when necessary, and she could also help me put the ponies in and out.

We spent the summer holidays riding, picnicking and playing with friends, both old and new. We had also joined the boys to the Pony Club, a lovely youth organisation for children with an interest in horse riding. So once the boys were members we were able to attend some of the teaching sessions, both mounted and dismounted. From here grew another friendship circle for the boys, needless to say mostly girls, with a small smattering of boys. One such friendship that grew during the summer through the Pony Club was with a little boy called Martin - he was going to be at Glapthorn School in September. Just over a year younger than the boys, his mother Nikki was keen for him to know some fellow pupils before he started. Unlike our year group the mothers hadn't particularly jelled, so there were no play sessions during the summer holidays. Although we had met Nikki and her husband Philip several years before, just after they moved to the area, we hadn't met again until we saw each other at the rally. Nikki asked me if I would bring the boys to tea so Martin could get to know them. Guy, Martin's little brother, was Michael's age, so they would be starting school the following year. It would be a good idea for them to get to know one another too.

Martin was a sweet little boy - one of those children who seem to be born adult; he oozed common sense and good behaviour. He was also one of those children that, as a parent, you're always pleased for your child to be friendly with. He was quite tall for his age, as tall as Ben and only a little smaller than Thomas, but not quite as tall as Christopher. Whatever he did he always looked neat and tidy, with his hair brushed carefully to one side. He was clearly a bright little chap who was full of good ideas and the boys immediately took to him. Michael and Guy had huddled together playing with Guy's farm all afternoon, and Nikki and I also seemed to have a lot in common. They too lived in a house that was in an offbeat place. They also had a little grey pony for their boys and Nikki, like me, had a chestnut mare that she competed. She was also very involved with the National Pony Club, being a key member of the educational committee. She taught prolifically at various pony clubs and also privately. My working life had started as a riding instructor, and before having the children I also taught for our pony club and had been on the instructors' and fund raising committees, so conversation flowed easily. Gradually the boys' friendship circles were growing - some friendship paths crossed and some didn't, but they were so lucky to have such a big social circle, which was now necessitating a separate calendar to keep up with their social engagements.

***

But before we knew it the autumn term had started and a new school year was ahead of us. The boys were moving up into Mrs. Poole's class. She was a lovely, gentle lady, with a soft voice and a very kind attitude. Her smile was wide, and the corners of her brown eyes wrinkled as she laughed, which made them dance and sparkle with delight when the children amused her.

Although everything seemed to be going well, I had begun to notice that Thomas and Christopher were beginning to bring home increasingly difficult reading books, even choosing the home read books from the school library, whereas Ben, on the other hand, was staying pretty well static. I started to become more concerned about his lack of progress, after all they were now six, and I really believed he was capable of more. I also knew what Ben was like. He was a past master at pulling the wool over people's eyes, and if anything he was now reading even more simple things than he had been in reception class. One evening I called Ben back to the sofa. 'Ben come here and sit with me for a moment,' I said, patting the seat beside me. 'I wondered if you'd like to have a look at Thomas' reading book.' He came over and climbed up next to me, snuggling up close as I opened the book. We started off by just looking at the pictures, and then I asked him if he could read any of the words. He looked for a second at the writing and then read fluently to the end of the book.

As I suspected, Ben had been pulling a fast one again. He'd completely duped this lovely natured lady into believing he could barely read. This called for some tactful action, so I put a note into his reading record book. I related to her that I had been looking through the pictures in Thomas' book with Ben, and much to my surprise he had read the whole thing to me. I then asked her if it would be possible for him to have something slightly more challenging, in light of this sudden advancement in his ability. Mrs. Poole met me outside school that evening. 'I think young Ben's been pulling the wool over my eyes, hasn't he. You're quite right, he was word perfect, so I've put him up a couple of levels. We'll see how well he copes, shall we?'

Not long after this incident Mrs. Poole came out to meet me at the end of the day. 'He's done it again,' she said, her eyes dancing with laughter. 'We had the Music Man in school today and he does this particular song with the children. They have to sing the words in the order of the musical instruments he has listed. The year two children are normally able to do it, but the year one children are just a bit too young, so I don't usually ask them to sing because there's really too much for them to remember. For weeks now Ben's been asking me if he can be the music man and sing. So today I let him do it, thinking that I would have to give him a lot of help. But, oh no, not at all. He was word perfect and reeled off a huge list of musical instruments. He never ceases to amaze me.' I laughed, 'Me neither, and I think he may just go on surprising us.'

Ben was also beginning to show a real leaning towards musicality, so mum offered to buy the boys a second hand piano for Christmas and give them some lessons. As an accomplished pianist herself, having earned herself a scholarship to the Royal College of Music at the age of thirteen, she was really keen for at least one of them to take up the piano. Thankfully, and not unsurprisingly, Ben took to it like a duck to water and even though his fine motor movement was way behind the other two, and his hand control nothing like as good as it should be, he streaked ahead with the piano, practicing at every opportunity until he was soon playing little tunes and even composing his own little ditties. In fact, he was well on the way to being ready for his grade one exam before he had been playing for six months.

MODULE 22:
THE SCIENCE OF WINTER SPORTS

During the school summer holidays our friends, Sarah and John, were keen to know if we would be interested in going on a skiing holiday with them and some of their friends. I was keen to jump at the chance, but approached Eddie with some trepidation as, apart from anything else, it was going to be an expensive exercise. We had always wanted to learn to ski. Well, to be more accurate, *I* had always wanted to ski, Eddie wasn't quite as keen. So we went and had supper with Sarah and John, to have a look at the holiday they had in mind, and to have a discussion about the cost and logistics of the exercise. After a persuasive supper and plans to use a child friendly holiday company, we decided that if we were going to give it a go, there was no time like the present. The holiday was to be in the Italian Alps. There was a nursery in the hotel, a ski nanny service and a private telecabin up to the base ski area. To keep the cost as low as possible we decided to go the week following the February half term, taking the boys out of school for a week. So we blindly committed ourselves to the challenge and paid our deposit.

The time went quickly and half term flew by as we prepared for the holiday, having shopped till we dropped. I looked on it as a challenge, getting all of us kitted out with the cheapest money could buy, but that didn't compromise our warmth and dryness, especially for the boys. Nothing would put them off faster than cold wet clothing. C & A's turned out to be the best option for all of us as we didn't want to spend the earth, just in case no one liked it. As luck would have it, half term seemed to signal sale time in the ski department, so I was able to buy us all we needed at half the normal price.

The packing began, but it soon filled me with horror as I methodically gathered everything in the upstairs spare room. Sarah phoned during the day as we both packed and unpacked our cases, trying again and again to re-arrange the order in which things went in. 'I can't get everything into the bags, so how on earth are you managing with all your lot?' she asked. 'I'm not,' I replied bluntly. 'In fact, I don't think I'm ever going to get it all in.' Slowly but surely I sliced by half the amount of clothes we needed, cutting everything down to the barest minimum, hoping for all I was worth we could manage without. But even after ruthlessly cutting the clothing allowance, we still had four large cases and a couple of small bags, plus a rucksack for each of us. As soon as Eddie got home from work, we loaded the car ready for our early start at 2.30am in the morning. We were flying from Gatwick and had to check in at 5am, ready to fly at 7am.

As the Mellors pulled up outside our house at 2.30, there was a gentle flurry of snow falling which added to the boys' excitement. John turned their car around and Will's little face peered out of the window from his car seat. Michael peered back and they waved at one another, pushing their excited little faces hard up to the windows, pulling faces at one another, misting the windows with their warm breath as they laughed. Once we arrived at the airport and unloaded the boys and the luggage, the enormity of what we were undertaking hit us. In fact, what the hell were we doing trying to take four little boys skiing when neither of us could ski, and none of the boys were really big enough to carry a case for themselves? It was nothing short of pure stupidity, but here we were at the point of no return. I managed to take two cases and my rucksack, and Eddie had the other two cases and his rucksack. The boys all had their own little rucksacks on and Christopher and Thomas valiantly struggled with a smaller case each, until we got to the terminal and managed to grab a couple of trolleys. The boys were uncontrollably excited, and would have run riot in the large, empty open space, had we let them. Somehow we managed to contain their excitement as we parked ourselves and the luggage near to the check-in, ready for its opening.

Gradually, the others began to drift in and the boys quietened somewhat as shyness took over. The desk opened promptly, so we were there ready to check-in in family groups. Eddie and I got our usual reaction as we handed over the passports. 'Ooh, how lovely – triplets, I've never met triplets before. Are you going skiing?' 'Yes' I replied, smiling back at her. 'Good luck' she said, grimacing, 'You're going to need it with this little lot.' I smiled nervously, and nodded in a knowing way, hoping she would think we had gone into this adventure with our eyes wide open, and that Eddie and I were experienced skiers who would ably tutor our little trainee Franz Klammers. As I walked away, having helped to put our luggage on the conveyor belt, I had that awful sinking feeling that you get when you realise you are totally out of your depth.

The flight was quick and we were soon in Geneva airport waiting for our luggage to appear on the carousel.

'Look after Will, can you, John, I need the loo,' said Sarah, then turned to me and whispered 'Can you keep an eye on Will too, you know what John's like?' She raised her eyebrows and grinned. John was just as likely to spot some interesting information to read and completely forget about watching Will, who in turn was just as likely to be found riding around on the carousel with the suitcases, laughing mischievously.

Once the cases were claimed and loaded onto the trolleys, we were ushered to our bus where a friendly girl in a pink jacket was waiting for us. 'Are these the triplets?' she asked, as we climbed the steps. 'Yes they are, and this is Michael, their little brother' I replied introducing all the boys, feeling very conscious of the fact that Michael mustn't feel the odd one out. She came round a little later to give us our lift passes and to book the ski school. 'I assume the triplets will be taking ski school as they're booked in with the ski nanny, and I see Michael is booked into the nursery.' 'Yes that's right,' I said, 'And Eddie and I would like to book ski school too.' She looked alarmed. 'Is this your first time too?' I started to have that same old sinking feeling again. 'Umm, yes it is,' I said hesitantly. The girl in pink looked sympathetically at me. 'Oh dear, well we'll try and help you as much as we can, I'm sure you'll be alright.' I was now beginning to feel certain that it wouldn't be alright.

After booking everything we were going to need, the girl in pink announced that there had been an amazing amount of snow over the last twenty four hours and over a metre had fallen. Because of this we were going to be dropped at the end of the road, so we would have to drag our cases up to the hotel. She promised that there would be plenty of staff to help us, and I have never wished so much that what she said was right. The thought of trying to get six cases and four little boys through thick snow was, quite frankly, horrifying. Thankfully, the girl was true to her word and there was an abundance of staff available so we only had to carry our own two cases. Then the lovely couple Thomas and Ben had been chatting to on the bus helped us with the boys. Simon picked Michael up and carried him, and Jo took Ben's hand to help him across the snow.

During the transfer we had watched with interest as Tom and Ben became engaged in conversation with this couple for a good half an hour. They were in our group and the cousins of one of John's old medical trainee friends, making them and us the only non-medical couples in the party. I had been able to overhear some of the conversation the boys were having with them, and it appeared that they had two boys about our boys' age, who also had a pony called Taffy. But their boys had been left at home with Granny, which I was beginning to think sounded a very sensible idea. It turned out that the couple had horses too, and they were really involved with their local point to point (the amateur form of steeplechase horse racing) as we were. As we chatted with them throughout the week we discovered we had many mutual acquaintances, and the coincidences between us were uncanny.

But the first morning still had to be faced, so we were down for breakfast early, with the boys dressed in their long johns and polo necks in readiness for the thick, all in one suits once we'd eaten breakfast. Sarah and I took Michael and William along to the nursery, which they didn't seem too unhappy about as they had one another. By the time we returned, Thomas, Ben, Christopher and Edward were all ready, warmly dressed in their ski clothes and standing with the two dads. They waited for us so we could all get into the little egg like pods together, to travel up the mountain.

The snow was still falling and as fast as the men cleared it the snow blew around, like packs of small white mice, in organised little flurries to cover the ground again. The ski nannies also came up with us to help, but it soon became a total nightmare. The boots were horrendously uncomfortable, and getting the right fit for all three boys was proving very difficult, as one pair after another were cast aside. Eventually the boys were all sorted, but we still had to have our boots fitted. The sweat began to pour down my back, as I became so hot with the effort of taking the boots on and off. Once we had the boots all sorted out, we then had to get our skis and poles measured up to fit us. These had codes on them which we had to write down in case the boys muddled up whose skis were whose. Then one of the ski nannies had the good idea of writing their names on a sticky label and sticking them on to the relevant skis.

Finally we emerged into the snow again, the children by now hot, bad tempered and grizzling, and not at all sure whether they wanted to learn to ski anymore. The boots were alien and uncomfortable, and the reality that we were about to disappear and leave them in the hands of an Italian speaking stranger was beginning to dawn on them. Edward started to cry and then Ben decided his ears were hurting. Tom's bottom lip was dropping and I was about ready to give up trying to learn to ski ourselves, feeling by now that it was going to be an almost impossible task. Sarah and John had gone, as they needed to keep up with their ski guiding group, leaving us with all the children to get into ski school. Just as I was about to give up, a ski nanny appeared. 'We'll take them to the ski school for you, you just go. We'll look after them.' She called some of the other nannies over for some reinforcements. 'Go over to that chair lift there and get on it without your skis on, it'll take you up to the adult ski school meeting area. Don't worry about them, they'll be fine, that's what we're here for. You just go and get yourselves sorted out.' With a feeling that crossed over between guilt and total relief, we did as we were told, trying to shut out the boys' sobs as we left.

But now there was the chair lift to negotiate. We struggled over to it, our arms filled with skis and poles, trying desperately to get used to the feeling of the concrete slippers on our feet. The chair lift operator gestured to us to step forward onto a cleared area. We stood there like unsuspecting lambs to the slaughter. DUUFF - the wood and metal chair had swept round the corner, taking us totally by surprise. 'Ahh, God that really hurt,' I cried out in pain as I flopped back on to the hard wooden seat. My legs had been completely taken out from underneath me. The chair then sped on its way up the mountain. Eddie and I both struggled to untangle ourselves and the skis from one another, as Eddie made a high pitched groaning noise, grimacing with the agony of being hit around the back of the legs with a plank of wood, travelling at high speed.

We had barely gathered ourselves and got the skis back into some sort of order, before we arrived at the dismounting pad. Not satisfied with trying to knee-cap us at the bottom of the mountain, the chair very nearly succeeded in decapitating us as we both dived out of its path, as we got off at the top. We stood gathering ourselves for a second or two, still damp with sweat from the previous hour's exertions, and now in severe pain from our tangle with the chair. The snow was now almost at blizzard proportions, as it whirled around us and into our eyes. There in the distance was obviously our ski group disappearing around the corner of a half buried small wooden shack. We quickly worked out how to put our skis on and shuffled rapidly after them, which caused yet more prolific sweating. As we rounded the corner the instructor was just starting to demonstrate the snowplough turn. I had been reading lots of little books on skiing before we left, so I at least had a bit of an idea about leaning one or other way to turn, and as an ex roller skating kiddie, I also had some idea of what it was like to have something with motion on my feet. Eddie, on the other hand, had neither read about it, nor had he any experience of the gliding motion, so it wasn't many minutes before he was on the floor.

After a few goes on the gentle slope the instructor decided it was time for us to try a slightly harder slope. I had severe doubts about this, as Eddie was barely able to stand up on his skis for more than ten seconds. But what else could we do other than follow the crowd? The next trick the ski instructor played on us was to take us on the pommel, or button lift, yet another masochistic device designed to trick any unsuspecting newbie skier. If, like Eddie, you thought you were meant to sit down on the little button that was on the end of the metal pole, it would then continue to sink to the floor. The long stretchy wire, which attached the metal pole on to the overhead wires, would lengthen downwards, carefully depositing you in a heap, ready for the next person to slide headlong into you. This would leave complete carnage with a mass of tangled bodies and skis to unravel.

At times I felt the operators sped the tricky conveyance up, just for a bit of a laugh to break their boredom. They watched us getting launched and lurched away from the start, until finally we had all made it to the top of the slope, only then to realise we were going to have to perfectly time our dismount, to slither down the little slope and on to the edge of the nursery run. Needless to say, many people didn't make it and lay sprawled at the top. Once we had managed to negotiate our way past all the hazards and dismount safely at the top of the 'easy slope' we were then asked to proceed crocodile style, in snowplough, back and forth across the slope after our instructor. But Eddie had never really caught up from our bad start, and having never mastered the snowplough technique properly was now really struggling. He had had several abortive attempts to grapple with the button lift before managing to get up to the top. Consequently, he spent most of his time playing catch up.

We all followed Walter, our rather small, plump instructor, in a slow and orderly fashion across the slope, turning to stand in line on the edge of the piste beside him.

I'm afraid in this situation self preservation kicks in and I was concentrating so hard on trying to keep upright myself that I hadn't looked around to see how Eddie was coping until we stopped. Eddie flew past us heading downhill at great speed - backwards! Like a champion figure skater he spun around and around, his skis crossing and uncrossing, nearly falling then recovering himself for a second, before sliding off again at great speed, until he finally fell in a heap. His skis slithered down the mountain behind him, having both come off with the impact of the fall. He was at least halfway down the slope, so we all made our way, crocodile style, slowly down the mountain towards him. The instructor picked up one lost ski and then the other, scooping down effortlessly to put one in one hand and the other in his other hand. Finally he pulled up next to Eddie. 'Eddie what a you doowin, you a tri to killa yourself. Remember sno plough, all the time sno plough.' Eddie by now was struggling to his feet. He had snow down his jacket and all over his hat, his goggles were also full of snow as he had skidded downhill face first. I could hear Eddie muttering under his breath as the instructor skied off. 'Twat, of course I remember snow plough, all the time snow plough. And if I knew how to do the bloody snow plough, I wouldn't be snow ploughing down the mountain on my face.' I couldn't help but have a little giggle at Eddie's angry mutterings.

After another hour our lesson came to an end and we were delivered back to the base station. I have to say I felt relieved to be back in one piece, and I was seriously wondering if we had done the right thing. I was worried about Eddie who was really not having a happy time, and there was no sign that tomorrow would be any better. After having left all the boys crying, I wasn't at all sure that they were going to be having a happy time either. I couldn't help but wonder how on earth they were going to cope with these hazardous devices that were the only route up the mountain. So after a quick lunch and a little practice on the small nursery slope, we decided to make our way back down to the hotel. By now the snow was falling in more huge feathery flakes, making it very difficult to see at all, and I guess we were both a little anxious about the children. We were keen to make sure they weren't sitting in the hotel feeling miserable, after all they probably would have struggled as much as us on their first morning.

We were met by Ben, still in his long johns and polo neck, and now wearing his tartan zip up slippers. He was rosy faced and laughing, and his fine blond hair bounced up and down as he was piggy backed along the hallway by Holly, one of the ski nannies. 'We're playing hide and seek, and Holly's helping me to find everyone. See you later.' With that he disappeared off around the corner with Holly. I could hear delighted laughter as they found one of the other children. 'Well he seems happy enough,' I said, turning to Eddie. 'Umm, perhaps we'd better go and see what Mikey and Will are up to', Eddie replied.

So we made our way towards the nursery, but as we walked past a window I could see them both in their snow suits with two of the nannies, sledging down a little slope in the garden. They too had rosy cheeks and were laughing, clearly having a lovely time. So we decided that we had to stop worrying about the children, and to concentrate on the fact that we needed to have some fun too. Soon the others appeared back from their day's ski guiding, obviously like us a little anxious to find out how all the children were. We all gathered in the dining room ready for tea, then the children were delivered back to join us. 'Can I play with you tomorrow, Holly?' asked Ben. He then turned to me. 'We're going to do cooking tomorrow and the chef said we could help him make the cakes ready for tea.' 'Oh good, how lovely,' I said, with a feeling of dread. I had an absolute terror that one day I was going to come across a baked bogey in something the children had helped to cook. My heart always sank when they did cookery at school because they always saved a cake or a biscuit for me, watching assiduously for my reaction as I tried it. But I knew where children's fingers sometimes went and I could picture the little candles that ran from the children's noses, knowing that everyone had a hand in the production of these delicacies. However, they were all clearly having a lovely time, so that was all that mattered.

The next morning we made our way up the mountain. The snow was still falling in huge feathery flakes and had amounted to at least another foot gathering overnight. We were up there nice and early so we could have a quick practice. There were hardly any people around. The heavy snow was keeping people in their beds. We headed over to the dreaded chair lift, this time determined to win the battle. We decided to try and get on it with our skis on, feeling just about confident enough to do so. The snow clearing men were working hard to get the standing pad free from the deep drifts, shovelling large piles of snow into a mound just beyond the front of the chair. Eddie and I stood waiting for the machine to start up, being the first customers of the day. The chair attendant beckoned to us, gesturing towards the cleared area just in front of the lift. We shuffled forward, this time ready and waiting for the beastly chair as it made its way towards us, slowly revving up speed as it rounded the corner, until it was at full throttle by the time it reached us. As much as we were ready for it, the speed and power it hit us with still took us off our feet, landing us in a grovelling heap on the hard wooden seat. 'Agh, you bloody thing,' grimaced Eddie, as we both hung on for grim death. The seat swept us at speed away from the starting block, only then to stab our skis hard and fuut into the heap of snow that had just been cleared. We lurched forwards, clinging on for grim death as we were pitched towards the pile of snow. Only sheer strength and determination kept us in the seat, as we hadn't yet had time to pull the safety bar down. We wriggled our bottoms back into the seat for the short trip up to the nursery slopes in readiness to dismount, then braced ourselves to stand up and slide away, but again the speed increased and we had to leap from the moving seat. I ducked as it swept over my head and Eddie was deposited in a groaning heap on the floor. He wriggled, quickly trying to get out of the way, as the next people were about to arrive. 'I'm determined to beat that ruddy thing,' Eddie said, as he brushed himself down. I was beginning to think it had a personal vendetta against us and I was pretty keen to avoid using it if we possibly could.

The snow was so deep now we couldn't see our skis at all, making skiing even harder. Things were getting worse and Eddie was doing an even better impression of a figure skater, as he spun and slid backwards down the slope, picking himself up time and time again. 'You haffa to getta yourself private lesson Eddie,' said Walter our instructor, as we stopped for a coffee break. The last hour continued to deteriorate and finally one of the group fell and hurt her knee. She was a pretty young woman and Walter wasted no time in offering to piggy back her down the mountain, giving her skis to a girl in our group who was more experienced. They set off, skiing in front of us, rapidly disappearing into the blizzard until they were little blurry dots way below us. We slithered and fell in our efforts to manage the difficult conditions, until finally we all took our skis off and trudged laboriously down the mountain on the edge of the piste.

We finally got down and had some lunch at the base station. 'Why don't you do what Walter suggests and have a private lesson,' I asked Eddie. 'Because it's yet more expense,' he snapped. 'I'm not going to pay out any more money, and I'm not going to ski school again either, that bloke's an idiot.' I had to admit that he did have a point, so we made the executive decision to practice on our own. It had to be better than the lessons which I was finding nothing short of terrifying. If nothing else I feared for Eddie's life.

That afternoon we took ourselves back to the slightly steeper nursery slope, gradually getting to grips with the button lift. Eddie still had a few involuntary dismounts, but he was slowly improving, although it didn't take much to dislodge him. Equally so, it didn't take much to upend him on the slopes either, as he seemed to have very little awareness of where his skis were pointing. I tried to help him, teaching him the very little I'd managed to learn, but we were soon getting pretty tetchy with one another. 'Just push your heels out,' I shouted to him as I followed him down the mountain. 'You know, the opposite to Charlie Chaplain, and then try to stay like that. If you lean one way or the other you'll soon find that you'll be able to turn.' But it just seemed impossible to teach him, and I didn't have the experience to help him any further. I pleaded with him. 'Please Eddie, do as Walter suggested and at least try one private lesson.' 'I'm not forking out for any more blinking lessons,' he said, in an irritable voice. 'Well please yourself then because I can't help you either,' I said as I skied off feeling very frustrated. But I was also aware that unless Eddie got to grips with this skiing lark, it was unlikely we would ever have another trip.

So I skied over to the button lift to have another practice down the nursery slope on my own, but Eddie had arrived before me, having had one of his uncontrollable whooshes to the bottom, inevitably ending up tangled in the orange netting. But I was still feeling really cross with him so I decided to let him get well in front of me, as it wasn't safe to follow him too closely up the button lift. As we travelled up I noticed a small boy flying down the mountain completely out of control, screaming as he went, until he finally fell at speed and slithered under the rope and onto the button lift track. As I looked up, I could see Eddie pulling the button out from between his legs and rapidly shuffling out of the way of the oncoming passengers. What on earth is he doing, I thought. It looked as if was going over to help the small boy, who was only just a little older than our own boys. Here he was, barely able to stand up on the skis himself, but still having a big enough heart to try and help this little chap. Suddenly all my anger melted away and I remembered just the reasons why I'd married him.

The next day we decided to have a secret peek at the boys' lesson. There was a large mound of snow which we could hide behind. Both Ed and Ben were reporting that the instructor was horrid, and that she was hitting them on their legs with her ski poles, so we felt it was a good idea to go and check on their reports.

Physical abuse had to be investigated, and John and Sarah were keen we should go and check that things were in order, especially after our experience with Walter, who was a less than caring ski instructor. Although the boys definitely weren't as triplety since starting school, there were still some very touching displays of brotherly closeness.

We watched as Tom and Christopher both encouraged Ben whilst he had his turn on the slalom, and they cheered him when and if he finished the course without falling. If he did fall and the instructor was otherwise engaged, they would shuffle quickly over to him in order to help him get up. It was clear there was still an incredible bond between them. The ski instructor, contrary to their reports, was also very sweet, helping them to their feet if they fell, brushing them down before giving them a little cuddle, and then setting them off again. She fed them sweets when they were resting and wiped their runny noses. In fact she was the epitome of care. Then we saw what the children were talking about. If they forgot which leg to lean on to turn, she gently tapped their boot with her ski pole to remind them.

On the other hand the two little ones were having a wonderful time. Being the eldest in the nursery group, they went sledging most days, and had trips into town with the nannies for a hot chocolate. They also went ice skating. In fact they couldn't have been any happier with their holiday.

Far too quickly the final day arrived and the boys went to their last ski school session, excited about the races and the badges they were going to be awarded. Eddie had finally agreed to have a private lesson, and the others persuaded me to go right up to the top of the mountain to ski back down with them, especially as the sun had finally decided to shine. It was a simply beautiful day and the warmth of the sun felt delicious as it wrapped itself around my exposed cold face. We travelled up the mountain on the chair lift, and underneath us I could see Eddie with his instructor. He was slowly following him across the slope, copying him just like the children had done, resting one hand on one knee to turn and then swapping to the other knee to turn the other way. He wobbled a little as we shouted out to him, and then waved for a split second. Then concentration fell over him again as he was determined, for our sakes, to get to grips with this very difficult pursuit.

As we continued on our journey up the mountain, beneath us was a line of very small children whooping as they bumped over the mounds of snow, their legs spread wide for balance and their little arms held out like small scarecrows, with the short poles dangling from their mitten covered hands. They looked like a little flock of migrating birds all in a row. In front was an instructor leading them over the small bumps, the children following her faithfully, just like the pied piper. Behind them was another instructor with an even smaller child between her legs, who was being steadied and balanced. As I watched, a familiarity became obvious - the matching snow suits, the C & A bright blue and yellow hats and yellow sun glasses, Christopher and Tom in the middle and Ben at the very back between the instructors legs, and Edward in his blue suit and red balaclava just in front of her. I felt so proud watching them, even now they were all far better than us. I felt so lucky to be there, watching my children in the snow with the beauty of the mountains around me, and in the company of some lovely people. It had all come to an end, as all good things have to, but we had met some new friends and enjoyed the company of our old friends.

Finally we were back at the airport, making hasty arrangements for the Marriages to come with their children to stay for Easter and our point to point races, before driving back home tired and happy.

***

We arrived home very late, as the flight had been delayed, but I sorted through the pile of post. In it was a letter from school telling us that there was to be a sponsored poetry recital on Monday and enclosed was the poem for the boys to learn. 'Oh crumbs, how on earth are they going to do this?' I said to Eddie, once the boys were in bed. 'They've only got tomorrow breakfast time to learn it.' So the following morning when they were getting up, I told them about the poem and asked them if they would like to wait until the following day to do it. But Christopher, not wanting to feel left out, was adamant he was going to learn it there and then. So we read and repeated the poem whilst he ate his breakfast, until he could recite it back to me. Then Thomas, not wanting to feel left out either, begged me to help him as well. Fortunately Ben didn't seem too bothered about it, so I sent a note explaining the situation asking for Ben to be excused until the following day.

That evening I arrived to pick them up from school. Thomas and Christopher came running along the pavement waving their little hand written certificates. 'We've done it, we remembered the poem,' Christopher said. 'Will you give us some sponsorship money, please mummy?' Then Thomas took over. 'It's for poor children in India. Do you know they're only as old as us and they have to go to work for hours and hours every day? They don't go to school at all, you know.' His eyes were wide with amazement. Ben had been chatting to Mrs. Poole, but was now making his way slowly along the pavement towards us. As he arrived he smiled then shouted out 'Surprise,' as he pulled out the certificate to wave in front of me. 'Well done Ben,' I said, feeling puzzled. 'Who taught you the poem. Did Mrs. Poole help you at school?' He shook his head. 'No, I learnt it this morning. I listened to you doing it with my brothers and remembered it.' I was incredulous, yet again he had amazed me with his ability to achieve more than I'd ever believed possible. By now Mrs. Poole had walked over to us grinning. 'He's done it again,' she said. 'Clever little boy.' We both shook our heads and laughed. He was certainly an achiever. I just hoped he would continue to have this sort of determination to do what he wanted to throughout his life.

MODULE 23:
ANIMAL HUSBANDRY AND FUND RAISING FOR CHARITY

The children were all excitedly gathering in the playground. Reception class, years one and two were having a visit to a local farm to see the lambing. Parents also gathered to help with the transportation - children were being allocated to various cars and the community mini bus was there for Mr. Palmer to drive. The farm was only a few miles away and, actually as the crow flies, only just at the back of our house. We sometimes rode the ponies through the woods to the farm and visited Andrew, the friendly farmer who lived there. Christopher ran over to me, his face glowing with excitement. He was in his element in this sort of social situation. 'Can David and Martin come in our car to the farm?' I looked across to Mr. Palmer, who smiled and nodded his approval. Michael was with me as there was no nursery. He was jumping up and down, tugging at the bottom of my coat. 'Can we go and see the lambs now?' I gathered my little troop and took them over to our car. We had swapped our old Granada to a seven seater - a Mitsubishi Shogun. Needless to say, the boys often wanted to have some friends home to play, and with the old car there was no room for any extras to travel safely and strapped in.

We pulled into the farmyard followed by the other cars and the little white bus with blue lettering on its side, announcing to all that it had been donated to the community of Oundle by the local Round Table. Farmer Andrew stood in the yard with his green overalls and gum boots, waiting to greet us. He had a friendly, weathered face, and there was a large L shaped tear in his overalls, which showed some of his hairy bare thigh which made the children giggle. He beckoned us to follow him to the sheds on the far side of the yard. The pens inside the sheds were full of sheep and their lambs; in fact everywhere we looked there were sheep. Andrew then took us to quietly peer into the lambing shed, a special barn designated as the 'labour ward' for the imminent births. In the corner was a sheep with her new born lamb, which she busily licked as it wobbled on its unsteady little legs. Its ears were still slightly crumpled from lying in the cramped womb with its sibling, which being a few minutes older was now nosing unsteadily around the mother looking for its first feed of milk. The children all quietly oh'd and ah'd, fascinated by the spectacle of new life.

We then proceeded into the indoor nursery where the slightly more vulnerable sheep and lambs were - the difficult births, the first time mothers who needed a bit of extra help and the orphans being adopted onto another mother who had lost her own lamb. There was a set of triplets who needed extra care, and a few orphaned lambs who were being bottle fed. At the end of the shed was a small pen with two new born lambs laying in the soft straw, still damp from their birth. Andrew called me over.

'These two have got your name on them. They're both one of sets of triplets born to first time mothers. It's too much for a young sheep to cope with triplets as her first lambs, so we usually take the smallest one away and leave them with twins. That way they all seem to do much better, but these two now need a new mum, so I thought the Arthey family would be the perfect answer.' He smiled the knowing smile of someone who knew they'd found a soft touch. Andrew knew that I was a complete sucker when it came to any little animal that needed some extra care or attention. Before I knew it, we were being bundled off with teats, bottles and lamb formula milk and, of course, the two lambs who were now safely contained in a large cardboard box. They were each wrapped in an old towel. I had to drop the children back to school and then I headed straight home, as we needed to make a warm pen in the barn for our new 'foster children.'

Michael skipped around excitedly as we unloaded them from the car, then he ran on in front of me, his fine blond hair blowing in the wind, whilst I carried the cardboard box towards the barn. 'Can I help mummy, can I make the lambs a pen?' His voice was full of excitement as I put the box containing the two new family members onto the straw covered floor. We rolled some bales over to make a pen in the corner, and then shook fresh straw into their warm little bedroom. Finally, we lifted our new little babies out of the box and into their carefully crafted home. They had no fear of us as they both nudged and nosed, looking for some milk as they were now hungry, having had only a tiny feed of the thick yellow Colostrum. So Michael and I went inside and mixed them both a bottle of milk, which reminded me of all the 18 bottles I used to make daily, when the boys were tiny. This set of twins would be a doddle in comparison!

We sat on the bales and I settled them, one at a time, upon my knee. They needed some encouragement to get them to accept the teat and then to suck. I tipped their heads back and stroked their throats gently to stimulate them to swallow. They felt so small and vulnerable, but their skinny little bodies were warm against my legs. Once they got the hang of sucking at the small red teats the milk soon disappeared. Then it was time to go to school to collect the older boys, who were eager to get home and see their new pets. 'What are we going to call them?' asked the boys. 'Well, let's think of some names on our way home,' I said. So we threw some names around the car as I drove back, the boys getting increasingly more silly with their suggestions as every mile passed, giggling at some of the ridiculous ideas. But eventually we settled on calling them Mint and Jelly. Not that we had any plans for these two to ever be accompanied by mint jelly. Being female they could re-join a flock and become mothers themselves when the time came, although I wasn't sure we would ever be able to part with them. They were soft and warm like small human babies, and we already felt protective towards them.

Like new human babies they needed feeding regularly, in fact every four hours, so for the evening feeds we had a large plastic sheet which we spread across the kitchen floor. Unfortunately what goes in has to come out, usually immediately after their feed, so we were able to take some precautions at which point the plastic sheeting came in to its own. Once the bodily functions had been completed it was pretty safe to let them play for about half an hour. We still had the original old carpets in the lounge and the kitchen, which was inherited when we brought the house, so the odd accident wasn't really too disastrous, and we always cleaned it up immediately. It was such a sight to see - boys, lambs and Basil the dog racing along the hallway and into the sitting room. The lambs sprang in the air, twisting their little bodies in excitement, as they rushed along with their gang of friends. If you ever watch lambs in a field in spring time, they gather in little groups, stop, and then all race with their friends from one point to another. They particularly seem to enjoy a mound to leap on and off. Our lambs were no different, and obviously thought the boys and Basil the dog were fellow lambs there to be raced with. They all ran together from one end of the house to the other, the boys shrieking with laughter and the lambs springing with joy. Basil the dog was always up for anything that included a bit of rush and tear, so he joined in for the sheer hell of it.

We were going out early one evening, so the lambs were in for their feed and a quick playtime. I was keen to get the boys all bathed early, so mum had come up to help with the boys' bath time, to have her supper with them, and to stay the night to babysit. She was supervising bath time while I did the lambs' feeds. We still, at this point, had the horrid sunken bath, again inherited with the house, which made getting any lingering boy out twice as difficult as it might have been with a normal bath. Tom, Christopher and Michael, at the prospect of lamb playtime had all got out quite willingly, but Ben, who was never as keen on the animals unless they were horses, was enjoying having the bath to himself. 'Come on Ben,' mum said. 'Time to get out, mummy's got tea ready now.' 'No, I don't want to get out yet.' He turned over in the bath to lie on his tummy, busying himself with the wind up frog. I could hear mum struggling to persuade him to get out, as we always left the bathroom door open. I could feel myself getting irritated by his failure to do as he was told, so I walked along the hallway to see what was going on. 'Come on Ben, don't be difficult for grandma, you know she can't lean in to the bath and pull you out and I don't want to have to get cross and pull you out either.' 'Just a little minute,' he said. 'I'm playing a game with Freddie frog and I can't get out yet.' I had a feeling a battle was about to begin. 'You've had lots of little minutes Ben, I've been listening to grandma asking you to get out for quite a while, so come on you're going to get out right now.' He started to kick in a petulant way, objecting to my instruction, sending water flying out of the bath and all over the floor.

At that moment the thundering of the herd came along the hall towards the bathroom before skidding around the corner, ending the stampede by the bedroom doors. But this time the lambs failed to turn, bounding headlong into the bathroom. Suddenly they saw the water in the bath and put on their brakes. Unfortunately, as Ben had now made a very slippery surface on the tiled floor, the lambs continued to slide headlong towards the bath which contained the reclining Ben. There was a loud splash as both lambs landed head first into the water and on top of Ben. He, in turn, in one surprisingly athletic leap, jumped out of the bath and on to grandma's lap. She was now sitting on the closed toilet seat waiting patiently with a towel resting across her knee for Ben to emerge, which of course he did slightly quicker than she had anticipated. She laughed at the look of horror on his face, having shared the bath for a few seconds with two lambs. Of course now we also had the lambs to dry as well before they could be returned to the cold barn.

We had so much fun with Mint and Jelly, and I think they too had had an equally lovely lambhood, playing with the boys and Basil the dog. But lambs turn into bigger lambs and when they started to escape from every pen and enclosure we made for them, heading relentlessly to Eddie's newly planted garden, this signalled the end of their days with us. Thankfully for us and the lambs, Sarah Mellor's father and brother were sheep farmers, so they found a place for them with their cade lambs. They would go on to join the adult flock in time and become breeding ewes.

Sarah and I delivered the half grown lambs to the Cambridgeshire farm, on a day when Michael and William weren't at nursery. We loaded the boys into their car seats in our Shogun, having folded the two back seats up to make a larger boot area for the lambs. By now they were quite a weight, having done very well on the formula milk, and then latterly on Eddie's plants. They both stood happily in the back of the car as we drove along the M11, watching with great interest as the cars passed by, occasionally turning round to look out of the back window. People passed us doing double takes, and even double double takes, as they looked in disbelief at our happy, but extraordinary passengers. Michael and William leaned round in their car seats to check on the lambs, giggling as they pushed their small hands through the gaps between the seats to let the lambs nibble their fingers. When we finally pulled into the farmyard Sarah's mother, Olive, came through the garden gate to greet us, her smiling face and rosy cheeks a picture of welcome and delight on seeing her youngest grandson and his little friend. Taking both by the hand, she led us to where we could put the lambs with their new play mates. I was convinced they wouldn't know how to mix with other lambs, having only ever played with children and an old, soft, collie dog, but they pushed their way through to get to the feeding trough, finding the lamb creep pellets irresistible for two constantly hungry and growing lambs. When I wandered out of the house half an hour later to check on them, they were rushing from pillar to post with a gang of other lambs, just as they had done with the boys and Basil.

Next winter Sarah reported that both Mint and Jelly were pregnant. Her father and brother had been moving the sheep one day, but our two had caused chaos. Mint and Jelly decided to turn back and investigate the humans who were at the back of the marching flock. They were being driven by the sheep dogs to their winter pastures near to the lambing sheds. As everyone knows, sheep are great followers, so the flock promptly turned back too. Mint and Jelly still naturally gravitated towards humans, as they had nothing but happy memories of time spent as honorary members of the species. Clearly they were totally unafraid of the snarling sheep dogs either, after all, their best friend

Basil had been a great and kindly playmate. The two continued to produce twin lambs for many years and finally died of old age, having more than earned their keep.

***

In the last few weeks before the summer holidays Mr. Palmer met me in the playground at the end of the school day. 'Oh Gill, could I have a quick word with you?' My heart did a little lurch. If my headmistress ever asked to see my mother after school, it was usually because I had been in trouble yet again, so I was conditioned to think that a request to see the head teacher was sure to signal problems. But Mr. Palmer was approaching me with a smile. 'Ben has come up with an inspiring idea and we would very much like to support him if you're willing to help.' I was a little taken a back and couldn't possibly imagine what 'idea' Ben could have come up with. But all became clear as Mr. Palmer explained. 'Mr. Tweddle, the vicar came to take assembly this morning as he does most Fridays. Anyway, Ben told Mr. Tweddle he would like to do something to raise money to help the poor people in Ethiopia or, in his words, Ethenopia.' Mr. Palmer gave a little chuckle. 'So we wondered what you thought about Ben's idea. He wants to learn to play the Snow Man theme tune on the piano, and he wants to get some sponsorship for doing so. What do you think, will he be up to it?' I hadn't got a clue, as I hadn't inherited my mother's interest or, sadly, her ability with music, so I told Mr. Palmer that I would consult with her, as she would no doubt have the responsibility of teaching him, even though he was now having lessons with a woman who lived next door to the school, and who was concentrating on Ben's grade one pieces.

Mum was rather horrified at the task ahead, but not wanting to dampen his enthusiasm, she set about finding a simple version of the music for him to try. Finally she managed to order a copy that was at about grade two level. He had been entered to take grade one, so Mum thought that with some concerted effort he would probably just about manage it. So the practicing began, as Ben picked out the notes laboriously on the black and white keys. He practiced and practiced until we could barely take anymore, until finally the tune began to take shape. As the tune started to sound more as it should, Thomas and Christopher began to hum along. This was their all time favourite video which they watched until it was nearly worn out, particularly over the Christmas period. Gradually the choristers started to sing the words too, which mum copied out for them. Finally Ben was ready, so Mr. Palmer set an afternoon aside for the performance. My mum and Eddie's mother were there with me, and Mr. Tweddle had also turned up for the occasion. Then the whole school started to file in and sit cross legged on the floor. The piano was placed at the front of the room, and Thomas and Christopher were both on a small raised platform next to the piano. As I stood there waiting I began to realise that my hands were shaking, in fact my whole body was shaking.

Ben began playing the familiar notes, as his fingers passed over the keys swiftly and fluently. Just under the surface his nerves were beginning to have an effect though, and his fingers started to trip over some of the early notes. Tom and Christopher slowed their pace accordingly and looked anxiously towards their brother until his familiar confidence returned, and away his fingers raced over the familiar keys again. The choristers quickened the pace again, singing faster to keep abreast with the notes. Finally it was over and all three took a bow. The whole school clapped and cheered their support. Ben was able to donate £100 to the 'Ethenopia' appeal, sent with a note of his achievement by Mr. Palmer and Mr. Tweddle.

***

Finally the end of the school year arrived - the boys' next year was to be the first of the final two years at Glapthorn. They were going up into Mr. Palmer, the head teacher's class, at which point they would be almost eight years old. But before breaking up for the summer we had the customary parents' evening just before the end of term. Mrs. Poole greeted us in her customary friendly manner, smiling widely, her eyes crinkled at the sides, sparkling and dancing in their usual way. We discussed the progress of each boy, having booked a triple time spot. Everything was going well and they had done their first ever SATs, being the guinea pig year, they were the first to experience the new performance testing. The boys all scored level two in maths, but Tom and Christopher had achieved a level three in English. Ben hadn't finished his English exam as he was a slow writer; therefore he had only managed a high level two. Mrs. Poole told us that we should feel very pleased with their results as it was all so new to the children, and also a step into the unknown for the teachers too.

At the end of the meeting Mrs. Poole, looking a little coy, said. 'Have you got a minute as I just wanted to show you this, it made me laugh so much.' She turned and reached into a box with some small blue exercise books in it. 'The subject I set for them was *my life so far*.' I'll read you Ben's first sentence.' She began. 'My life so far, by Ben Arthey. First of all I was just a little twinkling in my Daddy's eye.' She stopped and looked up at us grinning. 'Don't you think that's so sweet, he's got a really lovely way with words?' 'Just a twinkle in Daddy's eye' was a saying we used when we described the times before they were born or even thought about, but we hadn't realised just how literally they had interpreted it, so much so he had included it as part of his life history. She smiled with genuine affection. 'I'm really going to miss having them in my class, I've really enjoyed teaching my first set of triplets. I've enjoyed just how different they all are, but on the other hand just how special their close relationship is, and it's been so fascinating watching them interact with one another. I find it quite interesting that although they're so very different in character from one another, they all share their best friends. David and Martin are very definitely the favoured ones, and they all seem more than happy to share that friendship. There's never a glimmer of any jealousy between the boys, or indeed between David and Martin over the boys. It's been a real pleasure to have had the experience.' We, too, were sad that they were finishing in her class as she had been such a lovely teacher, but one door closes and another opens, and we were looking forward to Michael starting school and the boys going up another year.

MODULE 24:
EQUITATION AND HORSE
MANAGEMENT STUDIES

The summer holidays were upon us again and the boys
were attending their first pony club camp. I rushed around
in a frenzy, trying to make up four complete grooming kits
and put them into four separate boxes, ready for the early
start the following morning. The boys, on the other hand,
rushed around in a frenzy of over excitement, being of no
help at all. In fact, to say they got under my feet was an
understatement. Until the wonderful Auntie Pat, or
'Patience' Wallis, chugged into the yard in her blue
Diahatsu truck. She had arrived just in time to put some
order back into our lives. Auntie Pat, as several
generations of our family and friends have known her, or
Miss Wallis to those who knew her less well, was a district
midwife/health visitor during her working life, and I
remember her still doing her rounds while I was working
at the geriatric hospital in Kettering. To say children
should be seen and not heard was not quite Auntie Pat's
philosophy, as she loved to converse with all small
children, but her philosophies were of that ilk. She very
much believed that children should show respect to their
elders, and from an early age be made to accept their

responsibilities. She was quite tall with the beginnings of a limp as her hips began to trouble her, but she was still an active rider and had her own thoroughbred grey mare. Her hair, like her horse's, was grey, with a neatly curled perm. She was always very smart. In winter she often sported a tweed skirt and sensible flat leather lace up shoes, and in the summer she usually wore a floral print dress with sensible summer sandals unless, of course, she was around the horses, when she always wore hard shoes. She was the epitome of a country lady. Auntie Pat had been asked to teach Michael and another little boy called James at the camp for two out of the four days, gearing the lessons around a four year old's attention span and ability. This had very kindly been arranged for Michael's and James's benefit so they didn't feel left out. They weren't going to be expected to do the stable management lessons, but they could join in with anything they particularly wanted to do.

As soon as Auntie Pat arrived she gathered the boys into an orderly group, delegating various jobs to them. She soon had them putting their initials on the brushes with a black permanent marker, and gathering up buckets for the feeds and water, whilst constantly referring back to the list, neatly ticking off item after item. Next they were despatched to find some hay nets, and finally Auntie Pat supervised the tack cleaning, which I have to admit I usually did myself, fearing the watery mess that usually resulted if they did it themselves. But she was right, if they were to enjoy all the fun, then they had to do the less fun bits too.

The next morning Auntie Pat rolled into the drive promptly at 8.30 ready to help me load the final few bits and, of course, the boys and their ponies. Soon we were chugging down the road in the ancient old blue lorry we had recently purchased in order to transport our rapidly expanding equine collection.

The village where camp was being held was filled with lorries, cars and trailers. But, as luck would have it, we managed to pull up almost outside the farm. Children ran excitedly back and forth to and from their trailers and lorries, trying to carry armfuls of equipment. Whilst all the mothers looked harassed and tried desperately to keep the children focussed until everything was unloaded, then playing could begin.

We were allocated a huge stable for our four ponies as they were all used to one another. Adele, the kindly farmer's wife, whose son was also a pony club member and a participant in the camp, thought it would be easier for us to have everything in one place, which of course it was. The stable had been sectioned off into four little pens, with sheep hurdles and bales of straw as the dividers, but it wouldn't be too disastrous should one of the ponies break in with another as they were all friends. But the boys would still have their own stables to muck out, so there was no escaping the chores!! The children were allocated their ride instructors. Luckily, all three older boys were together, and Michael had his little ride of two with Aunty Pat.

Ben, Christopher and Thomas's ride had four girls in it, some of whom they already knew and some they would soon know. Chloe was already a friend as they had been to one or two rallies with her. They had also met Sasha, but Leo and Julia were new to them. Chloe was a year their senior and a real tomboy. She had rather wild, blonde, wavy hair. She was pretty, tall, slim, bronzed and athletic looking, and the boys liked her very much, especially her fun attitude to life. Leo was one of Chloe's family friends and was riding Chloe's big sister's pony; she had come up for the week from London. She, too, was a tomboy and full of fun, as was Sasha, who was a local girl. She was also plucky and had a very gung-ho attitude, so the boys were with three girls that could give them a good run for their money.

The fourth girl was two years their senior. She was, sadly, rather large and ungainly, with little or no conversation and she didn't smile once during the whole four days of camp. Her mother came in the mornings and dropped her off, then arrived back at four o'clock or sometimes even later, to pick her up. She knew no-one and had no help with her pony, and her mother clearly had no idea about pony management, and what it was all about. The children all tried to include her, as did the plentiful supply of parent helpers. But she skulked around on her own, never once trying to engage with any of the other children. As is often the case with children in this situation, the other children began to dislike her. One or two poked fun at her and taunted her, particularly when some of the brighter sparks realised she wasn't looking after her pony very well. On the other hand, all of us mothers were becoming increasingly concerned about her. She seemed to be so friendless even though we tried to encourage her to join in with the others, and we also tried to engage her in conversation.

It soon became apparent that she had absolutely no idea at all about how to look after her pony, so all the mums topped up his bed and made sure he had water and food. We had also found out that she had no energy giving feed for him in his little bundle of equipment, and only three small wedges of hay, which was only going to last for one night and not four days. We raided our own supplies to make sure that he was well fed, as Danny was such a sweet gentle and placid little pony, with large, kindly, brown eyes. He was heavier in build than most of the other children's pretty little Welsh ponies, but completely angelic in his nature. Julie could barely ride, but this lovely little pony looked after her as if she were the most precious thing he had ever had on his back. Slowly but surely we were all growing more and more concerned about Julie and Danny.

On the second day her mother dropped her by the gate and drove away in her fast sports car, without so much as a backwards glance. Julie wandered into the yard and took herself off to see her pony, but did nothing to look after him, other than giving him a half-hearted brush. Adele decided we would have to take over the care of Danny, as Julie clearly wasn't able to do it on her own. She had no idea about the correct application of the saddle and bridle either, and the first time she appeared ready to ride his tack was a complete mess. One of his ears had missed the head piece, and the brow band was somehow hooked over his head. The girth was twisted and the pad that went under his saddle was all ruckled up, making it very uncomfortable for him. So we made sure we were there to help her tack up, showing her and helping her to do it properly. Auntie Pat had taken charge of Michael, and if Ben played his cards right he got some help from her too. But Tom and Christopher were just about managing by themselves, having learnt to tack up on their own a week before camp.

On the third afternoon the boys' group were having a jumping lesson in the small jumping paddock. One at a time they rode forward from their stationary position in the ride, then trotted a circle before approaching the little cross pole fence at a steady pace. Some of them cantered slowly into it and some trotted, but all of them were holding tightly on to their neck straps for balance and to stop their lightweight little bodies being catapulted from the saddle should the ponies do a big jump. They all competently managed to negotiate the small obstacle.

Then it was Julie's turn. 'Hold the neck strap, Julie,' shouted Jane their instructor, as Julie trotted slowly towards the fence. Julie took no notice and held her hands high with stiff, out-stretched arms. 'Hold the neck strap, Julie,' shouted Jane again, but still there was no reaction. Danny arrived at the fence - Julie still held her arms stiffly out in front of her. For a second Danny stopped, then in slow motion he lifted his front end off the ground, carefully placing his front legs over the obstacle. Once his front end had landed, he jumped his hind legs carefully over the crossed poles. We all stood silently watching, as in slow motion Julie lurched forward with the impact of Danny's hind legs hopping over the fence. Danny stood as still as a rock hoping that Julie would re-gain her balance, but slowly and steadily she slid head first down Danny's shoulder towards the ground until, thud, she landed in a large and ungainly heap in front of her saintly pony. She lay there, not moving a muscle, as Danny bent his large head down to inspect her. We all stood silently for a second, waiting for her to move, or cry, or even yell - but not a thing. Leo turned to the rest of the ride, her eyes large and alarmed, and in her best jolly hockey sticks voice said, 'Oh God, I think she might be dead.' By now we were all running to Julie, stopping abruptly by her side. She looked up at us without a glimmer of emotion and held out her hands indicating she was waiting for us to help her to her feet, which of course we carefully did. It was most strange, her reaction, her pony's reaction and even our reaction to her fall. We were all used to children having the odd tumble, and indeed having a good cry, but never had any of us seen anything quite like this little girl's silent reaction. We took her back to the stables and un-tacked Danny, who seemed more than happy to return to his pile of donated hay, and then we took Julie into the house to sit quietly in the kitchen with Adele and her tea making team.

As we all arrived back into the yard half an hour later from the afternoon ride, Julie was sitting on a bale of straw outside Danny's stables. I went into the kitchen to warn Adele to expect the rush and throng of children and parent helpers, as we were now settling the ponies down for the night. But as I walked in, there was obviously something being discussed in a hushed tone. 'Do you know I just caught Julie in the farm office using the phone to call her mother? She said she felt fine and had gone out to see Danny, then two minutes later I walked into the office and there she was. When I asked her what she was doing in there, as cool as a cucumber she told me she was phoning her mum. Can you believe it? I don't mind anyone using the phone, but she might have asked. She really is a strange child. In fact I'm just a bit fed up with her mother, what does she think we are, a child and pony minding service? I mean, what a cheek. In fact I'm going to catch her tonight to tell her about Julie's fall and just see what sort of person she is.' It was most un-like Adele to get so hot under the collar. She was one of the warmest and most welcoming of people I'd come across.

That evening Adele kept watch, waiting near the gate so Julie's mother wouldn't escape her watchful eye. We had all gone before she arrived, because as usual she was late. I imagined her in her large Prada sunglasses, backcombed and loosely tied back, dyed blonde hair, as she swept into the yard in her convertible Mercedes.

The following morning we were all intrigued to know how Adele had got on with Julie's mother. But first the children had to be dealt with and the stables had to be mucked out, so some supervision was needed. I went to help Julie with the angelic Danny, leaving the boys to do their own stables under the watchful eye of Aunty Pat. But Christopher had other ideas and was busy playing around with Chloe, Leo and Sasha. Auntie Pat, as always, was a stickler for completing a task and keeping up with 'one's responsibilities.' As far as she was concerned, play could be resumed once the ponies had been looked after. I spotted Christopher being marched smartly across the yard, Auntie Pat's fingers firmly gripping his ear, whilst the girls all giggled at him. It was refreshing to see someone teaching the children some good old fashioned values, and I had no qualms in letting her do so. A pinched ear lobe never did anyone any harm, and probably taught Christopher a small but valuable lesson in responsibility for his future life.

As soon as the children rode out of the yard for their morning session, we all went inside for a coffee with

Adele to hear just what had happened after we had left the evening before. Apparently, Julie's mother was half an hour late to pick her up, so Adele had waited with Julie until she arrived, sending her off to check on Danny before speaking to the mother. It appears that she was very impatient with Adele and, in Adele's words, 'she looked at me as if I were something stuck on the bottom of her shoe.' Needless to say, Adele told her about Julie's fall, and then quite rightly pointed out that we were concerned that her daughter didn't interact with the other children, or indeed with us. She related the fact that Julie had helped herself to the phone without even asking permission. Adele continued to tell the tale, an increasing red tide of anger growing around her neck. It appears that the woman announced to Adele that Julie had a 'learning difficulty thingy' that affected how she interacted with others. She had omitted to fill this information in on her camp forms which, as Adele pointed out to her, would have made life far easier and less worrying for all of us had we known. In fact it was very irresponsible of her not to have told us.

Adele was so cross about the situation that she then decided to tackle her about the fact that she just dumped her daughter, and gave her no help with the pony, and did she realise that we had to help her with everything? Julie's mother looked at her in indignation and said, 'Well, that's what you lot are paid to do, I have no intention of paying for a service and then having to do it myself. Anyway, I told Julie if she wanted a pony she would have to look after it on her own, I don't even like the things.' By now the redness had crept from Adele's neck to her whole face.

We all sat there feeling indignant fury too, but also a great sadness for poor little Julie and the lovely Danny, as she continued to tell us more. 'So I'm afraid at that point she had to have a few home truths. Firstly I pointed out that we were all here principally with our own children, and that everyone who helped did so voluntarily. What she'd paid for was the use of the facilities and the instruction Julie was having, and nothing else. I told her that Julie had no idea how to look after Danny, and she was far too young for that sort of responsibility without supervision anyway. I also told her that thanks to the generosity of all you mums he was now being fed properly. The hay she had sent only lasted for one feed and not for four days, and if ponies are working hard they need more than just fresh air to live on. In fact by the time I'd finished she did actually look a little ashamed of herself. At this point she told me there was nothing she could do to help, as she had an 'important business to run', so we're obviously just another childminding service for her. It's Julie I feel so sorry for, I got the impression that she's constantly dumped on one school holiday organisation after another, and the pony is just another thing to keep her amused and out from under her mother's feet.'

I couldn't help but wonder what would happen to not only Julie but to the angelic Danny. They clearly had plenty of money, but I felt little love existed in Julie's life. I hoped that if Danny managed to survive in a family with no knowledge, he would be able to fill a gap in poor little Julie's life. We never saw them again, so sadly the answer remains a mystery to this day.

***

There was one more event during that summer holidays that caused the boys some excitement. It was something that to a lot of people could be of a rather controversial nature. As a country family who were involved in the equine world, and with Eddie being a farmer's son, country sports had been, and still were, part of our lives. Eddie had hunted as a small boy on his little pony, being encouraged by family friends who looked after him. He had then gone on to be the voluntary accountant/secretary for the hunt, so it had always been there in the background during the boys' early lives, and Eddie still hunted whenever he possibly could.

On the other hand I had only a few scanty experiences as a child, particularly as my parents weren't horsey and it was all they could do to cope with a daughter who was nothing short of obsessed, as they did their best to manage my first pony. Their only source of knowledgeable advice was from dad's old secretary and close family friend Aunty Iris and her husband Uncle Charlie. Both had a wealth of knowledge and I absolutely worshipped them. Uncle Charlie's beautiful horse, Greenways Fascination, or Sian as he was known, had qualified for White City in his day, to compete in a big show jumping competition. But Sian succumbed to an injury just before the event and was never able to take part. Even as a relatively inexperienced small girl I could appreciate what a wonderful horseman uncle Charlie was, as Sian danced around the arena with his high school dressage movements, a discipline Uncle Charlie focussed on after Sian's injury, which stopped him from being able to jump big fences. Uncle Charlie looked so slim and stylish on his beautiful, black prancing horse. People stopped in their tracks to stand and look on in awe, and I felt so proud that he was our friend. When some of my school friends, who rode at the centre where Sian was at livery, found out that he was my honorary Uncle, I was elevated to hero status which, when you're only twelve and the new girl at school too, felt very good.

Anyway, with our hunt kennels being located in the village, and with the arrival of a particularly friendly huntsman, the boys started to get an ever growing interest in the hounds, and to be honest the whole pageantry of it all. Ben and Tom really loved the theatre of it, and had made their own hunting outfits, using Ben's old red dressing gown and an old red cardigan of mum's for Tom. Mum then stitched on gold buttons and white collars so they look like the huntsman's own coat. Throughout the summer holidays it became a regular thing on a Sunday morning for the huntsman to walk the hounds up through the park to our house, usually arriving at about seven thirty in the morning. The boys always woke in time for his arrival and as Eddie and I stumbled out of bed, often after a late night, the boys were spilling out into the front paddock, more often than not in their blue stripy pyjamas to help with the hounds.

As the summer passed and autumn approached, and the summer holidays were drawing to a finale, the huntsman suggested they should come on hound exercise on their ponies. He was on his bike, but the boys, with the exception of Michael who was just too young, were all mounted. It was the start of an interest that grew as fast as their father's had at that age, and it wasn't long before they had persuaded us to let them go to the pony club meet during the October half term. With Auntie Pat on hand to lead one of them from her horse, Eddie another, and a friend called Jane to take the third, we were all sorted. But Michael was also desperate to go with his brothers, so I went on foot to walk with him on little Taffy. It was a huge success and for the time being satisfied the early encouragement they had been given by the huntsman.

MODULE 25:
THE EARLY DETECTION OF
LEARNING DIFFICULTIES

The small, striped pencil flew across the room, hitting the television before bouncing back to land in front of us, frustration having yet again got the better of Michael. He rolled over on to his back and made an angry little grunt, as he kicked out at thin air. He had been lying on his stomach on the floor whilst I knelt beside him, his right arm propping him up, his left hand gripping the pencil. His tongue poked between his closed lips. He was deep in concentration as he desperately struggled to copy his name, which I had written in bold black letters on a large white sheet of paper. I tried in vain to encourage him to get up off the floor and to come and sit up at the table. 'You'll find it much easier if you sit up here, Michael, you can't be comfortable trying to write lying down on the floor.'

It was now the fourth afternoon we had been through this ritual and it always ended on the same note. He was such a lovely, placid natured child, and yet this one thing seemed to bring out the very worst in him. Nursery had asked me to have a concerted effort at home to get him writing his name. It was his last term at nursery before he was due to start school in September. The older children had all been given a little felt bag with a work book inside. They were all starting to learn to recognise the letters of the alphabet and Canning House nursery set themselves a target to teaching every child how to write their own name, before they left at the end of the summer term. The boys had done the same in their last term and, although Ben had struggled a little, especially with his hand control and co-ordination, he at least had learnt how to write his name before leaving. At this rate Michael wouldn't, and somehow he seemed to be a little different to the other boys. Although they had all progressed at different rates, they had all done things pretty well in the same way. Michael, on the other hand, had perfectly good hand control and could manipulate tiny Lego pieces to make fairly intricate models. He could also draw simple pictures well, and he could now do some pretty complicated jigsaws for his age. But he showed no interest in, or even the ability, to learn to write his own name. He also showed no recognition of any letters or numbers, and learning the days of the week and the order in which they came in had no significance to him at all. Whereas Ben, from a very early age, amazed nursery by always knowing what day of the week it was.

So after having a week of Michael's increasingly difficult behaviour, I decided to speak to the staff at Canham House about it. They were really sorry that it was causing so much anxiety to Michael and equally so to me, and told us to stop immediately. 'He's probably just not ready yet, we've got a little while to sort it out before he leaves. We'll give him a break for a few weeks and then have another go. And of course don't forget he does appear to be favouring his left hand, which always makes things much harder.' So I went away feeling a bit happier. Of course the left handedness would be the problem, and as he was so verbally bright there couldn't be too much wrong.

In fact he had been the source of great amusement with his observations and linguistic skills over the past year. The first was in September when he was just three and a half. Auntie Pat had come over with her sister Diana, who was staying with Pat in Northamptonshire whilst visiting from Scotland. Pat had asked me if I would like them to take Michael for a ride on Taffy, whilst I went to fetch the boys from school. Michael was, of course, highly excited at the prospect of having Auntie Pat and her sister all to himself, especially as they were going to take him out for a ride. It was one of those lovely, warm autumn days that often occur in late September, and as I drove out of the drive I could see in my mirror the two ladies, one each side of Michael and Taffy, disappearing into the woods and down the mown grassy ride by our house, as the lowering sun shimmered through the branches of the trees. They were keen countryside enthusiasts, both from an ornithological as well as a botanical point of view. The ladies were extremely fit, and thought nothing of walking for several miles. Soon after I had arrived home with the boys, Auntie Pat and her sister Diana arrived back with Michael. The two ladies were staying for tea so they could see all of the boys. Diana was always very interested in them and their progress. As soon as the boys finished their tea they asked if they could go out and play for a while. I started to clear the table whilst Pat and Diana chatted to me. Then Pat, eager to tell me without Michael in earshot, related with great delight the conversation she had had with Michael on their ride. Apparently as they had turned down the bridle path which headed back towards home, Michael asked if they could stop and pick some blackberries for 'a little minute.' As he picked and ate one or two of the ripe berries, he stopped to closely study the one he gently held between his fingers. 'Auntie Pat,' he said, 'Isn't it abs'lutely incredible how there are lots of little teeny tiny berries that make it into one really big berry?' She was not only incredulous at his observation, but also at his linguistic skills.

The second time was when we went to church on Christmas morning. A pigeon had flown into the building to take refuge, probably from the awful cold weather outside, and was sitting high up in the rafters. The vicar announced that the visitor was there and any attempts to expel it had been unsuccessful, so as God's house was a welcome home to all we would just have to ignore its presence. At first we heard nothing from the church's avian squatter, but as the singing escalated it started to flap and flutter around the rafters. Michael seemed fascinated by the bird and tipped his head back. His large, round, blue eyes became even bigger, as he looked to see where the fluttering was coming from. The church quietened as the vicar prayed, then he asked for a few moments of complete silence, whilst we reflected upon the miraculous birth of Christ. The pigeon continued to flap and flutter until Michael's curiosity got the better of him. 'Mummy,' he said, in what I can only describe as a very loud stage whisper. 'Is that the Holy Ghost up there?' Needless to say, it caused great amusement amongst the surrounding congregation who were within earshot.

The third incident came on a family trip to the swimming pool. Eddie had the three older boys with him and I had taken Michael into the changing room with me. We were both a little cold from an hour in the pool, so I quickly wrapped my towel around myself and then cuddled Michael up in his big, blue, soft fluffy towel. As I looked along at the cubicle doors to see if there was an empty one available to change in, it became apparent there were none. It was in the days where communal changing areas were becoming more popular, so I put aside my modesty and popped Michael up on the bench to dry him before drying and dressing myself. As I rubbed him with his towel I became aware of him standing up on tip-toes to look over my shoulder. Following his gaze I could see he was staring at a beautiful Mediterranean looking girl, who was changing just a little way along the bench. He smiled at her and she smiled back. 'Michael,' I said in a quiet but sharp tone. 'Don't stare at ladies getting undressed, it's very rude.' But he took absolutely no notice of me and continued to stare, craning his neck, and even dodging around me as I tried to block his view. The girl, who clearly had no inhibitions, poured her slim body into the tight black swim suit and zipped up the front to enclose her very ample bosom. As she walked past us to go to the pool she smiled in a flirtatious way towards Michael. He smiled back at her, then he turned to me and said with heartfelt sincerity, 'Oh mummy, she's got the most lovely boobies.' Needless to say, it was the last time he ever came into the changing rooms with me.

***

Michael stood at the front of the house waiting for me to take his picture. Like the boys, we wanted to have a photographic record of his first day at school. He was so excited to be going, and for Michael it was one step nearer to his ambition of catching up with his big brothers. 'Brothers, brothers look at me, I'm just like you now with my new school clothes on!' He shouted out to them.

Going to school was never going to be an issue for Michael as he had his best friend Guy there and, of course, his brothers too, even though he had severely jeopardised his first day by getting Minnie Mouse's foot stuck up his nose the day before. We had been for the pre-school booster at the doctor's surgery, and as he was so good I brought him a present of his choice - a kinder egg. Inside the egg was a toy, in this case a Minnie Mouse in kit form, ready to be made by the child. He very expertly put her together while we were in the car on the way home, so I never gave Minnie Mouse another thought, that was until lunch time. Sue had come to visit us and see Michael before he started school, so we all sat around the table about to eat lunch. Suddenly I caught sight of Michael with his finger stuck up his nose. 'Don't pick your nose, Michael, it's not very nice, especially when you're at the meal table.' He looked at me with a worried expression on his face. 'But I have to Mummy, I need to get Minnie's foot out!' 'What!' I exclaimed as I lay him across my knee, whilst Sue went and fetched a torch so we could see better. There it was, about as far up his nostril as it could possibly be. I tried in vain to get it out with the tweezers, but quickly realised that I was more likely to push it even further up if I poked and probed any more.

There was no other answer, we would have to go to casualty. The doctors all laughed when I told them what Michael had got stuck in his nose, but they soon looked serious when they saw just how far up it was and just how jammed in it was. The nominated doctor tried again and again to get a grip on the slippery plastic, but with no success. By now he was looking concerned as he and his colleagues searched through a drawer of instruments. Finally he brought out some vicious, crocodile jaw-like tweezers, with what looked like teeth all along the edge of them. 'If these don't work, we're going to have to take him down to theatre,' the doctor said. 'One last chance. Keep your fingers crossed everyone.' By now we had a cubicle full of nurses cooing over Michael, who now looked rather small and vulnerable. Obviously, Casualty wasn't that busy as several more doctors had gathered, all fascinated by the challenge their colleague faced as he tried to extricate the slippery foreign body. I held Michael tightly on my knee to keep him as still as possible. The doctor went in again, the pincers clinked as they locked on to the slippery plastic, then slipped off it again with another clink. I was holding my breath, desperate for it to work. He tried again – clink went the pincers, then the doctor started to gently pull, and pull and pull, until suddenly Michael did a half cough, half sneeze as he screwed his eyes up. The plastic foot shot out on the end of the tweezers and then pinged free, as it catapulted across the room and under the trolley. It was out and a cheer went up in the cubicle, at which point Michael started to cry. 'You've lost Minnie's foot,' he said, as the large tears rolled down his face and blobbed on to his T-shirt. The gathering of doctors and nurses all laughed, but the nurses were very quick to find him a lolly as consolation for losing the appendage. I was just very grateful that we could go home and get things ready for the next day.

***

Michael's first term at school went well and he was back in dear Mrs. Green's class, but sadly only until Christmas, as she was retiring. He brought home the same reading books as the boys had started with, and he appeared to be starting to read and at no slower pace than the triplets had. He was beginning to write his name and could certainly recognise the letters in his name. In fact I gave myself a sharp tap on the wrist for being so worried. He was a bright little chap, why on earth would he have problems?

That was until one evening near to Christmas and near to the end of his first term and, of course, the end of his time with Mrs. Green. We were sitting in the kitchen, having had supper. The boys were learning their spellings for the test next day. Michael, not wanting to feel left out of the homework session, asked if he could have some paper because he wanted to practice writing his name. He sat there carefully forming the letters, as I concentrated on the boys. 'Done it Mummy,' he shouted. 'Look I've done my name.' I looked across the table and smiled at him. 'Well done Michael.' I was on auto-pilot, which often happened at the end of a busy day. But then I did a double take. Something had caught my eye as I looked back at his writing. There on the page was what looked vaguely like his name, but something was very odd about it. I walked around the kitchen table to have a better look. In front of me was what I had a strong suspicion was a mirror image of his name. The only way to find out for sure was to go and fetch a mirror. As I held up the paper and looked at the image reflecting back at me, there was a perfectly written image of his name. It was neat and tidy, in fact it was beautifully written, just back to front. Again the alarm bells began to ring so I decided that the next day I should ask Mrs. Green what she thought. 'Well dear,' she said. 'He's actually done it a few times in class. Very clever really, I couldn't do it could you?' I shook my head in agreement as she continued. 'Don't be too concerned yet, I've had children do this on the odd occasion before. Most grown out of it and never looked back, but I do think it would be wise to keep an eye on things.' I so wished she wasn't retiring. Mrs. Green would know what was to be done. Would the next teacher be as experienced as her? I very much doubted it.

***

We were also having a spot of bother with Ben and Tom too. Although it wasn't really too much to worry about, it was just proving difficult to be one step ahead of them. As I've already said they had an increasing interest in the local hunt and, as most Tuesdays the hunt seemed to be around our house, or certainly within the vicinity, Tom and Ben quickly cottoned on to this fact. Suddenly they became experts in what we as a family call, 'swinging a leg,' as they feigned illness. Ben was the first to hook us in with his acting abilities.

I went in to wake him one Tuesday morning, only to find him looking pale and wan, complaining of feeling terribly sick. So I told him to get up and see how he felt once he was out of bed. He came into the kitchen in his dressing gown, which was an ominous sign, instead of getting dressed as I'd anticipated. He sat down to breakfast, still looking rather pale. 'I can't eat anything, mummy,' he said, hanging his head, 'I feel far too sick.' So I took him back to bed thinking we were in for another horrible school bug, which all the boys would no doubt go down with, and then just as a parting gift, Eddie and I would get it. Eddie took the other boys off to school and I quietly got on with the jobs, letting Ben sleep. He had gone back to his bed with a bucket just in case, so I didn't want to be too far away should he need me. But at about ten he appeared in the kitchen again, suddenly looking much brighter. 'I feel fine now mummy, my sick feeling has gone away, can I have some breakfast now?' How odd I thought, as I got him his toast ready. Oh well, at least now I could go outside and get on with the ponies, and feel happy to leave Ben watching television in the lounge.

Not long after I had gone outside, Ben suddenly appeared, fully dressed in his jodhpurs. 'And just what do you think you're doing outside, young man?' I asked. 'I feel better now so I thought I could come outside and help with the horses, and perhaps I could ride Taffy?' he said, tipping his head sideways, giving me one of his angelic and pleading smiles. 'Oh no, I don't think so, I think you can go back inside because you're off school and poorly.' 'But I don't feel poorly anymore,' he answered, with a little grin on his face. I told him I was very pleased he felt better now, but he could still go back inside as he was off school because he'd felt poorly, and those were the rules.

He walked back into the house with his head hung low, his shoulders rounded, looking a picture of utter misery. Just as I was finishing the morning's work with the ponies, I heard the familiar sound off the hunting horn calling to the hounds. Here they were again, the second Tuesday in a row around our house. I suppose because we had all the woodland beside us, it was inevitable it was going to happen. The ponies all lifted their heads from grazing and trotted to the fence to peer enquiringly into the woods. Suddenly the huntsman appeared on his lovely, big, grey horse, rounding the corner onto the grassy ride with a few hounds behind him. 'Morning madam, and morning young sir.' He touched the peak of his riding hat as he grinned. I turned around to see Ben standing behind me in his old red dressing gown, with its sewn on white collar, the arms at half mast up to his elbows, as it was now completely outgrown. He had put his ready tied stock on, having velcroed it around his thin neck. The tiny hunting whip he had had for Christmas was held efficiently in his small hand, the lash and thong coiled expertly round his fist. He looked so cute with his skinny little legs poking out from underneath the dressing gown, and at the end of his feet were his slightly large, shiny black jodhpur boots. There wasn't much I could do about it now, and I guess I was a soft touch really if I'm honest, so I allowed him to stay outside and watch the hounds until they finally moved on.

Two weeks later Tom got up looking rather pale and sickly. He told me he couldn't possibly eat any breakfast. In fact he repeated virtually the same exercise as Ben, managing to completely pull the wool over my eyes and gain himself a day off school. This time the hunt was meeting in the village and was coming straight up the track and into the woods beside the house. I had been out and mucked out early on this particular morning, this time deciding to keep the ponies in because the hunt was coming. I didn't want them tearing around the field and churning it up. Consequently, I was back in the house before there was any sign of them. Basil the dog started to bark, signalling the hounds' approach, so I walked to the large French windows to see what, if anything, there was to see. I did a double take as Tom appeared on the drive, dressed in his little tweed hacking jacket, pony club tie and jodhpurs. There he sat on dear little Whisky. Unbeknown to me, Tom had sneaked out of bed, gone outside and tacked up Whisky in readiness to join the hounds when they passed through. I opened the French doors. 'And just what do you think you're doing? You can go and put Whisky back and come inside immediately.' He turned and grinned at me. 'I will in a minute, but the hunt's here now and I need to help the huntsman if any of the hounds are naughty. He'll need my help because I know all the short cuts through the trees.' Well, what could I do? It was just all too late to clamp down on him now and make him come back inside and, as Ben had got away with much the same only a couple of weeks earlier, I couldn't be any different with Tom.

The following week the hounds met in the village where the boys' school was. Much to my surprise the whole school was there too. Mr. Palmer approached me. 'I thought I was going to have a mutiny on my hands this morning. Ben and Tom both arrived at my desk first thing this morning to tell me that the hounds were meeting in the village today, and they thought it would be a very good idea if the whole school came to the meet. They wanted to introduce me to their friend the huntsman.' He raised his eyebrows and grinned. 'It wasn't quite what I had planned for the morning, but there was something about the look on their faces, that told me they would be going anyway, whether I agreed or not.' He laughed as I looked embarrassed by my small boys' behaviour. 'It's fine, a little diversion from the school day never hurts, and the children often study far better after some extracurricular activity.' He smiled kindly at me, and I realised we were so lucky to have such an understanding and open minded head teacher, although at times I wished there was a little more structure to the school day, with maybe some sort of timetable being adhered to. But we couldn't have it all ways, and Mr. Palmer's wonderfully random way of making school interesting was part of its appeal. But I did feel it was time to point out to him what the boys were up to. I told him that there was a bit of hoodwinking going on when the hounds were around. I told him about both boys' recent hookey days from school, so that he would be up to speed should any future deceptions occur.

Not long after telling Mr. Palmer about the boys and their little plans, I was called to school to fetch Ben as he'd been poorly. It was a Tuesday again, but a quick look at the meet card revealed that the hounds were the opposite end of the hunt country, so nowhere near to home and nor were they likely to be. I felt pretty certain that Ben would have been aware of this, unless of course he had accidentally looked at the wrong Tuesday. Anyway, there was nothing for it other than to go to school to fetch him. When I arrived Ben sat looking very sorry for himself in the secretary's office. 'Oh Gill, Mr. Palmer wants to see you before you take Ben home,' Mrs. Ball said. 'He feels a bit guilty and wants to explain what's happened.' I sat waiting, looking across at Ben who was extremely pale.' 'I really am poorly Mummy, I promise,' he said, in a dejected little voice. Mr. Palmer came into the office whilst Mrs. Ball sat with his class. 'I must apologise, Gill, but you know the conversation we had the other week about the boys and their mystery illnesses on Tuesdays?' 'Yes I do,' I said. He continued. 'Well of course today is Tuesday, so I automatically assumed Ben was trying it on when he came to my desk and said he felt really sick. So naturally I told him to go and sit back down and that I was aware of his little game. Poor little chap came to me three times to tell me, and each time I told him to go and sit back down. Anyway the fourth time he came up to me, and before I could say anything, he was sick. So I feel I owe you both an apology.' Obviously I told him that he didn't owe either of us an apology, and that he wasn't to worry in the slightest as no harm had been done. In fact it was a good lesson to both Ben and Tom in the consequences of crying wolf.

MODULE 26:
SWIMMING INSTRUCTION AND
PHONETICS

With the new spring term came the arrival of two new teachers. A supply teacher to cover for Mr. Palmer whilst he did some extra work, and Michael's new reception class teacher, who brought with her a new reading system. It consisted of a whole new set of reading books. Mrs. Green's good old tried and tested ones had been consigned to the bin. There were some very specific instructions that came home with the new books. We were to read them through to our children first, and then they were to read them back to us. Mrs. Green, on the other hand, had used a combination of word and picture recognition, with the use of some phonetics. This had been very successful for the boys and appeared to have been working for Michael as well. But I had to admit that the new reading books did look a lot more interesting, and they had some fantastic illustrations. So only time would tell how good they would be.

The supply teacher, Mrs. Wyatt, was to be with the older children which included the triplets for the first half of the term. Mr. Palmer was involved with some administrative and future planning work for the school. Because of this it was decided that, for the consistency of the children's education, it would be better to employ a supply teacher to cover Mr. Palmer's busy time. To say she was like Miss Trunchbull from Roald Dahl's Matilda is probably a little harsh - on Miss Trunchbull of course!! She was positively terrifying. Her hair was like wire wool, with eyes too close together and slightly crossed as they peered through milk bottle thick lenses, framed by thick, black plastic rims. Her teeth looked as if she had borrowed them from a horse, like big, crooked, yellow tombstones, they sat in higgledy piggledy disorder in her mouth. And just as a finishing touch, she had several large hairy moles dotted over her face. Poor woman couldn't help what she looked like, but she could help her manner, which was even less attractive than her appearance. She bellowed and shouted at the children, and any mother that dared to approach was nearly eaten alive. I witnessed one poor mother calling her Mrs. White instead of Wyatt. She grew puce red, as a tide of angry blood rose steadily up from beneath her collar and into her face, turning her almost scarlet before she exploded into a furious tirade of curses. Somewhere along the line, through all the rantings, she informed this poor, unsuspecting mother that she was not White, and never had been White, she was Wyatt and she expected to be called Wyatt. The terrified mother scuttled out of the playground and back to her car, looking anxiously over her shoulder as if she were expecting this gargoyle of a woman to be pursuing her along the pavement. We all avoided her like the plague, and the whole dynamics of the playground changed. We often used to gather at the end of the school day to have a chat, sometimes for half an hour or more if there was something to talk about and the weather was fine, and the children were happy chasing one another around the playing field. But since Mrs. Wyatt had been there, no one dared. We all collected the children and fled, just on the off-chance she may appear, keen to chastise us for hanging around and gossiping.

The first swimming lessons of the new term had arrived and Helen, David and Laura's mother and I both turned up as usual at the pool to help. We had been weekly helpers since the children had all started to swim and, if I'm honest, although we grimaced at the thought of it, we actually quite enjoyed it. Our older children had been swimming for some time now, and Laura, David's younger sister, was pretty well swimming alone. Helen and I prided ourselves in being extremely good helpers. We were the only ones who turned up every week come rain or shine, and we could now accredit several children's swimming certificates to our early tuition in frogs' legs. We often had several children at once holding on to the rails, practicing along the edge of the pool.

The pool felt cold as we descended down the steps. 'I bet they turned the heating down over Christmas,' I muttered to Helen. We both winced as our bodies submerged into the cool water, goose pimples immediately pricking our skin. 'Poor little Gordon's taken up his usual place,' I observed as the small boy clung grimly to the edge, his little hands already blue with cold and his face contorted with terror. It was now his second year of swimming lessons and his fear still hadn't subsided. The trouble was, it was always poor little Gordon. It was poor little Gordon who at least once a week stood in the playground as he waited for the school bus, with a plastic bag clutched in his little hand containing his damp pants and trousers, while he wore an over-sized pair of borrowed jogging bottoms to go home in. It was poor little Gordon who was sick with terror in the swimming pool the first time he ever went, causing the pool to be evacuated and closed down for two days whilst it was cleaned. And it was poor little Gordon who ate rabbit poo off the grass in the school playing field because someone (I'm ashamed to say that someone was Ben) told him they were currants growing. We had all tried to help him to swim, but anybody brave enough to approach him was kicked - even bitten, and his ear-piercing screams could be heard at the other end of town, so everyone had now given up trying. I always felt sorry for him, but there were so many other children who were desperate for our attention and help, and he had now become rather overlooked.

I set off again across the pool with Laura, encouraging her by just having my hand placed gently under her tummy, now only for her confidence as she was definitely just about to swim alone. Suddenly I heard Mrs. Wyatt's booming voice. 'You - mother over there, leave that child and come here. She can swim, come and help this one.' I looked up to see her gaze falling upon me as she pointed her bony finger down towards Gordon. I carefully looked over my shoulder, in the hopes that she was looking at someone else. 'Yes you, the mother in the blue and red suit, leave that child and come and get this one away from the edge.' I looked over at Helen and mouthed that I was sorry to leave Laura. Helen smiled sympathetically and came to take over from me, in order to help Laura, who was still just lacking a little bit of confidence. 'Don't worry,' she muttered as we passed in the water, 'And good luck, you're going to need it.'

As I approached Gordon his screaming began. Mrs. Wyatt still had her eyes firmly fixed on me as I smiled nervously at her. Gordon was by now at full throttle, screaming and kicking viciously towards me. 'Don't pussy-foot around and get hold of that child,' she shouted at me, and then turned to Gordon. 'GORDON, BE QUIET.' She emphasised the QUIET. He must have found her just a little more terrifying than the water itself and instantly fell silent, allowing me a moment to grab him and prise him away from the edge. In one swift move he turned from the edge of the pool to clamp himself tightly around my neck. He squeezed so hard it took my breath away and he wrapped his legs tightly around my body. Gordon was a small boy, who was definitely a little behind for his age. I don't think he would ever be the brightest light on the Christmas tree, but he had a very sweet way with him. He reminded me of a little mouse. His ears were slightly large and stuck out at right angles to his head, he had thin, fair hair that always had wild sprouts sticking up at the back, and a cow's lick at the front. His narrow, pale face had a light splattering of freckles and his teeth were rather too large for his small mouth. He was very thin and as he got cold his skin always became blotchy and blue, especially as he spent every swimming lesson hanging onto the edge of the pool for an hour. As we moved away from the edge he let out a high pitched whine, while I tried to bounce him around and jolly him out of his terror. I spent the whole hour with him tightly attached to me, like a limpet to a rock. His grip was relentless, but by the end of the session he was managing the odd little giggle as we played in the water. I splashed Christopher when he swam towards us pretending to be a monster for Gordon's benefit, which made Gordon chuckle. At the end of the session I popped him on to the steps and helped him out of the pool. He turned and smiled, giving me a shy little wave before trotting off to get changed. I, on the other hand, had bright red marks all around my neck and sides, where he had been tightly clamped for the last hour.

The following week Helen and I walked along the edge of the pool towards the steps. 'Are you going to help Gordon again this week?' Helen asked. I shrugged my shoulders. 'Probably not, I expect someone else'll get the job this week. I think I'll keep a low profile and steer clear of Mrs. Wyatt.' Helen laughed and we both decided we would get ourselves as far away from her as possible. But there in his usual spot was Gordon, holding tightly on to the rail. 'Hello,' his little voice called as we approached. 'Will you come and swim with me again?' he looked directly at me. In a funny way I felt quite pleased, even flattered that he wanted me to help him again, so of course

I told him I would. His little face lit up as I walked through the water towards him, and he quite expertly transferred himself from the edging rail to his clamped position around my neck. But he wasn't crying, and I don't know if it was my imagination but he didn't seem to be holding on quite so tightly.

Gradually, as the hour progressed I managed to get him off my neck until he was just holding on to my hands, while I towed him through the water. The faster I went the more he laughed, and I think I could safely say he was enjoying himself, as his confidence slowly grew. Each week he was waiting for me and each week we made a little more progress. He laughed and giggled his way through the lesson, barely realising that every time he got into the pool he was getting closer and closer to being able to swim on his own.

Finally the day came. We had been going back and forth across the width of the pool, my hand only gently resting under Gordon's stomach. Now there was nothing more needed than confidence. We set off again as I chatted away to him, constantly distracting him away from the fact that my hand was no longer underneath him. We finally touched the other side of the pool. I scooped him up and out of the water. 'Well done, Gordon, you're so clever, I think that someone is going to be getting their swimming certificate today.' He grinned at me, but looked a little bemused, knowing that he should be pleased but not really quite sure why. 'Did you know that you've just swum a whole width without me holding on to you?' Still grinning he shook his head. 'Do you want to try it again?' Gordon nodded his head so we repeated the width, this time with Mrs. Poole as our witness. Everyone stood to one side to watch and Gordon grinned from ear to ear when a cheer erupted as he reached the other side of the pool. I was so proud of this little boy. He had conquered his biggest fears and achieved something that everyone had given up hope of him ever doing. Although Mrs. Wyatt was a gargoyle, one thing she had done was made us deal with something that everyone wanted to avoid and, as a consequence, one small boy had achieved something that made him have a huge pride in himself.

***

During the half term Mrs. Wyatt held her reign of terror the children became more and more unsettled. Mr. Palmer greeted me at the school gate one evening. 'Can I have a little word with you, Gill?' he asked. I had a feeling, as I always did whenever any teacher wanted to have 'a little word' that there was trouble afoot. He asked me to come into the office for a few minutes, something he had never asked me to do before, so I felt my stomach turn in anticipation of what he was about to tell me. He began, 'I thought I'd better talk to you about a situation that has arisen today.' Oh no, this is sounding very ominous, I thought. 'Christopher and David have led a - how shall I describe it?' He sighed, as he thought about how he should word what he was about to say to me. 'A verbal petition to tell me that the class doesn't like Mrs. Wyatt and that she is being, in their words, 'very horrid' to them. It's a situation we are aware of, and between you and me, she isn't any more popular with the teachers than she is with the children. Sadly, she was the only supply teacher available for the length of time we needed someone, so we had no choice, but I can assure you we won't ever be having her again.'

I was flattered that he felt it necessary to share this information with me and I apologised for Christopher's outspoken behaviour. I told him that I would have a word with Christopher and explain that there was nothing the school could do about it, and that she would be gone very soon. There were only another three weeks to go and I was sure that they could manage to tolerate her for that short time. Mr. Palmer was clearly upset that he had landed Mrs. Wyatt upon his treasured class and was obviously dying to get back to the helm to rescue them from her. I assured him that I didn't think it would mentally scar them, and they would soon return to happiness once he was back. In a funny way I felt quite proud of the fact that Christopher and David were prepared to stand up and speak for the rest of the class, and that they weren't afraid to be outspoken, but on the other hand they had to have respect for their elders and the decisions they made. Not all teachers, nor indeed work colleagues in the future, would always be just to their liking. Tolerance was a great attribute that must be nurtured. They would have to be aware of the difference between being tolerant when necessary and speaking up for justice when it was appropriate to do so. Mrs. Wyatt's time there was short lived and, in fact, Mr. Palmer finished his other business quicker than expected, so the children were pleased to have him back with them sooner than had been predicted.

***

Michael's first year was going well and he seemed to be enjoying school, getting involved with as much as he could. I had completely relaxed about the reading and writing as he now seemed to be making good progress. His writing book was filling up with the letters of the alphabet, written in rows, as he practiced again and again to perfect his writing skills. And he was now on level three of the new reading system, so there no longer seemed to be anything to worry about. One day a friend called in to see me. Her children were slightly older than ours so she had brought some bags of outgrown clothes for us. As I unpacked them some reading flash cards fell out. I smiled. Liz was always keen to encourage her children to achieve, and I was sure she would have spent many hours with these well worn pieces of card. I put them to one side as I continued to unpack the clothes and books.

That evening I sat down with Michael to do his reading homework. It always took a little while to settle him, as he was keen to be outside playing with his brothers. Finally I got him sitting down with me on his own in the living room. The other boys continued playing outside in the ever lengthening daylight. We were close to the longest day, and I was having an increasing struggle to get them in for bed. Michael wriggled and fidgeted as always. He still wasn't really comfortable reading, but he was resigned to the fact that at some stage in the evening he would have to do it. I did the same thing as usual and read him the book. He then repeated it back to me which, as always, he did pretty well. 'Michael, I've got something to show you,' I said. 'We've been given some special cards with all the words you're reading in your books. Shall we have a look at them and you can see how many you can read to me?' Michael looked less than enthusiastic, but nodded in agreement. I found an easy one to start with - THE. He looked at it and showed absolutely no recognition. A blank expression appeared on his face. 'Come on Michael, I know you know this one. You've just read it to me in your book.'

He continued to look blankly at the word, so I thought I'd better find another easy one - ON. Perhaps he was just playing around. He looked at it and again the blank expression appeared. I could feel a rising surge of irritation as I was sure he was being difficult. 'Come on Michael, I know you know this one, stop being awkward.' He looked up at me, tears welling in his eyes. 'I don't know what those silly words are.' He slid down the settee and pouted as he fought back the tears. He really didn't know. I could see he wasn't pretending, so I sat him up on my knee and comforted him. 'It doesn't matter Michael, don't worry about the flash cards. We'll have another look at your reading book instead.' He cheered up and opened his book again. This time I covered the picture and asked him to read the words to me. The blankness appeared again and it became obvious that he was unable read any of the words, but as soon as I uncovered the picture he reeled them off in perfect order. Could it be that he had remembered the words by recognising the pictures? I couldn't really believe it, but there was no other explanation for it. We were aware that he had an amazing visual memory. Even before he was three years old he was unbeatable by any of his brothers at the game 'pairs'. He was quite incredible, memorising where any card that had once been upturned lay. The older boys found it so frustrating that, try as hard as they might, they could never beat him.

The following evening I waited behind to see Michael's teacher, Mrs. Richards. I went into detail about the flash cards and then his inability to read any words in the book once the picture was covered. 'Are you trying to say he's got to this level of reading by memory alone?' asked Mrs. Richards. 'Well, yes I suppose I am.' I replied, realising that she clearly thought I was talking complete and utter rubbish. She was a kindly woman really, but she could have a rather abrasive attitude when upset and I could see she didn't really take kindly to me giving her this information. I think she thought I was implying that she hadn't done her job properly, which I suppose in a roundabout way I was. 'Don't be silly, he can't possibly memorise all the words at this level. I'll have a proper look tomorrow and I'm sure we'll get to the bottom of the situation.' In her gruff way she was trying to reassure me, and I wished I had the same confidence that Mrs. Richards had.

The next evening Mrs. Richards was outside waiting for me. 'Oh Gill, could I have a word?' I walked over to her, as she distanced herself from the hubbub of mothers, whilst they gathered their children. 'Well it appears you're right. He does seem to have memorised all the words by the pictures. I really don't know how he's managed to do this but he has, and it appears he has no recognition of the words at all.' In fact, she was repeating exactly what I'd told her last night. I wasn't churlish enough to say 'I told you so' but I felt that way, particularly when she told me that she didn't want me to read with him anymore as they were now having to teach him phonetically. I felt like saying that if I hadn't identified the problem in the first place, we may not have known about it until he started in his second year. It was rather irritating as I now felt as if I were being blamed for the problem, rather than being patted on the back for actually identifying it. So Michael was put back on to good old Mrs. Green's tried and tested reading books (clearly someone had had the sense to hang on to one or two copies!), and I pretended to not be reading with him during the evenings.

Finally the end of term arrived and we had parents' evening a few days before breaking up. The triplets were doing well, although Ben's behaviour had been in question a few times of late. He was frequently found wandering around the class room, often not applying himself to his own work, preferring to help others with theirs. There had also been an incident which, although Mr. Palmer hadn't mentioned it, his embarrassed brothers had. Mr. Palmer had planned to do drama one afternoon - one of Ben's favourite lessons, but for some reason he changed his mind after lunch and decided to do art instead - one of Ben's least favourite lessons. After huffing and puffing in a noisy complaint, he then proceeded to sit at his desk with a scowl on his face, his two fingers in a rude v as he rested his head on his hand and aimed it towards Mr. Palmer, supposedly as a surreptitious gesture of his irritation. But as an experienced teacher, something like that wasn't going to be missed, so Ben had a thorough dressing down and was sent to read in the corner for the duration of the art lesson. In general he had been more wilful just lately and for no real accountable reason. The amateur psychologist in me decided it was just Ben trying to assert himself. All I knew was that it wasn't very pleasant, and the sooner he got out of this phase the better, particularly before he made himself thoroughly unpopular. Again we found ourselves learning how to deal with the difficulties that arise as a parent. The trouble was that there was no dress rehearsal, it was just in at the deep end and sink or swim.

Michael was our real worry though, so we were

anxious to hear what Mrs. Richards had to say. Although she could see that he was making progress now that he was learning to read phonetically, she was still very non-committal when I asked again if she felt that Michael may be showing signs of dyslexia. She kept on telling us that 'boys were often slower than girls to get started,' and 'it was far too early to say if there were any real signs of a learning difficulty.'

The following evening, just two days before the end of term, I arrived to pick up the boys from school. Michael was first to the car, having seen me pull up he had run out of school and along the path to greet me. He opened the door and jumped in. 'Mummy, Mrs. Richards has given me a letter for you. Can you open it and tell me what it says?' I opened the letter as the other three boys meandered lazily along the path towards the car, chatting with their friends. I opened the letter and glanced over it before sharing the information with Michael. As I read my eyes grew larger and I could feel a tide of anger rising within me. There in black and white, printed on school headed paper, was a letter informing us that Michael was to be held down for a year in the reception class. As he was the youngest and the smallest boy in his year and because of his problems with reading, it had been decided that he, along with two of the youngest girls in the class, would be kept back. This was so out of the blue, after all it was only last night that we had been at the school talking to his teacher, and she hadn't mentioned a word to us.

Clearly I couldn't tell Michael what it was about, so I made some excuse up about the times for the end of term concert. Until I had been and at least talked it over with Eddie, I didn't want Michael to know anything about it. My gut feeling was that, like me, he would think it a very destructive thing to do to our smallest boy. Michael was constantly trying to keep up with his brothers. By doing this to him it would psychologically make the gap between him and his brothers even bigger. He would, therefore, feel he had to struggle even harder to catch up. Verbally he was still so forward, and as he was so used to playing with children older than himself, holding him back a year, I felt, would take him backwards.

Eddie sat behind his desk as we walked in to the garage, so I told the boys that they could all go over to see Cockney Gordon in the service reception and get themselves a hot chocolate from the machine - this was always viewed as a special treat, especially as the vending machine added loads of sugar to the powdery mixture, which was not encouraged at home!! I needed at least a couple of minutes with Eddie alone so he could read the letter and we could have a quick discussion about the situation.

Eddie read quickly and I waited for his reaction. 'No, no this isn't right,' he said, as he looked down at the white printed paper, his eyebrows furrowing in irritation. 'They can't do this to him. Poor little boy is always striving to catch up with his brothers, this can only be destructive to his confidence, he'll feel even further behind them if they keep him down.' I felt relieved as he said, 'I'll phone the school now and reason with them.' I was really glad that Eddie and I were once again singing from the same song sheet, so I kept the boys amused while Eddie phoned the school. Mr. Palmer was, as always, completely reasonable about the situation and the problem was sorted out immediately. He saw straightaway what we were saying, and agreed with us that it could only be destructive for Michael's confidence. 'I must admit I was only half convinced by Mrs. Richards's idea, but we're struggling a bit for space in the class, as this year and the previous year have been big intakes.' Mr Palmer told Eddie. 'Anyway, that's not your problem and I think Michael will get along very well with the new teacher we have starting in September.'

So the situation was resolved for the time being and we could look forward to another school year with some optimism. I was going to work hard with Michael on his phonetics during the summer, and we had a full summer social programme too. There were two camps this time, as the triplets were going to intermediate camp this year, and Michael and Guy were going to attend the junior camp at its new venue.

The end of year concert was of its usual high standard, and I couldn't believe that it would be the triplets' turn to stand up with their class at the end of next year's school concert. They would be reading their leaving essays about what the school had meant to them. Time was rolling on so quickly but, as it sped by, was I any nearer to becoming a qualified parent? On the whole I felt that I was, but just when a sense of security fell over us and we had a time of calm, something else would come along to challenge us, teaching us yet more about the intricacies of parenthood and this most complicated Masters degree from the University of Life.

MODULE 27:
TIME OUT TREATMENT FOR DIFFICULT BEHAVIOUR, SEPARATION ANXIETY

The weather had been amazing, with the sun shining every day and this continued throughout the whole summer. It became probably, the summer I will most remember as being so totally idyllic for the boys. They spent more and more time with the Herbert boys, leading an Enid Blyton's Famous Five type of existence. They were either at our house or theirs, building dens in the wood next to us, or in the woods next to the Herberts'. We went on picnic rides with the ponies, again at either venue. It was after one of these rides that the boys cooked up a plan to have a few days camping at the Herberts' house in their paddock. They set up tents and built a camp fire a little way away.

The tents were pitched at the bottom of the paddock and next to the stream, but conveniently situated so they were in full view of Nikki and Philip's bedroom, and the patio where they spent most summer evenings relaxing after supper.

Their home was in as equally an idyllic spot as ours, and they looked across a grassy valley with a stream bubbling through the bottom of it. The prospect of so much fun all became too much for Ben to resist, and finally he got over his fear of sleeping away from home and was brave enough to stay over and sleep in the tents, on the condition that he could go and stay in the house with Nikki and Philip if he became afraid. Even Michael and Guy joined in as they had their own little tent, which worked wonderfully well, until one night they were nearly frightened to death. As the camp was so near to the water, a flock of Canada geese had settled there for the night. Michael and Guy had either woken, or had never actually gone to sleep, when they heard muffled talking. They lay there convinced it must be kidnappers which, when you're only five and a half, and nearly six, is pretty terrifying. Too scared to move, they clung to each other, until they dared themselves to quietly call to their older brothers in the larger tent next door. Martin and Christopher eventually heard them and went to see what the problem was. 'We can hear kidnappers outside, they're talking. Can you hear them?' The two little boys, with their large scared eyes, whispered to them. 'We're really frightened, can we come in your tent?' Martin and Christopher stopped and listened hard, and then Christopher laughed. 'You silly things, it's only the geese chattering to one another.' 'Oh' said the two little boys, looking over tired and rather surprised. 'Well we still want to come in to your tent just in case.' So they swiftly moved into the main tent and immediately fell into an exhausted sleep.

The boys cooked bacon and eggs over the camp fire every morning, and barbecued most evenings. They swam every day in the pool and paddled in the stream, trying unsuccessfully to catch fish with bent pins tied to cotton, so they could cook them on the camp fire. If Nikki had to go out teaching I would fetch them and they would spend time doing much of the same at our house. In fact I wished I were their age again and could join in. Having spent most of my early years up to the age of eleven, with the exception of a year in Africa, mainly living in suburbia, it seemed to me to be a very appealing life that the boys were leading and one that I would love every child to be able to experience. It was all about the freedom, the fresh air, the sense of adventure, and the ability to think for themselves that was so very important. I realised at this stage of my 'degree in parenting' our children were very privileged to have the sort of life style and freedom that they were able to enjoy.

The only down side to this idyllic summer was Ben with his bad temper and utter wilfulness. If he didn't want to do something there was nothing on this earth we could do to make him do it. It was a trait I have to admit he had always shown, even from the early days in the special care unit when he consistently pulled his feeding tube out. He made it quite clear, even at that early stage, that he wanted to be fed by us and to feel the closeness and warmth from another human being. He knew that it was far more preferable to just lying in an incubator, while a syringe pumped milk into his tiny stomach.

Ben pushed the boundaries left, right and centre throughout the summer. If we had friends over for tea he refused to play with them, but would insist on loitering around me whilst I tried to chat with the visiting children's mothers. We always had an old playgroup friends' get together every holiday in order to have tea and a play, while we mums could all catch up with one another. But Ben was nearly driving me mad, so Eddie and I decided it was time to use the 'time out' method. If I asked him to go and play with his friends and he refused, I would then tell him he would have to go and spend time in his room. I told him that I needed time to talk to my friends, without him hovering around listening all the time. If he didn't want to play with his friends then that was up to him, but I had to have time alone with my friends. So the battles ensued. Every time friends came he started to behave badly. No matter who it was he did the same old hanging around thing, even hiding behind doors, furtively listening in to our conversations. As soon as I saw him there I would ask him to leave and go and play with his friends. If he refused to go, or went for a few minutes and then re-appeared, he would be marched promptly to his room for five minutes of 'time out.'

One afternoon he had been particularly difficult and I had marched him back to his room for the fifth time. 'You bugger,' he shouted after me, as I walked away from his room, much to the amusement of the gathered mothers, who were all exceptionally supportive over the whole situation. In fact we even got invited back, which was nothing short of a miracle. 'Ignore him,' I said, as I looked down the hall way to his room which, being a bungalow, was on the ground floor. The boys' bedrooms, unfortunately, looked straight down the hall to the kitchen. He leant against the frame of the door waiting to see what I was going to do about it. When he realised that I was continuing my conversation, and taking no notice of him he tried again. 'Bugger, bugger, bugger.' I could feel my blood pressure starting to rise, but all the others told me to 'ignore it, don't react or he'll know he's got the better of you.' So, with their support I managed to get through the afternoon without letting him see that he was having any effect on me at all.

Finally they all left, at which point I told Ben he was going to have an early night. I was very fed up with his showing off and his bad behaviour. With that he stormed off down the hall and slammed the door into his bedroom. He clearly hadn't realised his own strength, as he slammed the door so hard it fell off its hinges and dropped to the floor. 'Oh no' he said, panic suddenly overwhelming him. 'Oh please don't tell daddy, will you mummy. He'll be really mad with me.' I suddenly realised that if I handled this situation carefully I could have the upper hand. 'Well Ben, I don't know about that. I think you've been really naughty this afternoon so you tell me why I shouldn't tell daddy? How do I know that you're not going to be as bad the next time we have friends for tea?' He looked thoughtful for a moment. 'I promise I won't be bad and horrid anymore if you don't tell daddy.' I took hold of both his hands, looked him straight in the eye and said, 'We'll have a deal, shall we Ben. I'll try and mend the door so daddy won't know, if you promise me you'll be good for the rest of the holidays. But if you break the deal for even one moment, I'll have to let daddy know just how naughty you've been and I'm sure he'll have some big punishment for you. And that'll be something like not going to a pony club rally, or over to the garage to help Mike.' Mike was Eddie's young sales man. Ben loved nothing more than going with Eddie to work on a Sunday morning to help Mike. Mike had made him his own special badge with 'BEN Sales Assistant' on it. The thought of that made Ben's eyes grow wide with horror and fill with tears, so he promised on 'God's honour' that he wouldn't be naughty, and that he wouldn't swear anymore. So we had a fragile truce which just about held throughout the rest of the holidays with the exception of the odd raised eyebrow, or an occasional stern look.

MODULE 28:
MEMOIRS, INHERITED TRAITS AND
AN IDYLLIC LIFESTYLE

I sat outside on the patio in the warm afternoon sun. Mum
had come up for a cup of tea. I started to discuss with her
our dilemma with Ben, which I had to admit was really
beginning to worry me. Was it something we were doing
wrong? 'Why is he so difficult?' I asked her. 'I really don't
know where he gets this wilful streak from. I'm sure it's
not our side of the family,' I said with a grin, Eddie and I
always used to blame one another's side of the family

when one of the boy did something wrong – tongue in cheek, of course. She raised her eyebrows. 'Well, you probably don't remember when you were just a little younger than Ben, we had a pretty difficult time with you too?' Oh no, here we go, I thought, I was obviously about to hear exactly where Ben got his difficult streak from whether I wanted to or not. Mum continued. 'Well it all started when we were on the ship sailing out to Africa. You must remember having chicken pox?' I nodded, in fact how could I forget it? I was confined to the isolation hospital for just over a week, which also coincided with us crossing the equator. There was general partying going on, but I was only allowed out for a short time to watch the celebrations from a distance. All the children, excluding me of course, had to queue up to have a dollop of face paint, and get a signed certificate given to them by King Neptune himself.

It was so boring in the isolation hospital, and although mum and dad tried really hard to keep me amused it was very difficult for them too, as they couldn't be with me twenty-four-seven. At first there were two other children in the unit, but their pox was several days ahead of mine, so when they went I was all alone. It did have some advantages though. I had made friends with a lot of the ship's crew before becoming ill, and they frequently called to visit me, usually bringing gifts when they came; in fact I collected an enormous family of Trolls thanks to their generosity. There was the waiter that used to carry me on his shoulders to tea, and then there was the steward and stewardess husband and wife team, who looked after our area of cabins on the ship. Later on in the journey mum and dad had an evening out with them both when we docked in Aden. This was in 1965 and during the times of conflict - I can remember standing on deck with Dad watching gunfire streaking through the dark night sky.

Then there was the cocktail waiter from the cocktail lounge. I think I had a little crush on him. He had red hair and dark brown eyes, and was very good looking, probably only in his early twenties - he was always full of fun. He used to make me my own little cocktail with mixed fruit juices, and fill it full of all the fruit that went into the glasses of Pimms. Because I really liked the cocktail cherries, he would fill a cocktail stick full of them and place it on top of the glass. So with visits from all of these people at some stage most days, the time passed reasonably well. They usually had a minute or two to play a game of snap, or read me a story. I also used to wander along the deck outside the isolation hospital to sneak through the barrier and into the staff area. There was a parrot in a cage along there, which I spent time talking to and feeding peanuts. It was on one of these occasions that I was very privileged to see an enormous whale appear at the rear of the ship, blowing a huge shoot of water from its blow hole, high up into the air. Dad had just arrived and spotted me wandering along the deck and out of bounds, so he caught up with me and we were able to stand and watch the whale for some time before it disappeared into the deep.

Then there was the evening when a swallow landed on the ships railings, exhausted from its journey. It sat almost next to me, too tired to fly away, so we observed one another for some time. We gazed deep into one another's eyes, me into his black little beads, and he into my blue eyes as we sailed into the hotter weather. I slowly wandered back into my room but to my amazement the little bird flew in after me. There was a large fan up high on the wall in order to keep the air circulating, as by now it was very warm. I was terrified my little friend would perish in the blades of the fan, so I climbed up to the top bunk in my effort to catch him. He took off from the edge of the fan so I leaned over to try and grab him. At that moment I managed to over balance and fall from the top bunk to the floor. As I scrambled to my feet one of my visitors called by on her way back to the staff quarters, only to see me looking down at a huge gash in my ankle, which was just beginning to ooze blood. She rushed off to get the ship's doctor. But as I was terrified of doctors, when she ran one way, I ran the other and out of the hospital. I had a fair idea where mum and dad's cabin was, so I ran along the outer deck to the port hole that I was sure was theirs, jumping up so I could see inside. I jumped up again and banged on the glass, bringing them inquisitively to the window. When I looked back along the deck I could see a trail of blood all the way from where I had run, and now there was a growing pool gathering by my foot as I stood waiting for them.

Mum and dad quickly came round and hurried me back to the isolation hospital, only to arrive at my room just as the doctor arrived with his nurse and the worried stewardess. Fortunately the cut wasn't as severe as it had looked, although there was a large v-shaped tear. The doctor placed a giant padded dressing over the wound, as I sat on the bottom bunk bed, which then had to be re-dressed for several days. Although stitches were seriously considered, I think the look on my face, and the fact that I drew my knees rapidly up under my chin and clutched my arms tightly around my legs at that prospect, was quite enough to put the doctor off even trying. My little bird had by now flown out and was sitting back upon the railings again, cleverly hitching a lift to the ever approaching coast of East Africa.

Finally Mombasa was in sight and the point at which we were to disembark. The plan had been to fly from there to Dar-es-Salaam, where we were going to stay for a month in order for dad to do some work in the book shop. Mum continued with her tale. 'You were awful about having to see doctors, a legacy from our trip to the hospital for tropical diseases, I think. Anyway, they wouldn't let us fly unless a doctor from shore gave us a certificate to say you were clear of the virus. I don't quite know how, but you got wind of the fact that he was coming out to the ship in a small boat, in order to see you. With that you decided you weren't going to be around when he came. Whilst we were waiting for the doctor to arrive, you crept off and hid.'

As she related the tale I could remember standing in the isolation unit looking over the ships railings, waiting to spot the doctor leaving shore in his boat. I remembered seeing him walk down some steps on the harbour wall in the far distance, and then get into a little white speed boat. At this point I made myself scarce and found a cupboard in the isolation hospital to hide in. Mum continued. 'We searched high and low for you. In fact we had just about all the staff that knew you, and some that didn't, looking too. Needless to say, he could only stay for a while, and when we couldn't find you he got back on to his little boat and went back to shore, so obviously we didn't get the certificate we needed. Quite why they wouldn't allow the ship's doctor to sign the certificate I don't know, but they wouldn't, so we had to find another way of getting from Mombasa to Dar-es-Salaam. That's when Dad called his colleague Janet Clark to see if she would come and fetch us. We were so cross with you, although also somewhat relieved when you re-appeared a few minutes after he'd gone, looking very pleased with yourself. I don't think you had any idea how much upheaval and panic you had caused, not only with everyone searching for you but also having to find another mode of transport. That was just the start of the six months from hell. We had a terrible journey in Janet's Mini Clubman Estate, sliding around on the mud roads in the rain. We couldn't stop for fear of getting stuck, and as you were being car sick every half an hour we were on tenterhooks, as the ruts in the mud roads were getting deeper and deeper. We had you hanging out of the car window to be sick; Dad had to cling on really tightly to you.'

'After that you seemed to pick up every illness that was going. First a nasty tummy bug in East Africa, then soon after we arrived in Salisbury you got Impetigo, swiftly followed by an undiagnosed illness that caused your glands to swell in your neck. They tested you for TB but never really did find out what was wrong, but you had to swallow some large tablets twice a day for several weeks. You just became more and more difficult about the whole thing, until you suddenly decided that dad and I were a witch and a wizard, who had disguised themselves as your parents. You thought that the witch and wizard had kidnapped you and taken you away from England. You refused to take the tablets, and if we did manage to get them into your mouth, you used to hold them under your tongue, or in your cheeks until we had gone out of the room, then you would spit them out. In fact you were generally very naughty.'

The weather was very hot and humid which I don't think you enjoyed much, and you didn't like the school much either. In hindsight I think you were really very unhappy to start with, far more than Dad and I realised at the time. You missed your friends, and you definitely missed the family and your pets. And living in an apartment didn't suit you either. You were such an outdoor child so you were constantly asking me to take you to the park or to the swimming pool.'

It was a difficult time for all of us, and it only improved when we moved on to the Cape, where we had a bungalow with a lovely big garden. We could go to the beach every afternoon when you finished school and it was only then that you finally settled down and became our little girl again.' Mum telling me this made me wonder if there was an underlying problem that was bothering Ben, so I asked him if there was anything worrying him. He furrowed his brow for a second, lost in thought, but then dismissed my question with an abrupt 'no' before running off. But there was something about his face that made me wonder, just by the way he looked into the distance, his eyes glazing over for a second as he paused to think. I was sure

278

something would become apparent before much longer.

***

The summer holidays were drawing to a close, but we still had one more treat to look forward to before the start of term. The family that lived in the big house and owned the estate and land adjacent to our property, had issued an invitation to several families, which also included the Herberts, to join them for an end of summer holidays barbecue.

The barbecue was to be held on the August bank holiday Monday, which was a couple of days before the children returned to school. The weather had held throughout the summer and we were still having some lovely warm days, although the evenings were noticeably cooling down. We were invited to arrive at five thirty to help carry the salads and plates up to the clearing in the little spinney just behind the lake. The boys were in high spirits; they had met Dodo's twin grand-daughters riding in the park, and the girls told them that we were having barbecued Muntjac for supper. Their mother, Diana, hadn't contradicted them, so the boys believed it to be genuine and, for what it was worth, so did I. They were so wonderfully eccentric that nothing would have surprised me. I was always quite partial to the little Muntjac deer (of the living variety), as they were so small and dainty, that was until a friend's dog was attacked by one and left needing hundreds of stitches. Apparently they have fang-like tusks that are razor sharp, and will use them without hesitation if they feel threatened. The boys' fascination was the same as the fascination they had with the 'cow's tongue' my mother-in-law cooked and pressed one summer. The fascination was of the morbid curiosity kind, so when they were offered a taste of it, they all re-coiled in horror, which I suspected would be their reaction to eating Muntjac.

There was a huge fire burning in the clearing, with garden chairs of all varieties surrounding it. Dodo's three little Pekinese dogs, Lulu, Sophie Woo and Junior were snorting and snuffling around and yapped excitedly as the children ran by. Bess, her beautiful and gentle brindle Lurcher, greeted all the people she recognised, trotting up to them with a doggy grin, lifting her long elegant nose to expose her white, pointed front teeth, and wagging her long whip-like tail. The children chased one another in and out of the trees and bushes and at the side was a halved oildrum with hot embers at the bottom of it, glowing red and white as the meat slowly cooked over it. The Muntjac took the form of small steaks, much to the disappointment of the boys, who expected to see a whole Muntjac slowly turning on a spit over the fire, like a suckling pig with an apple in its mouth. There were marinated chicken pieces and chops, kebabs and salmon steaks, cooking alongside the Muntjac, giving off an amazing aroma as they sizzled away. We all set out the salads and puddings across the long trestle tables.

The children were having a marvellous time, as most of them knew one another. Although there were three pony clubs represented, most of them competed at the same competitions, particularly as they had all just started to represent their pony clubs in the teams. If they didn't know one another, they certainly did before the end of the evening. There was one particular guest who the children all seemed rather fascinated with - Jeremy Hilton-Brooks by name. Poor chap had a drink problem, but of course the children had no concept of this and to them he was just a fun and friendly man. He sent them on errands to find certain plants, feathers and leaves from the surrounding garden, giving an element of competition by awarding a ten pence piece to the first back with the given task. He was a tall, strongly built man with a thinning crown, but with thick salt and pepper curls around the side of his head. His face, needless to say was rather red and bloated and his nose was almost purple. He wore a multi-coloured Hawaiian shirt with bright red trousers which matched his flamboyant character and face. I felt sorry for him and his little wife, as clearly his drinking had ruined their lives. They were now tenants in a small flat within the big house, having lost their own home which, by all accounts, was as big as the Hall they were now housed within. His wife, a thin woman who had a deep and profound relationship with nicotine, clearly adored him, and I could see why as he had a very charismatic personality. He had obviously been a very handsome man in his youth, before drink and age had changed his appearance leaving him bloated and red.

Finally the embers in the big fire started to die out, and the tea lights that hung in jam jars from the trees dwindled as the flames drowned in the melted wax. There was a chill in the air and it was now completely dark, so we carried everything back through the large garden, past the lake and back to the house. The children had long since disappeared, having gone back to the house to continue playing. So had Jeremy, probably to find a whisky bottle as the wine supply had dried up. But as we walked in through the back door, we were confronted with a throng of children crowding around the sink, Jeremy at the centre of the mêlée. In the sink was a hedgehog being bathed in warm soapy water, the children giggling as Jeremy held it gently with his thick rubber gloves. He turned to all of us as we entered the kitchen and said, 'Poor Mrs Tiggywinkle's got fleas - she doesn't like having fleas, does she children? So we thought we'd better give her a bath.' He returned to the serious job of bathing the poor little hedgehog who probably thought its number was up, watched by the fan club of adoring children.

This was the final big treat, as we now had to concentrate on acquiring new shoes and replacing outgrown or worn out school clothing on our last few days of the holiday. We traditionally always went to the cinema on the last day with the Herberts. It was an attempt to cheer them up before starting back to school the next morning. They sat along the row of seats with glum faces. Usually Nikki and I were the only ones that really enjoyed the film. It was never very nice, the return to school, and I always felt a little sad for a day or two after they had gone back. The house always felt so quiet and empty, but soon life became busy with my own things again, and the boys got used to the routine of school once more.

MODULE 29:
THE CRUELTY OF CHILDREN,
VERBAL REASONING, DYSLEXIA AND
THE STATEMENTING PROCESS

The kitchen was full of laughter and chatter again, as the boys sat at the table eating their tea. We were two days into the new term of the boys' final year, and a few weeks off their ninth birthday. Thankfully Ben suddenly seemed much happier with his school and home life. Michael clearly adored his new teacher Mrs. Tomlin, and he was excited by the new work they were doing. His reading had made a little progress through the holidays but I wouldn't say he was out of the woods by any means. So I planned to go in and see the new young teacher at the end of the first week, just to give her our support and to tell her that anything she felt would help Michael to make progress, we would be happy to do.

'Can we leave the table, Mummy, and go and play for a little while?' asked Christopher, as he left his seat and was on his way out of the door. 'Ok, off you go but only for a little while. Don't forget you've got spellings to do tonight.' With that they were gone, so I turned back to the sink to wash up the grill tray; cheese on toast always made a terrible mess when the cheese melted on to the bottom of the pan. I scrubbed away at the charred matter, enjoying the few minutes of quiet. Suddenly a little voice cut into the silence. 'Mummy.' I turned to see Ben was still sitting at the table. 'Yes Ben, what can I do for you?' 'Tom Evans isn't at school anymore.' 'Oh really,' I said in surprise. 'Why's that, has he gone to a different school?' 'Ummm, I think so,' said Ben quietly. 'Oh dear, are you sad about that?' I asked. 'No, I'm not at all sad. I'm really pleased. He wasn't very nice to me. He liked Thomas and Christopher but he didn't like me very much.' He continued to sit at the table looking thoughtful. 'Mummy?' 'Yes Ben,' I said. 'What's a spastic?' I walked away from the sink, drying my hands on the tea towel and sat down at the table with him. 'Why do you ask me that Ben?' Ben stared down at the table, worry written all over his face. 'Well, Tom Evans told me last term that his mum said I was a spastic, and that's why I was a bit odd. So what is a spastic and am I a bit odd? He told me that his mum said that's why I tripped over lots, and why I wobbled my head, and why I used to have crossed eyes. Is that true Mummy, am I a spastic?' He looked so sad as he chased a few toast crumbs around the table with his index finger.

I got up and lifted him from his chair to sit him on my knee. 'First of all Ben, I'll tell you that calling people a spastic is a very old fashioned, cruel and disrespectful thing to do. It's what people with cerebral palsy used to be called. People that suffer with cerebral palsy can have what is called spasticity in their limbs, causing the limb or limbs to spasm and curl up. This makes it difficult for them to use their arms or legs properly. Now tell me if you think that applies to you?' Ben shook his head. 'No.' 'Well I think that Tom and his mum are very unkind to say that.

You did have a little bit of brain damage when you were a baby, but you know all about that don't you. You also know that's why your eyes had to be corrected, because your illness caused your muscles to be weak and floppy. It's also the reason why your head can be a little wobbly and you sometimes fall over. But you're getting much better all the time, and you hardly ever fall over now do you?' He looked round at me. 'So I won't die then?' 'No Ben, of course you won't die. Did Tom tell you that too?' He nodded. 'Is that why you were so naughty all summer. Were you worrying about the nasty things Tom had said to you?' He nodded his head again. 'Oh Ben, you should have said something to us. A problem shared is a problem halved, you know.' I told him that if anything else ever worried him again he was to come and tell one of us immediately so we would be able to put his mind at rest. Ben hopped off my lap. 'Can I go and play with my brothers for a little while now?' I smiled at him and nodded.

So that was why he'd been so difficult, Mum's little story did have some relevance after all. Ben had been unhappy, and he was worrying all summer about it. I expect all the hanging around listening to my conversations was in the hopes that he would hear something that would give him a clue to what was worrying him. I couldn't believe that a supposedly educated woman could have been so stupid to say something like that to her son. Not only was it misleading him, but I also suspect he had elaborated the story to further upset Ben. It was an incredibly naive attitude to have in this day and age. I felt really sad for Ben because he had had such a horrid summer, I was glad he had finally spoken to me about it, and now he knew that he could discuss his worries with us at any time.

***

At the end of the first week back at school I went in to meet Michael's new teacher. I just wanted to see what her opinion was about Michael's reading problems, and to ask her for any advice that she could give us to help him with his work. She was really lovely and clearly very passionate about her career in teaching, for which she had just qualified. She reassured me. 'Oh I don't think you need to have any worries about Michael. He's one of the youngest in the class, but he's way up there with the second year children when we have class discussions. His general knowledge and language abilities are wonderful. I'm sure his reading will suddenly click, but I'll keep in touch with you over it.' I felt somewhat happier having talked to her. She seemed to really have her finger on the pulse and clearly already knew the children in her class, even though she had a two year age group to contend with.

It was Monday morning again. I looked at the boys playing on the drive, as they waited for me to call them to get ready for the journey to school. I could hardly believe that this was their last year at junior school before embarking on the next educational stage at the middle school. They had grown so much. Thomas was now nearly as tall as Christopher, and Ben was putting a little more distance between himself and Michael, who at one stage looked as if he was sure to catch Ben up. They were all still fair, although Christopher had thicker, much wavier hair, which was probably a tone darker than his other two triplet brothers. But Michael was the one who had changed the most. As a very small boy he had straight, fine, almost white blond hair, very similar to Ben and Tom, but within a year his hair had changed to look much more like Christopher's. It had suddenly thickened and developed a distinct wave to it, again a tone darker than the other two. He was beginning to look just like a smaller version of Christopher, and I wondered if as adults they would look as alike as the identical two did at this present moment.

There were one or two things we needed to address

though. One of which was the boys' mathematical progress, which we had noticed was a little slow. Eddie did the times tables on the way to school, but maths books were never part of their homework. It was clearly not a favoured subject in Mr. Palmer's wonderfully varied and interesting timetable which, in every other way, we were delighted with. We had visits to the zoo, talks about Natterjack Toads, visits to dinosaur exhibitions and trips around museums. They made models of Stonehenge and the Parthenon, and frequently went to school dressed up as a child from another age, none of which we would have wanted to change for one moment as it increased the children's curiosity, but maths fell quietly by the wayside.

We decided that this was something we could sort out for ourselves, so we employed a home tutor to come one evening a week. He came in the form of a rather strange man called Mr. Tynan or, as the boys called him, Mr. Thailand, who advertised himself in the local paper under the heading of EDUCATION. Other than his thin, dyed brown hair, he looked just like Jimmy Savile, even down to the horrid, brightly coloured shell suits. His false teeth didn't fit properly, and rather embarrassingly they shot out of his mouth one night as he said goodbye. He picked them up off the floor and scuttled away, ramming them back into his mouth as he went, which caused the boys to fall into helpless giggles. He smelt of women's perfume and I'm afraid I never allowed him to teach the boys behind closed doors, neither did I leave them alone in the house with him, which I have a strong suspicion he rather hoped I would. The boys hated every minute of his lessons and after several weeks, just as we were wondering how to tell him we didn't need his services anymore, he stopped coming.

We breathed a sigh of relief but we were faced with finding someone else. I didn't fancy answering an advert again, so we decided to phone the lady who coached several of the children from school who were sitting entrance exams. She came with very good credentials, and although we had no plans to sit entrance exams, she was sure to be able to coach them with their maths in readiness for the middle school. As so often seemed to happen in our lives, the lady coincidentally turned out to be the mother of one of my old school friends. I did wonder when I learnt her name was McCormack, but I'd never given it any more thought until I spoke to her. In fact I had even stayed with them over night when I was 13 so that Lynne, her daughter, and I could go to the youth club disco. She had very little space to fit them in, but luckily because they could all be coached together she was happy to make a couple of hours a week free for them. It was the best thing we could have done as far as their education was concerned, and as it turned out, it changed the whole master plan we had mapped out for them.

Mrs. McCormack was a small and efficient, no nonsense sort of woman, and the boys loved her immediately. There was no getting up and wandering around for Ben, that was knocked on the head the moment he even started to slide his small, skinny, little buttock off his chair. A choice of two sweets from the jar at the end of the lesson was eagerly awaited, and for exceptional work a chocolate bar was awarded. They responded better than we could have hoped, although Mrs. McCormack confirmed that she felt they were rather behind for their age. I was so keen for maths not to be the thorn in the side it had been for me - maths had left me dead from the neck up after about the age of eight.

***

Just a few weeks into the new term, I had a call from school to tell me that Mrs. Tomlin wondered if I could call in and see her when I picked the boys up. She wanted to have a quick chat about Michael's progress. I asked the boys if they would go and play in the play ground and look after Michael, whilst I chatted with Mrs. Tomlin. She was clearing away the afternoon's activities and smiled kindly towards me as I entered the mobile class room. 'Thanks for coming in. I just wanted to have a little update with you after our chat the other day.' I smiled back. She continued. 'Having said I wasn't too worried when we spoke last time, I've been watching him closely. Like you, I now definitely feel there is a problem. On one hand he seems so bright, but then on the other hand – well, I'd like you to have a look at this.' She went and fetched a little exercise book. 'This is Michael's news book. They write any interesting bits of news from home in this. The others in his age group are writing simple words and having a go at some more complicated words, obviously spelt as they sound, but this is what Michael is producing.' She opened the little brown book to reveal pages and pages of random letters, all moving diagonally from right to left down the page. 'As you can see there are no recognisable words here, and the letters aren't even moving in the correct direction.' This, as far as I was concerned, was conclusive proof that things were amiss. 'I hope you don't mind,' she said looking slightly embarrassed. 'But I've asked the school inspector to have a look at him when he comes in next week. He's really good with learning difficulties, in fact it's his area of specialism, so I feel he might be able to give us some advice.' I was very grateful to her, and thanked her profusely for her interest.

The following week I had a call from Mrs. Tomlin at lunch time 'Are you picking the boys up tonight, only I wondered if you would mind popping in to see me again? I've seen the school inspector today, and he's told me some interesting things that I'd like to discuss with you. Also I want to show you something else that Michael has astonished both of us with today.' It seemed a long couple of hours until it was pick-up time. As I drew up outside the school I had butterflies in my stomach, as it was so important for us to find out how we could help Michael.

Only a few days before, he had appeared in our bedroom at 6.30am. He climbed onto our bed, sat himself between the two of us and perched up on our pillows in his Mickey Mouse pyjamas. 'I don't want to go to school anymore.' Large tears rolled down his cheeks from his equally large blue eyes, as he looked the epitome of desolation. 'Why Michael, what is it, what's making you so sad? I don't like seeing you this unhappy. I thought you loved Mrs. Tomlin.' He looked back at me through his water-filled eyes as the tears spilled down his face. 'Oh I do love her, but I don't like all the horrid words and letters that I don't understand. Yesterday I had to go and do bark rubbing with Mrs. Nolan, the dinner lady, and all the not very clever children, instead of doing story writing.' I comforted him and told him that very soon we would get him some special help with his words and reading, but we would have to see an expert teacher before we could do that. He seemed happy with my explanation, but it left me feeling upset and very adamant that we would have to sort this problem out, sooner rather than later. The fact that he even realised he had been sidelined during the story writing lesson told me that he was bright; most five year olds would have seen it as a lucky escape from lessons and nothing more.

Mrs. Tomlin was waiting for me. 'Come on in,' she smiled her warm smile as I closed the door behind me. She began. 'Well today's been very interesting, and I can tell you that the school inspector is certain that Michael has definitely got some level of dyslexia. He's done some simple tests with him which has revealed that he's cross lateral. This often goes hand in hand with learning problems.' I looked puzzled. 'He's right eye dominant, left handed and right footed.' This was quite true, we had just started to do triathlon with the pony club and although it was really for the older boys, Michael also wanted to join in. He had been learning how to shoot the air pistol, and although he held the gun in both hands, it was his left eye he automatically shut as he took aim with his right eye. It was also true that he kicked a football with his right foot, yet he was very definitely left handed.

Mrs. Tomlin continued. 'He, like us, feels that Michael is a very bright little boy, but clearly his reading and writing is holding him back. He feels if we don't deal with it quickly it could lead to frustration and even disruptive behaviour, although I can't imagine that can you?' I smiled, Michael was about the last little person I could imagine being disruptive and certainly at the moment was the perfect image of a rather small, angelic boy. Mrs. Tomlin continued. 'Anyway, I must tell you what happened next. We've been doing some work with addition and subtraction on a number scale. With the scale the children can count forwards to add, and back to subtract, giving them the answer if they count accurately. Unfortunately, Michael has struggled with this too, and his numbers are often back to front and in wrong columns, but we've now got some new work books with the number scales at the top of each page, and with different little exercises to do. One of the exercises has drawings of a squirrel with piles of nuts waiting to be put into a bag. The idea is to either add or take away from the pile. The school inspector was with Michael whilst he worked on some of these problems. Suddenly he called me over to watch. Michael was able to look at the problem, then either subtract or add the amount of nuts in his head by using his imagination. He visualised it by picking up the relevant number of nuts, either taking away or adding to the squirrels' bag, by pinching his fingers together over the book. He dropped the imaginary amount of nuts into the bag, then he could tell us the answer. At this age we wouldn't expect a child to be able to do this sort of sum in their head and, what's more, he got every single one right.

I, like them, felt that we should try and deal with the problem sooner rather than later, so I asked what the next step should be. 'Firstly we have to start the statementing process with your permission, and then we should be able to get some funding so the school can get some extra help for him. Specially trained teachers will come in and do some one-to-one work with him, so hopefully with some specific strategies in place everything will become easier for him.' So, obviously I gave my permission for the statementing process to begin.

But then only a fortnight on, I had a distressed sounding message left on our answer phone by Mrs. Tomlin. 'Can you come in tonight and see me. I need to talk to you urgently.' My heart missed a beat as I listened to the message.

I walked quickly towards the mobile classroom and Mrs. Tomlin met me at the door. 'I'm so upset,' she said, as I walked into the classroom behind her. 'I started the ball rolling in order to get Michael's statementing process underway immediately after the school inspector had been, and after I had discussed it with you. But Mr. Palmer has come in to see me this afternoon with some upsetting news. He's told me that it will now have to wait until Michael is seven before we can do anything to help him.' 'Really?' I said looking shocked. 'How come?' Mrs. Tomlin continued. 'Well apparently schools are only legally responsible for statementing children after the age of seven. You see the theory is that children, particularly boys, can be late developers and a lot can happen between five and seven. It's not until they're seven and still having difficulties that the schools are responsible for their extra tuition, and then the statementing can begin. The school does get funding every year to spend on this sort of thing, but they can also allocate the money to be spent elsewhere, particularly if there's no one with a problem in the school, and this year the money has already been spent. So you can now see why schools are none too keen to get anyone statemented. I'm just so angry, it's really not fair on him, or any other children who need help for that matter. Is there any way that you could find someone out of school to help him, I hate seeing the affect it's having on him?'

She really was an exceptional and dedicated teacher, and her worry was absolutely genuine. I reassured her, and told her that I would be on the case, we would find someone as soon as possible. In fact I did have someone in mind who I knew gave learning support part time at a senior school just into Cambridgeshire, so I decided to phone her. If she couldn't do it herself she was sure to know someone who would.

Somehow this brought everything to a bit of a head. Ben was still being quite disruptive within the class, much to the embarrassment of his brothers. It wasn't anything really bad, just little incidences mainly due to the fact that he really wasn't being challenged enough. I think he'd realised he could get away with things, often pulling the 'I'm not as able as my brothers,' card out, which made me angry with him, but even more angry that he seemed to be getting away with it. One evening, after the boys' lesson, Mrs. McCormack offered me a cup of tea; her next pupil had cancelled so she had some time for a chat.

I spoke to her about my concerns and filled her in on the latest information about Michael's dyslexic diagnosis, which she had been following with interest. Another thing that was slightly concerning us were the increasingly frequent reports that the new head at the middle school was very anti-competitive sports. Then, just recently, during a conversation with a friend whose dyslexic daughter was at the middle school, it was revealed that there was little or no help provided for children with dyslexia in the school, and that Northamptonshire was one of the worst counties to be dyslexic in. One mother told me that her son had finished his maths book, and he was told that he couldn't have a new work book until the others had caught up with him.

As we chatted I discussed the possibility of her keeping the boys on as pupils throughout their time at the middle school. But, as she rightly pointed out, it would just lead to more frustration if they were to be working at one level with her, and another at school. 'Look Gill,' she said. 'They're bright boys and they'll soon get bored and frustrated if they don't have any challenges in their schooling.' I gazed into my tea, feeling for once completely helpless to know where to turn next. She continued. 'You've seen what's happening with Ben and his slightly disruptive behaviour, and all because he's able to get away with it. Consequently, he's allowed to work at a lower level than he's capable of, and that will only get worse.' She was right with what she was saying. If it were only Thomas and Christopher, I wouldn't have been quite as worried. They were playing mini rugby at the local rugby club now, fulfilling their need for competitive sports. They also didn't carry a label in quite the same way as Ben did with his former problems. We felt this was probably why he was able to cleverly pull the wool over the teacher's eyes, because he knew they expected less of him.

Michael was also another worry, as obviously there was going to be little or no support for his dyslexia. Mrs. McCormack looked thoughtful for a moment. 'You haven't thought of going out of the county for their education have you?' I looked up from the depth of the tea cup. 'Not really, why?' I said with a quizzical frown. 'Well it's just a thought, but my grandchildren all go to the boys' grammar and the girls' high school in Stamford, just into Lincolnshire. They would have to take an exam, just to make sure they would be up to the level of work necessary for a Grammar education, but we could soon get them ready for that. I think the exams are usually in February. Why don't you and Eddie have a chat and go and have a look. We're really pleased with it and the sport, music and drama are of a really good standards too. They also have a resident special needs teacher, which would be wonderful for Michael's problems.' I drove home, mulling the whole idea over. We had done so much forward planning with the boys' schooling and it had seemed, up until a few months ago, that we had everything cut and dried. I didn't know how Eddie would feel about us travelling twenty miles to school and back twice a day. Obviously, if we continued with our original plans, they would be at school very locally, only fifteen minutes away from home, and a few moments walk from the garage should they have after school activities.

I tentatively broached the subject with Eddie that evening, after the boys had gone to bed. He sat looking thoughtful, as I repeated the conversation I had had with Mrs. McCormack. 'Well she does have a point, and I must admit I'd like the boys to be able to have the opportunity to play all the sports I enjoyed at school.' Funnily enough it was the sport that seemed to be the main thrust for Eddie – he'd enjoyed and excelled at sport as a boy when he went to his local Grammar school. It had then given him a healthy social life after he left school, playing cricket and social rugby. He felt that for young people working in a new area away from home and friends, playing a sport could instantly give them a source of meeting people with a similar interest, and an introduction into a friendship group.

I, on the other hand, was anxious that they should be settled in an educational system that would last them throughout their school days. Although I wouldn't have swapped my varied and ever changing education, principally because my father moved around so much, I knew how disruptive it had been to my learning. The Grammar system had been ended in Northamptonshire some years before, but it was still very active in Lincolnshire. There was also an infant school that fed into the boys' grammar school, dependant on passing an exam at the age of eight. This would enable Michael to move at the same time with the boys, going into the infant school, where he would have the dyslexic support he needed. At thirteen they would then move on, much as they would do if we stayed in the present system, to the senior part of the school. The boys' joint best friend, David, had just been given a place at the choir school in Peterborough and Martin, their other joint best friend, had already moved to Kimbolton School, soon to be followed by his brother Guy, so Michael would also be losing his main friend too. All of this was quite alright, as at their age they would soon make more new friends, but it did also have some bearing on our final decision.

***

I picked up the phone and dialled the number, feeling a little apprehensive. Angie answered the phone. 'Hi Angie, it's Gill Arthey, I hope you don't mind me calling you but Eddie and I have been becoming increasingly worried about Michael's reading and writing, and I'm told you're the person to speak to.' She laughed, 'I've been expecting a call from you. Dawn told me you were having some worries.' Dawn was her sister in law and also had a son called Michael who, coincidentally, had some very similar problems. He was a few years older, but Angie had been helping her nephew for a while and he was now making good progress. I told Angie our tale, and the school inspector's diagnosis, but I was mainly concerned with trying to get him some help sooner rather than later. 'I'd love to help him, Gill, but I'm chock-a- block in the evenings.' She was clearly genuinely sorry that she had no vacancies, as she racked her brains to think of someone else who may have some space for him.

Suddenly an idea occurred to me. 'Would you have any room for him one afternoon a week if I could arrange with the school for him to have the time off?' Angie sounded enthusiastic. 'Yes, I could do that if you're able to sort it out. I have Wednesday afternoons free and I'd be more than happy to help him then. I'll wait to hear from you.'

The next day I went in to see Mr. Palmer, who I think thought I might be on the war path about the statementing. He looked slightly worried as I waited outside the classroom for him. But we weren't troublesome parents and we would never have made a fuss. So I told him about Angie and the problems she had with fitting him in during the evenings. I then broached the idea about taking him out of school for the afternoon every Wednesday. He looked thoughtful. 'Well, I can't see any reason why you shouldn't. I know Mrs. Tomlin would be delighted, as she's very keen for him to have some help sooner rather than later.' So with that all sorted out, Michael started his 'special lessons' with Angie two days later. I fetched him at lunch time and took him home for something to eat, before setting off to travel the few miles to Angie's house.

Angie was a warm and motherly lady, who had a really calm aura about her. She was quietly spoken and she suited Michael down to the ground. They soon had a lovely rapport. I would often turn up to find him sitting on the large chair by the Aga in the lovely, warm farmhouse kitchen, having his drink and a biscuit whilst he chatted away ten to the dozen with her. She, like Mrs. Tomlin, felt that Michael was quite bright, but that he was very definitely showing strong dyslexic traits. Unfortunately, he was too young to have an assessment with the dyslexic institute, they preferred to wait until the children were a little older than his five years and eight months. She also felt that our thoughts about the Stamford Grammar school option was a very good idea and should be investigated. She, too, had heard that the help for children with specific learning difficulties was sadly lacking in the Northamptonshire school system at the present time. Soon after Christmas we made the decision to go and have a look around Stamford school.

The boys all seemed highly excited about the meeting, as they piled into the back of the old Mitsubishi Shogun. It quite surprised me, as I thought we may have a bit of objection about leaving their friends, although as I've already said their special friends were going, or had gone elsewhere anyway. We were to go to the headmaster's office at the senior school first, he would then take us around the school and tell us how the three tier system worked, and what would be expected of the boys in the exam. I have to say I was a little worried about the exam. We knew their maths was still a little behind and they had never done a verbal reasoning paper in their lives. But Mrs. McCormack told us that she was very happy to do some papers with them so they could practice.

The school was situated in the lovely old historic town, with a lot of the school being housed in parts of the original old buildings. But first we went in to meet Mr. Timm, the headmaster, in his office. He was a man with a clear air of authority, although he struck me as very kindly. He warmly welcomed the boys and us into his office. He had grey hair and was of a solid frame, although not plump; I should think he had played his fair share of rugby in his time. He invited us all to sit down, but straight away focussed on and directed all the conversation towards the boys. He had a large, old fashioned map of the school grounds on a small coffee table in front of him. 'Who can tell me where we are on this map?' As quick as lightening Christopher said, 'We're here,' and pointed to a building on the map. Mr. Timm looked impressed. 'Well done Christopher, you're right, that's exactly where we are.'

The meeting continued to go well and, much to my surprise, Michael, who was usually fairly reserved in these situations, chatted away to Mr. Timm as if he had known him all his life, even asking him questions as we walked around the school grounds and buildings. We decided we definitely wanted the boys to sit the exam, after all we had nothing to lose by trying. The exam was to be held in early February. Michael, on the other hand, was able to go to the infant school without sitting an exam. Mr. Timm told us, 'We usually ask the children to have a very simple maths and reading test at Michael's age, but because of his current difficulties it may be too upsetting for him. He'll have to sit an exam before he comes up to the middle school, as he really will have to cope with the level and pace of the work by then, but he'll have had eighteen months of dyslexic tuition by that stage, so he should be in a better place to cope with it.' I couldn't believe how accommodating and helpful they were being, and having been fairly ambivalent before we had been to see the school, I now felt desperate for them to pass the exam and be accepted. The school was lovely, the facilities were fabulous and the boys were clearly very excited about the prospective possibility of going there.

The entrance exam day in February dawned, and we had to be at the school for 9.30am prompt, armed with pencils, rubbers and rulers. They each had three pencils and a sharpener in a pencil case. Eddie took them, while I stayed at home with Michael to do the ponies. The morning dragged, and my mind was constantly drifting to the boys sitting the exam, until finally Eddie drove in with them at lunch time. They bounced out of the car and came running in to tell me all about it. They all seemed fairly confident that it had gone well, but most children of that age think they're invincible, so we would have to wait a whole two weeks to see if they were right.

The results day came, and Eddie was on a day off. As usual our post was late, in fact it had been increasingly unreliable of recent weeks. By lunch time the post still hadn't arrived and I had to almost physically restrain Eddie from phoning the school there and then. But when it hadn't arrived by four I was near to bursting too. 'That's it,' said Eddie, 'I'm going to have to ring them. I can't wait another day to find out.' He was put through to Mr. Timm's office. 'What would you like to hear me say?' asked Mr. Timm. 'Well I'd like to hear you say that they've all passed and they have a place with you.' Mr. Timm laughed, 'That's very good then, because they have all passed and we're very pleased to be having them. They'll have some catching up to do but we're happy that they'll cope.'

The feeling of relief now we were settled was something I couldn't have anticipated. The biggest worry had been the scenario that one or even two may get in, but not all three. Obviously we were particularly worried about Ben because of his past history. We had also made the decision not to mention anything about his past problems to the school, as we didn't want it to compromise the expectations of his potential. We wanted him to achieve what he possibly could, although all we expected was his best. It could always be mentioned at a later date, should it be necessary. We had begun to notice that more and more, his best often wasn't being reached because most of the time the expectations of him were lower than the expectations of his brothers. But now we were settled, all we had to do was continue the extra lessons throughout the summer and they would hopefully be nearer to the level they needed to be, ready for their new start in September.

MODULE 30:
INDEPENDENCE AND A GRAMMAR
SCHOOL EDUCATION

We went to meet the boys at Moat Farm. It was mother-in-law's day to go to school, as she always did once a week, before taking them back to her pretty farmhouse for tea. We arrived with my mother just as tea was being served and the boys were all sitting around the circular kitchen table. A large vase of colourful flowers sat in the middle of it upon the equally colourful table cloth. 'Well boys,' said Eddie, 'We have some news for you.' They all looked up inquisitively, their faces eagerly waiting to hear what Eddie was about to tell them. 'I've just spoken to Mr. Timm at Stamford school and guess what, he told me that you've all passed the entrance exam so you will all be going to Stamford this September. What do you think about that?' Their faces opened up into smiles, Christopher let out a big 'yeeehhh' which stimulated them all to jump up from the table and danced around, Michael included. I think he understood what was going on and that he, too, would be moving schools. We had been to see the infants' school after seeing the boys' school, and he seemed to really like it. He told us that he wanted to go there, but I wasn't quite sure if he understood that he would be at this smaller school on his own, rather than with his brothers as he had been at Glapthorn. Anyway, the main thing was that they all seemed hugely excited, which had to bode well for the success of this venture.

After a few days a letter came, just to confirm in writing the fact that the boys had been given a place at the school, and with it an enormous list of school uniform and sundries that we would have to purchase. At first it all looked very daunting and, I have to say, worryingly expensive. But as I read and re-read the information, it soon became clear that an awful lot of the clothing could be purchased from other sources, rather than just at the school shop. Grey shirts could be found anywhere, from John Lewis and Marks and Spencers, to ASDA and Littlewoods. So could the dark grey trousers, grey jumpers and even the blazers. The school very kindly sold blazer top pockets with the badge embroidered on them, especially for those parents who chose to buy a cheaper blazer and put the pockets on themselves. The only thing that couldn't be found elsewhere were the school tracksuits, which had embroidered school emblems and a Latin motto on them, and the house tie according to which house they were affiliated to. Our boys were to be in Cecil, which was populated by boys who lived to the south of Stamford.

Michael's uniform was slightly different and his blazer and cap had to be bought from the school shop, although at his age the winter tops were a red polo neck, of which we had a plentiful supply due to our immense and growing ski wear collection.

Not long after the initial letter we had another one to invite us to a new parents' evening. Our letter had a specific note just for us, which asked us to speak to the boys about their preference on how they wished to be placed in their classes. There was a choice, as there were two parallel classes. They could either stay together and go into one class, or one of them could separate away and go into a class on his own. There wouldn't be three parallel classes for another two years. As I read the letter my gut feeling was that they wouldn't want to be separated. They had all been quite happy together at Glapthorn, so I didn't anticipate that they would want to be apart until the classes split into three. But how wrong I was. Tom immediately leapt at the opportunity to be in a class alone. I felt irrationally sad, I was so surprised by his reaction about being separated. Although they weren't as triplety as when they were small, they were still very close to one another. They appeared to enjoy every minute spent together, so I couldn't understand why he should want to be separate.

When we were alone I asked him again why he had made that choice. 'Sometimes my brothers embarrass me especially when Ben's naughty, and because I look like him I'm scared the teachers will think I am him. I'd also like to make my own friends and not have to always share them with my brothers.' It made complete sense when he articulated it that way. Christopher was always the self-appointed spokesperson and was always very popular at school, which none of the others seemed to mind at all, but I could see that Tom may, by now, feel that he wanted to assert himself and establish his own independence. Ben, on the other hand, was now so much his own person and so very comfortable in his own skin, I don't think it mattered to him one iota whether he had brothers with him or not. So that was the decision we went with and I respected Tom for speaking up and for knowing what he felt was right for him.

This surprising show of independence began a bit of a trend during that summer term. The first time was early one Sunday morning. The light was breaking through the curtains in our bedroom, so I had tucked down even further under the duvet. I wanted to linger in that lovely sleep that only comes by knowing there is nothing to rush out of bed for. Something that we were very rarely privileged to be able to experience. With Eddie working most weekends, school during the week and horses to do, interspersed with pony club competitions or horse shows at the weekend, we had very few lie-ins. Anyway, it was only 6am, so there were at least two more hours of slumber to enjoy before having to climb out of bed and get on with the animals and the day ahead. Just as I was dropping back into a lovely, restful sleep, Eddie sat bolt upright in bed. 'I can smell bacon!' he said. I opened my bleary eyes and propped myself up on my elbow as I sniffed the air. 'No I think you're imagining it. It's just wishful thinking, tuck down and have a little longer in bed for once.' Eddie snuggled back down and rested his arm across my waist as we took on the shape of two spoons in the kitchen drawer.

No sooner had we got comfortable again than Eddie was bobbing his head up and out from under the duvet. 'Oh, for goodness sake, what's the matter now?' I asked in an irritable voice. 'I can definitely smell bacon cooking. Sit up and smell it, you can't miss it now.' I sat up, as by now lying in had completely gone out of the window. I sniffed the air. 'Yes, I think you're right, I can smell bacon too.' With that Eddie shot out of bed and trotted down the stairs from our upstairs bedroom. We had moved up there earlier in the year, as at nine years old we now felt the boys were old enough to be downstairs alone. After all, they were only just at the bottom of the staircase and through the kitchen. I was out of bed too by now to follow Eddie down the stairs. As I rounded the dog leg of the stair, I saw Eddie rush towards a smoking frying pan which, from where I was standing, appeared to have the plastic spatula melting in it, like a grey soft cheese. As Eddie rushed across the floor to rescue the pan and its contents before it burst into flames, he stepped in a large pool of cooking oil that the boys had obviously spilt. Both of Eddie's legs shot out from under him as his naked body made a loud SPLAT, hitting the quarry tiled floor heavily. 'Ughhh, you little b*****s,' he groaned. 'What the hell are you doing?'

By this stage I had bypassed the oil and Eddie's writhing body, and had reached the melted plastic mess and rescued the charred, smoking bacon from the grill. Eddie was slowly getting to his feet as he grunted with the pain, rubbing his oily side where it had taken the full impact of the fall. I held my hand out to help him to his feet, and stifled my desire to laugh at the comic sight, as I realised that it wouldn't be very diplomatic at this present moment. I could now hear the boys in the bathroom, so I gave Eddie the small kitchen hand towel to wrap around himself to protect his modesty. We peered round the bathroom door to see the other three boys huddled around Thomas who had his hand under the cold tap. 'What are you up to boys, the kitchen was nearly on fire?' They all turned to face us. 'Thomas has burnt his hand, look there's a big blister on it.' They all looked most concerned and showed us a large fluid filled lump on Tom's hand. 'The fat jumped out of the pan and burnt him. We wanted to surprise you and cook you breakfast,' said Christopher. They all looked so sweet standing there in their pyjamas, surrounding their injured brother, so how could we be cross with them? We congratulated them for their first aid skills and for their enterprising ideas, but we suggested that I should give them a few cookery lessons before they tried to surprise us again.

A few weeks after this incident, and again very early one summer morning, I awoke. I didn't quite know what it was that had woken me, but something had, and when I looked at the clock I could see it was only 5.30am. I turned over and tried to go back to sleep, but there was something that kept on gnawing into my consciousness and I couldn't settle. In fact, something was telling me to get out of bed and go and have a look outside. I stumbled sleepily to the window and gently parted the pink curtains to peep out, not wanting to wake Eddie. I cast a glance around the yard and across to the field. It was a beautiful, sunny early June morning and not a cloud was in sight, only a few fading vapour trails wisped across the clear blue morning sky.

Everything seemed to be in order, so I quietly let the curtains fall back together and started to walk back towards the bed. But wait a minute – I walked back to the window and parted the curtains again. My eyes frantically scanned the paddock. Where were the ponies? I looked backwards and forwards, making sure my eyes weren't deceiving me. 'Eddie, Eddie, wake up, I think someone's stolen the ponies.' I called out to him as I stood by the window hoping to see one of the fluffy little greys wander round from the back of the field shelter, which was the only part of the paddock we couldn't see from the bedroom. Eddie appeared by my side as he put his glasses on, blinking hard to focus his sleepy eyes. 'You're right,' said Eddie, 'They've gone. I think we'd better get dressed and go and have a look for them, they must have got out and gone into the woods.' That could be only marginally better news than them being stolen, with 500 acres or more to search through, and after that acres and acres of fields. Needles and haystacks sprang to mind.

We both crept downstairs as we didn't want to wake the boys and alarm them, at least until we knew a bit more about their ponies' whereabouts. I walked out to the yard to go into the paddock for a double check, but as I walked past the tack room I noticed the door was open. I briefly paused to look inside, but as I did I could hardly believe my eyes - all the ponies' saddles and bridles were missing. We both peered in through the door, dumb struck, not knowing what to do next. 'I just wonder,' said Eddie 'Let's pop in and check the boys are still in bed before we phone the police. I think we need to make sure the ponies' disappearance isn't closer to home than we think.' I ran inside, my heart beating hard. All the beds were empty.

We had our answer, but where had they gone so early in the morning, and were they safe? This was the first time they had been out riding on their own like this, and although they knew the woods like the backs of their hands, what if something had happened? Other than going out and wandering around the woods in the hope of finding them, there was nothing we could do other than put the kettle on and wait for their return. After about an hour, by which time Eddie and I were sitting outside at the garden table in the warm, morning sun with yet another cup of tea, we heard the cracking of the branches in the woods. We jumped up and walked to the ditch at the edge of our garden. There, coming through the trees, with Ben in the lead, were the boys and their four grey ponies. They had bits of leaves stuck in the tops of their hats and twigs clinging on to their jumpers. The ponies had leaves and twigs in their manes and tails too. They all had rosy cheeks and the ponies even seemed to have smiles on their faces. It had been a worrying hour but they were all safe and very happy. They were incredibly lucky to have the freedom to be able to take themselves out into acres of woodland, and not to have to go anywhere near a road. They had been having such a wonderful time. So we suggested that if they wanted to ride really early in the morning again, they might plan it in advance and then we would know where they were.

This never happened quite so early in the morning again, but they did start to ride out into the woods a little bit more on their own, after telling me where they were going. They often took themselves off to the bit of the wood they called 'Africa' as it was a clear area with long, yellow grass that looked like the African veldt. On other occasions when they really wanted an adventure they took themselves to the bit of the wood they called 'The Black Death'. This was a dark and dank piece of woodland, which they dropped down into after negotiating a steep slope. Once down there a little stream meandered its way along a mossy bank, with lichen covered trees running by the side of it. The boys imagined there had been a lost village at the bottom of this hill, as there were one or two crumbling stone walls and buildings now all covered in the green slippery moss. They decided the population had been wiped out by the 'Black Death' which they had been learning about at school.

June also heralded Eddie's 40th, so we decided it was time to have a party. We had lots of friends to invite, with so many people having supported us when we had the triplets, and then there was the ever growing circle of friends we were meeting through the children. A couple of days before the party, the marquee went up in the garden. This caused some hilarity when a fox came into the empty marquee and pooed in the middle of the dance floor.

Billy, who was our best man and also Christopher's godfather, along with his brother in law, Thomas, who was Thomas's godfather, decided to organise a 'This is your life' for Eddie. We were going to surprise him with it, so the boys were under orders to not mention a word. This was a concept that Ben struggled with, he couldn't quite help himself, the words just seemed to burst forth from inside his mouth. Whether it was not letting on about a secret present or a surprise day out, or the score from a football or rugby match, the information just seemed to leap from his lips, swiftly followed by his hand being slapped across his mouth as if to slam the door shut, unfortunately after the horse had bolted. So although the other boys knew, we were reluctant to tell Ben for fear of the secret escaping in front of Eddie.

The only trouble was, I had written a poem for the boys to recite during the 'This is your Life' performance, and I needed Ben to learn his lines and to practice before the night. I talked to him about his difficulty and asked him if he felt it would be at all possible for him, just for once, to manage to keep his mouth sealed. Ben looked thoughtful. 'Well I could really try very hard, but I don't think you'd better tell me yet as I need to think about it. Perhaps you could tell me the secret very near to Daddy's party, and then there won't be as long for me to keep it shut up in my mouth.' I couldn't help but laugh - at least he was honest. In fact that was the trouble, he was so honest that he viewed keeping a secret as not telling the truth, and the truth always had to be told. Perhaps if I could change his view on the situation it would make it easier for him. So I explained to Ben that the thing we were organising was for his Daddy to really enjoy, and it would spoil it completely if he were to tell him. Keeping a secret wasn't deceiving his Daddy at all, and he should look on it as looking after something that would be a very special present for his Daddy to enjoy. If he wanted to join in with the surprise, and not be the only one who didn't take part, he would have to manage to keep a secret. 'Let me think about it all night and I'll tell you tomorrow if I think I can keep it in.' He looked very sincere about it and I felt I might have got through to him at last.

The next morning Ben came into the kitchen. 'Mummy, I've thought all night about what we talked about and I've decided that I can do it. I think I can keep the secret.' So with a severe warning about a fate worse than death if it were to slip out, I read him the poem. His eyes lit up as any kind of performance was just up Ben's street. This is the poem that they learnt, each of them having their own little part to recite:

OUR DAD

Well Dad, what a to-do and all of this is just for you.
Mind you we think you're worth it,
All the ranting and swearing and rushing and tearing,
We haven't minded, not one little bit.

A Masters In Motherhood

As a boy you led a happy life,
You didn't have too much trouble and strife.
The O's and the A's left you in a daze,
The accountancy exams were more like a maze.

Then on to Smith Millington, you've lots to tell,
Then you got married – was it hell?
A few years later we were a twinkle in your eye,
You didn't put a bun in the oven, just a bloody great pie.
We weren't quite the 4 and 20, but by Jove we were plenty.
Mum thought you might do a flit
But you hung around to do your bit,
Even when we did a ------ dirty nappy

Oundle then beckoned and you and John reckoned,
That you would make a pretty smart pair.
Customer service was part of the plan, to help to make a
happy clan. There is just one complaint, and that's the
smell in the Office that makes us all faint.
Who is to blame? No one knows,
Probably the one who face just glows.

Then along came Michael, the jewel in your crown.
He makes us all laugh and never frown.
After him you had the chop,
You knew you both just had to stop.

When Mum was stuck at home with us
And you went hunting, we made a fuss.
One day she said 'I know, we'll join him.'
So now we're all ponied, dressed and shod,
We think you think it's a bit of a sod.
Because into your pocket you have to dig deep
For all our ponies you have to keep.

Anyway Dad there's nothing else to say,
Except to have a Happy Birthday.

The party night arrived and Ben had kept his part of the deal. 'This is your life' went just as planned, with Billy and Thomas as compères, inviting people from Eddie's life to come up and say a few well-rehearsed words, to the gathering of friends and family. There was a lot of laughter throughout the performance, and the boys' birthday poem to Daddy was left until last. They were word perfect and everyone laughed, clapped and cheered as the boys did their bit all very professionally, waiting until the laughter had stopped before continuing with their words. We all fell into bed in the early hours of the morning. Happy, a little worse for wear, and very satisfied with how the party had gone.

But now the end of term was upon us and the boys' final day at Glapthorn was here. I had brought various presents for the boys to give to their teachers, and I had found an extra special one for Mrs. Tomlin. She had been such a good and supportive teacher to Michael and had helped him, and us, with Michael's learning difficulties, even speaking directly to Angie, in order to find out what things she could do to help him in class. She was a teacher in a million and we had been very lucky to have her at such a crucial time.

I quickly brushed my hair and bundled it up into the plastic clip holder that contained my wilful blonde curls, tucking them into a neat bun at the back of my head. My hair was so thick and allowed its freedom was unruly and wild, so I almost always tied it back or controlled it in some way. A quick sweep with the mascara, as a token effort in the makeup department, found me ready to go to school. I looked at myself briefly in the mirror, now almost ten years on from the boys' birth. Hum, not too bad I thought, I wasn't wearing that badly for thirty-five years old. No grey hairs yet, not too many wrinkles, no middle age spread at the moment, and a nice bit of colour from the outdoor life that I was leading whilst looking after the boys' ponies. We'd been through quite a lot over the last ten years, and it wouldn't have been surprising if we had both been showing signs of wear and tear, but maybe, on the other hand, parenting had suited us. We had both survived this first ten years incredibly well. Eddie's hair was perhaps a little thinner, and his middle was perhaps a little wider, but overall we hadn't changed too much. I couldn't help but wonder if the next ten years would be as kind to us.

There was one other thing that had occurred to me over the last few months, and that was the fact that I was slowly morphing into my mother. The first sign that it was beginning to happen was when I found myself unconsciously trilling away to the music being played through the supermarket radio. It used to embarrass the life out of me when mum insisted on singing along with the music she heard played in any public place, and I used to shush her immediately. Now here I was doing just the same. Not long after this, Tom had a smudge of tomato sauce left on his cheek from a lunchtime bacon butty. We had left home in a hurry and I hadn't been round with the flannel. They were all smart in their best clothes, and as we arrived at the christening I noticed the offending saucy smudge. Quickly I pulled out my handkerchief and licked the edge of it to use as an emergency flannel. Tom screwed up his face in revulsion at what I was doing. I felt awful as it was the one thing I couldn't stand my mother doing to me, and here I was doing just the same to him. I expect all of us have traits of our parents, and it's only natural that we're going to emulate the things that they have done with us, even licking a handkerchief to create a makeshift flannel. I had had an extremely happy and interesting childhood, and if I managed to do half the job my parents had done, I wouldn't be far short of the mark. Eddie had also had a lovely childhood growing up on a farm, having a similarly free life populated by ponies, just like the boys were enjoying. I really hoped I would manage to succeed with this 'degree' even if I had momentarily lapsed by using saliva on my handkerchief.

***

There was a buzz of excitement as I walked into the school. The children were preparing for the end of year concert. Reception class children were finishing having their faces painted as animals for their parts in the show - years one and two were preparing for their musical percussion arrangement. Year three children were having a quick read through their poem 'Albert and the Lion' just to remind themselves of the words, and the year four leavers were getting ready to read their compositions after singing a few lively songs for the audience.

Eddie arrived and we took our places, sitting at the back of the room on the tiny chairs. As usual the concert was of an excellent standard, as one year after the other performed, until we got to the moment we had been waiting for. The year four children all filed in to take up their places in alphabetical order on the stage. After singing their songs, one after the other the children read their little essays, which were mounted on big bits of cardboard. The audience was very attentive and at least the boys, being the first letter of the alphabet, got their bit out of the way early on. The essays were really lovely, and it made me realise what a happy time the boys, and indeed all the other children, had had at Glapthorn. They described the things they had enjoyed, and related funny little tales from some of the many outings they'd been on. The time when the frog jumped out of Clare's hands and nearly went down the front of her jumper, and how Henry lost his wellington boots in the pond when they went pond dipping.

The audience giggled, as one after the other the children read their essays. I was surprised that I didn't feel a little more sad, but as I looked around the room it was the reception class children's parents who looked tearful, much as I had done at that same stage. Suddenly I began to realise why I didn't feel sad anymore - the children were ready to move on. The next challenge was in front of them and Glapthorn had done an admirable job. The children were all confident and well-rounded young people, ready to go out and enjoy the next stage of their education and lives. Nothing would quite match the wonderfully varied time they had experienced at Glapthorn, and the school alone could take the credit for giving the children inquisitive and enquiring minds.

As the stories continued my mind drifted. I reflected upon what I had learnt and achieved over the last ten years, whilst studying for the most complex of Masters Degrees, awarded from the University of Life. I think I could safely say that I had now completed my studies there couldn't be too much else I would need to learn. We had learnt about the wonders and mysteries of the miracle of birth. We had learnt more than most about childhood illness and the process of recovery. National health systems that worked well, and some that didn't. The education system and some of the extracurricular activities available. Learning difficulties and the complexities of the human brain.

We had also learnt to follow our instinct - to listen, to understand, and to be tolerant and selfless. The subjects had been many and varied, but now I felt we could give ourselves a pat on the back. We had learned so much in a relatively short space of time. I pictured myself in my gown and mortar board, walking up the steps and climbing upon the stage on my way to receive my degree certificate. Turning to the clapping, cheering audience I take my bow, before carrying on to receive my award from the Dean of the University of Life. The clapping continued - my day dream came to an end, and I was back in the class room on my tiny chair. The leavers were all smiling on the little stage, enjoying the enthusiastic appreciation from the audience.

I looked at the boys. Ben was still slightly smaller than his identical brother Tom, who in turn was slightly smaller than Christopher, who was the third tallest in the class. They still all had their lovely blond hair and large blue eyes and, although I was obviously very biased, they were all nice looking little boys who, I was sure, at some stage would probably break a few hearts. I felt a surge of pride when I looked at Ben standing there alongside his brothers - he had achieved so much from such a sticky start. I wondered if in some little way our determination to help him achieve had been a factor, or was it in fact, his own complete and utter gritty determination. But maybe, on the other hand, having two brothers of the same age had given him something to strive for. They were there to show him the way and encourage him along and there is no doubt they had done just that. I am sure we would not have had such a happy outcome had this not have been the case. But we could all feel proud of his achievements, and he could feel so very proud of himself. I couldn't help but feel excitement at what the future might hold for them, and simultaneously a surge of relief. Surely now I could begin to relax.

But, just as these thoughts passed through my mind, a little voice called to me, cutting into my subconscious, invading my thoughts. 'So you think you've finished do you? Well you can forget your daydreaming, this is just where the studying really begins. Around the next corner, eagerly awaiting is 'The PHD in Parenting!!'